Teach Yourself VISUALLY™

Chromebook®

Guy Hart-Davis

Visual
A Wiley Brand

Teach Yourself VISUALLY™ Chromebook®

Published simultaneously in Canada

Copyright © 2021 by John Wiley & Sons, Inc., Indianapolis, Indiana

Wiley publishes in a variety of print and electronic formats and by print-on-demand. Some material included with standard print versions of this book may not be included in e-books or in print-on-demand. If this book refers to media such as a CD or DVD that is not included in the version you purchased, you may download this material at booksupport.wiley.com. For more information about Wiley products, visit www.wiley.com.

Library of Congress Control Number: 2020946175

ISBN: 978-1-119-76296-6

ISBN; 978-1-119-76297-3

ISBN: 978-1-119-76298-0

Manufactured in the United States of America

Trademark Acknowledgments

Contact Us

For general information on our other products and services please contact our Customer Care Department within the U.S. at 877-762-2974, outside the U.S. at 317-572-3993 or fax 317-572-4002.

For technical support please visit https://hub.wiley.com/community/support.

Sales | Contact Wiley at (877) 762-2974 or fax (317) 572-4002.

SKY10021816_102020

About the Author

Guy Hart-Davis is the author of more than 150 computer books, including *Teach Yourself VISUALLY iPhone 11, 11 Pro, and 11 Pro Max*; *Teach Yourself VISUALLY MacBook Pro and MacBook Air,* 5th Edition; and *Teach Yourself VISUALLY Word 2019*.

Author's Acknowledgments

My thanks go to the many people who turned my manuscript into the highly graphical book you are holding. In particular, I thank Devon Lewis for asking me to write the book; Lynn Northrup for keeping me on track; Kim Wimpsett for skillfully editing the text; Doug Holland for reviewing the book for technical accuracy and contributing helpful suggestions; Debbye Butler for proofreading the book minutely; and SPi Global for laying out the book.

How to Use This Book

Who This Book Is For

This book is for the reader who has never used this particular technology or software application. It is also for readers who want to expand their knowledge.

The Conventions in This Book

① Steps

This book uses a step-by-step format to guide you easily through each task. **Numbered steps** are actions you must do; **bulleted steps** clarify a point, step, or optional feature; and **indented steps** give you the result.

② Notes

Notes give additional information — special conditions that may occur during an operation, a situation that you want to avoid, or a cross-reference to a related area of the book.

③ Icons and Buttons

Icons and buttons show you exactly what you need to click to perform a step.

④ Tips

Tips offer additional information, including warnings and shortcuts.

⑤ Bold

Bold type shows command names, options, and text or numbers you must type.

⑥ Italics

Italic type introduces and defines a new term.

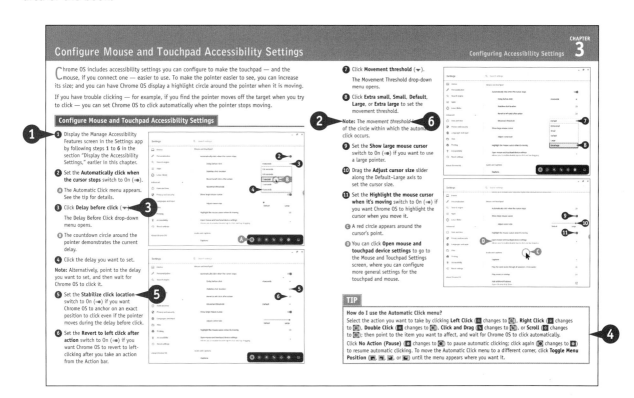

Table of Contents

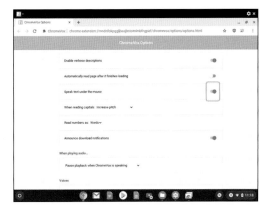

Table of Contents

Chapter 6   Running and Managing Apps and Extensions

Chapter 7   Managing Your Files and Folders

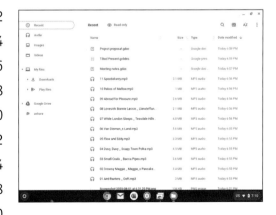

Table of Contents

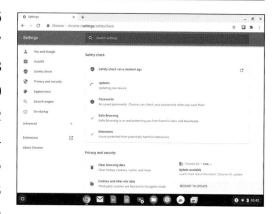

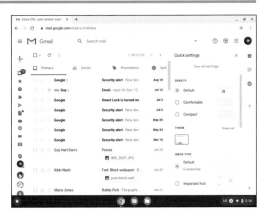

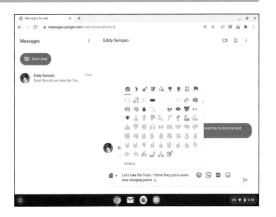

Table of Contents

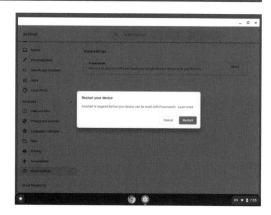

CHAPTER 1

Getting Started with Your Chromebook

In this chapter, you get started using your Chromebook. After a quick exploration of the Chromebook concept and the different types of Chromebooks available, you set up your Chromebook and sign in to your Google Account. You then learn to use the touchpad and the keyboard, connect to Wi-Fi networks, give commands, and work with windows. You also learn to lock your Chromebook, put it to sleep, sign out and in again, and shut it down.

Understanding the Chromebook Concept

A Chromebook is a laptop computer that runs Google's Chrome OS, a lightweight operating system designed to work well on low-end hardware. Chromebooks and Chrome OS are designed for ease of use, portability, and easy administration and management. Chromebooks are suitable for home use, but they are also widely used in schools and colleges, organizations, and companies. Each Chromebook receives operating-system updates for a fixed period.

This section explains the key features of the Chromebook concept. The next section illustrates the various types of Chromebooks available as of this writing.

Choose Chromebook Hardware

Like other laptop computers, a Chromebook is a self-contained unit that includes a built-in screen, keyboard, touchpad, speakers, microphone, and webcam as well as the system board, processor, memory, and storage.

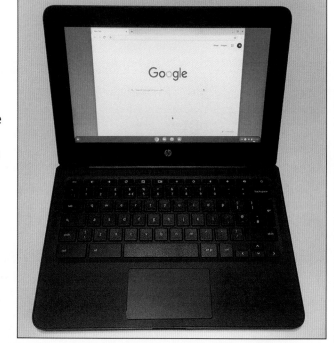

Chromebook models are available in a wide range of prices and capabilities, from inexpensive and modestly equipped models built to survive usage by children up to $1,000-plus models with powerful hardware and high-resolution screens designed for professional use.

When choosing a Chromebook, you will normally want to get a model suitable for the type of usage it is likely to receive. Here are three examples:

- For elementary or junior high school use, you might choose a heavily armored Chromebook with a small screen, and perhaps a reduced-size keyboard; a modest processor; minimal memory, such as 4GB; and a small amount of storage, such as 32GB.

- For college use, you might choose a Chromebook model with a good-size screen, such as 14" or 15", so that the student can view more data at once; a moderately powerful processor and enough memory to run more demanding apps, such as 8GB; and enough storage — perhaps 64GB or 128GB — for however much data the student needs to store.

- For a power user, you might choose a tricked-out Chromebook model with 16GB of memory, 256GB of storage, and a 4K high-resolution screen.

Identify the Strengths and Weaknesses of Chromebooks

Compared to other laptops, such as Windows PCs and Apple's MacBook models, Chromebooks have various strengths and weaknesses.

Chromebooks' key strengths include the following:

- **Online storage.** Chrome OS is designed to store data online, normally in your Google Account's storage. Storing data online gives you automatic backups and the ability to access the data from anywhere. Other operating systems, including Windows and macOS, also provide online storage, but not to the same extent as Chrome OS.

- **Easy updates, recovery and replacement, and administration.** Chrome OS automatically receives updates to keep the operating system secure and to add new features. Because the Chromebook stores your data and settings online, you can easily recover from hardware or software problems, or even move seamlessly to a replacement Chromebook. And for administrators, Google provides powerful administration tools, such as the Google Admin console.

- **Low exposure to viruses and malware.** Chrome OS includes built-in protection against viruses and malware.

- **Cost.** In general, Chromebooks cost less than Windows laptops and Apple MacBook models.

  The key weaknesses of Chromebooks are as follows:

- **Dependence on an Internet connection.** Because a Chromebook is designed to store most of its data online, it requires an Internet connection to perform its full range of actions. However, some apps do enable you to work offline.

- **Limited choice of software.** The Chrome Web Store provides a wide range of software, and all recent and current Chromebooks can run many Android apps as well. But widely used apps such as Microsoft Office are not available on Chromebooks.

- **Not suitable for all purposes.** Generally speaking, Chromebooks are not good for gaming or for applications such as video editing.

Understanding and Determining a Chromebook's Auto Update Expiration Date

Google provides a set period of support and updates for each Chromebook model, starting from the model's release date and running until its Auto Update Expiration date, or *AUE date*. As of Fall 2020, each Chromebook receives six-and-a-half years of upgrades; but from 2020 onward, most new Chromebook models will receive up to eight years of updates. The update period for any Chromebook ends in June of the relevant year, so — for example — a Chromebook first released in December 2020 would receive updates until June 2028, giving a total of seven-and-a-half years.

You can look up the Auto Update Expiration Date for a Chromebook on Google's Support website; try https://support.google.com/chrome/a/answer/6220366?hl=en, or go to https://support.google.com and search for **Chromebook auto expiration date**.

For a Chromebook with the Chrome Education Upgrade or the Chrome Enterprise Upgrade, an administrator can also find the Auto Update Expiration date in the Google Admin console: From the Home page, click **Devices**, click **Chrome management**, click **Devices**, and then look at the Auto Update Expiration column.

For a Chromebook managed through G Suite, an administrator can find the Auto Update Expiration date in the autoUpdateExpiration field in G Suite Admin SDK.

Explore Different Types of Chromebooks

Two main types of Chromebooks are available. The first type is a Chromebook with a typical laptop-style design and a built-in screen that is not a touchscreen. The second type is a convertible Chromebook with a touchscreen. A convertible Chromebook has a 360-degree hinge that enables you to position the lower part as a support for the Chromebook, or fold the lower part underneath the screen, and use the touchscreen for input.

Apart from these two types of Chromebooks, you can also find other Chrome OS devices for specialized purposes. This section briefly covers such Chrome OS devices.

Laptop-Style Chromebooks Without Touchscreens

The standard type of Chromebook has a laptop-style design with a built-in screen that is not a touchscreen. The illustration in the previous section shows such a Chromebook.

You use this type of Chromebook just like a laptop, using the touchpad to move the cursor around the screen and to click, and pressing the keys on the keyboard to enter text or to invoke keyboard shortcuts.

Convertible Chromebooks with Touchscreens

Convertible Chromebook models with touchscreens tend to be more expensive than laptop-style Chromebooks, but they give you greater flexibility for computing or for consuming digital media.

Like other Chromebooks, convertible models come in various sizes. For example, screens may be as small as 10 inches or as large as 15 inches. The example Chromebook shown here has a 15-inch screen, which means the lower part has space for a numeric keypad on the right of the keyboard. The touchpad is centered below the main part of the keyboard, so it appears offset to the left relative to the keyboard as a whole.

The 360-degree hinge on a convertible Chromebook enables you to rotate the lower part of the Chromebook either partway around, using the lower part as a support or stand for the screen, or all the way around, giving a tablet-like configuration with the keyboard and touchpad pointing downward. For example, a tent-like configuration, such as that shown here, can be useful when you are using the Chromebook as a display device.

Rotating the lower part of the Chromebook to a position in which you cannot sensibly use the keyboard and touchpad causes Chrome OS to disconnect the keyboard and touchpad, so any keypresses, touches, or clicks do not register. This means the touchscreen is the sole means of input.

You can also fold the lower part of the Chromebook under the screen, as shown here, and use the Chromebook like a thick tablet. Holding the Chromebook in this configuration, with your fingers resting on the keys on the underside, can feel strange at first, but most people get used to it fairly quickly.

Other Types of Chrome OS Devices

While most Chrome OS devices are Chromebooks, some Chrome OS devices use these two other form factors:

- **Chromebox.** A Chromebox is a free-standing Chrome OS computer to which you connect an external keyboard, mouse, monitor, speakers or headphones, microphone, and other accessories.

- **Chrome tablets.** A Chrome tablet is a tablet computer that runs Chrome OS. The touchscreen is the primary means of input, but you can also connect an external keyboard and mouse, if necessary. Examples of Chrome tablets include Google's Pixel Slate tablet.

Set Up Your Chromebook

The first time you power on your Chromebook, Chrome OS automatically walks you through a routine for setting up the Chromebook and signing in with your Google Account.

During setup, you can change the language in which Chrome OS displays the user interface. You can change the keyboard layout, if needed. You can also configure accessibility options for use during setup and thereafter. For example, you can enable ChromeVox spoken feedback, display the large mouse cursor for easier visibility, or make the screen magnifier available. See Chapter 3, "Configuring Accessibility Settings," for in-depth coverage of the accessibility features.

Set Up Your Chromebook

1 Press **Power**.

The Welcome screen appears.

2 Verify that the Language button shows the language you want to use, such as English (United States). If so, and you want to use the default keyboard layout for that language, go to step **14**.

3 To change the language or the keyboard layout, click **Language** (⊕).

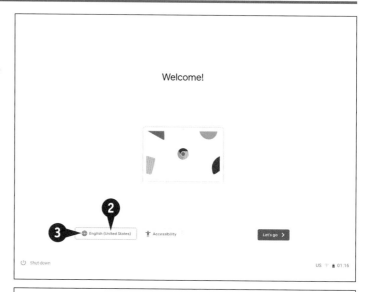

The Language & Keyboard screen appears.

4 To change the language, click **Language** (▼), and then click the appropriate language.

5 To change the keyboard layout, click **Keyboard** (▼), and then click the appropriate keyboard layout.

6 Click **OK**.

The Welcome screen appears again.

7 If you want to configure accessibility, click **Accessibility** (🛉). Otherwise, go to step **14**.

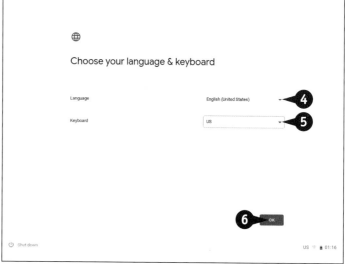

The Accessibility Settings screen appears.

8 Set the **ChromeVox (spoken feedback)** switch to On (◉) if you want to use ChromeVox.

9 Set the **Large mouse cursor** switch to On (◉) if you want to display the large mouse cursor.

10 Set the **High contrast mode** switch to On (◉) if you want to apply a high-contrast color scheme.

11 Set the **Screen magnifier** switch to On (◉) if you want to enable the screen magnifier.

12 Set the **Select to speak** switch to On (◉) if you want to enable the Select to Speak feature.

13 Click **OK**.

The Welcome screen appears again.

14 Click **Let's go**.

The Connect to Network screen appears.

15 Click the Wi-Fi network to which you want the Chromebook to connect.

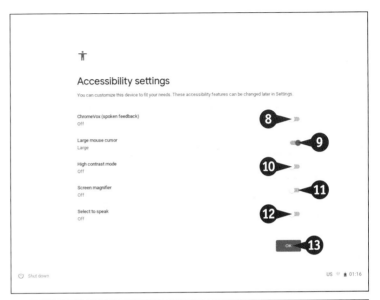

TIP

If I change the keyboard layout during setup, must every user use the layout I apply?
No. The keyboard layout you apply during setup becomes the default layout for the Chromebook, but you can add other layouts afterward, as needed. As long as you add the keyboard layouts needed, any user can change the current keyboard layout from the Sign-In screen. So even if your initial keyboard layout returns different letters than those shown on the Chromebook's keys, each user will be able to apply their preferred layout and type their password without a problem.

continued ▶

During the setup routine, you connect the Chromebook to a Wi-Fi network so that it can access the Internet and contact Google's servers. You then log in with the Google Account that you want to make the owner account for the Chromebook. The owner account is the administrator account for the Chromebook and can access and change key system settings that other users cannot change.

You can change the owner account for a Chromebook by "powerwashing" it and then setting it up again. See the section "Powerwash Your Chromebook" in Chapter 12 for details.

Set Up Your Chromebook (continued)

The Join Wi-Fi Network dialog box opens.

Ⓐ The SSID box shows the *service set identifier*, abbreviated to *SSID*, for the Wi-Fi network.

⑯ Click **Password** and type the Wi-Fi password.

Ⓑ You can click **Show password** (⊙ changes to ⊗) to display the password characters.

⑰ Click **Connect**.

The Join Wi-Fi Network dialog box closes.

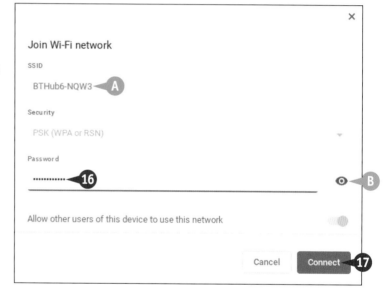

Chrome OS attempts to connect to the network using the password you provided.

Assuming Chrome OS succeeds in connecting to the network, the Google Chrome OS Terms screen appears.

⑱ In the System Security Setting area, set the **Optional: Help make Chrome OS better by automatically sending diagnostic and usage data to Google** switch to Off (   ) if you do not want to share anonymized diagnostic and usage data with Google.

⑲ Click **Accept and continue**.

The Checking for Updates screen appears.

If updates are available, Chrome OS may download and install them.

Next, the Sign In to Your Chromebook screen appears.

20 Type the email address or phone number for your Google Account.

C If you find you need to create a new Google Account at this point, click **More options**, click **Create account**, and then follow the prompts.

21 Click **Next**.

The Hi screen appears, prompting you for your password.

22 Type your password.

23 Click **Next**.

The You're Signed In! screen appears.

24 Look at the sync options, such as Chrome Sync and Personalize Google Services.

25 If you want to review the sync options after setup, click **Review sync options following setup** (☐ changes to (☑).

26 Click **Accept and continue**.

TIP

Why is the Allow Other Users of This Device to Use This Network switch disabled?
While you are setting up the Chromebook, the Allow Other Users of This Device to Use This Network switch in the Join Wi-Fi Network dialog box is set to On but disabled so that you cannot set it to Off. This is because all users of the Chromebook will need to use this Wi-Fi network to sign in to the Chromebook until you add other Wi-Fi networks, which you can do once you complete setup.

continued ▶

During setup, you can choose whether to back up data to Google Drive and whether to allow apps and services to access data about your Chromebook's location.

If you have a phone running Google's Android operating system, you can connect it to your Chromebook so that the two can work together. If you prefer not to make this connection during setup, you can make it at any point later. This feature works only for Android phones, not for other phones, such as iPhones.

Set Up Your Chromebook (continued)

The Google Play Apps and Services screen appears.

27 Click **Back up to Google Drive** (changes to) if you do not want to back up data to Google Drive.

28 Click **More**.

Further options on the Google Play Apps and Services screen appear.

29 Click **Use location** (changes to) if you do not want to allow apps and services to use your Chromebook's location.

D Select **Review Google Play options following setup** ( ) if you want to review your settings for Google Play after setup ends.

30 Click **Accept**.

The Connect to Your Phone screen appears.

E The Select a Device list shows the Android phone or phones associated with your Google Account.

31 If you want to connect your Android phone to your Chromebook, verify that the Select a Device list shows the correct phone, click **Accept & continue**, and then follow the instructions in the section "Connect Your Android Phone to Your Chromebook" in Chapter 4. Otherwise, click **No thanks** to skip connecting your phone.

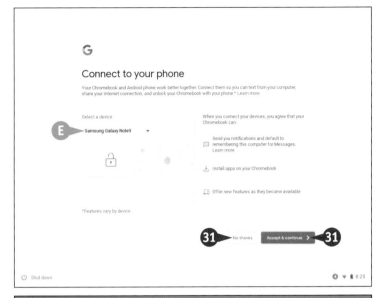

After you connect your phone or after you choose to skip connecting your phone, the Howdy dialog box opens.

F You can click **Close window** (✕) to close the Howdy dialog box without taking the tour.

32 Click **Take a tour** to view an introduction to Chrome OS.

Note: To shut down your Chromebook, press **Power**. In the Power menu that appears in the middle of the screen, click **Power off**.

TIP

Should I back up my data to Google Drive?
Backing up your data to Google Drive is normally a good idea, because it enables you to protect your data from accidental loss, work on the data from any device that has an Internet connection, and restore your data if a problem occurs. However, it is vital that you protect your Google Account with a strong password and two-factor authentication to prevent malefactors from taking over your account and accessing your data. If you work with ultra-sensitive data, or company or organization policies forbid the use of online storage, you may need to use removable storage, such as microSD cards or USB drives, instead.

Start Your Chromebook and Sign In

When you are ready to begin a computing session, start your Chromebook and sign in to your Google Account. After you start your Chromebook, Chrome OS loads and automatically displays the sign-in screen. On this screen, you click your user name and enter your password to sign in.

If you have just set up the Chromebook, your user name may be the only one on the sign-in screen — in which case, Chrome OS selects your user name for you, so you do not need to select it.

Start Your Chromebook and Sign In

1 Press **Power**.

Your Chromebook starts, and the sign-in screen appears.

2 Click the account you want to use.

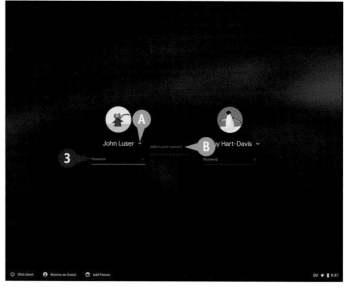

The account becomes selected.

A If you need to see more information about the account, including the email address, click **Expand** (˅) to the right of the user name.

B The pop-up panel displays information about the account.

Note: Displaying more information is especially helpful when the sign-in screen includes two or more accounts with the same user name, and the icons do not enable you to distinguish the accounts.

3 Click **Password**.

The Password field becomes selected.

④ Type the password for the account.

⑤ Click **Sign in** (→) or press Enter.

Chrome OS verifies your credentials and signs you in.

The desktop appears, and you can start using Chrome OS.

Chrome OS will not accept my password. What could be wrong?

Caps Lock might be on, or Chrome OS might be set to use a different keyboard layout than you believe you are using.

Look first to see if Caps Lock (🔼) appears on the right side of the Password field. If so, press Alt + 🔍 to turn off Caps Lock, removing the symbol.

Next, click the status area in the lower-right corner of the screen to display the system menu, click **Keyboard** (🖥) to display the Input Methods menu, and then click the keyboard layout you want to use. For example, you might click **US** for a standard US keyboard layout.

Explore the Chrome OS Desktop

Your Chromebook runs Google's operating system called Chrome OS, which is designed to be easy to use and to run well on computers with relatively modest hardware. The Chrome OS desktop, which appears after you sign in to your Google Account, is the area on which you open apps and windows.

The key components of the Chrome OS desktop are the wallpaper that forms its background, the control strip called the *shelf*, and the system menu that gives you quick access to settings.

Explore the Chrome OS Desktop

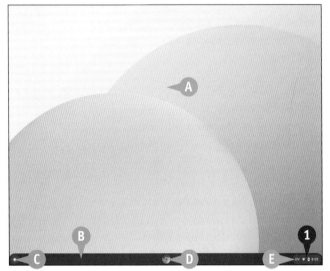

Ⓐ The wallpaper forms the background to the desktop.

Ⓑ The shelf is a control bar that initially appears across the bottom of the screen.

Ⓒ The Launcher icon (⊙) appears at the left end of the shelf.

Ⓓ Icons for "pinned" apps and running apps appear on the shelf. In this example, only the Chrome app icon (◉) appears.

Ⓔ The status area shows reference information, such as the time and the battery status.

❶ Click the status area.

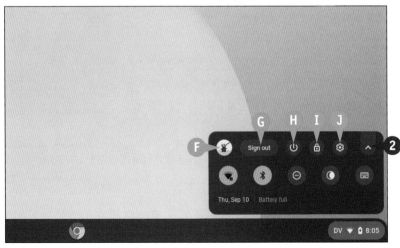

The system menu opens. Normally, the system menu opens in its collapsed form at first.

Ⓕ You can click your account icon to display account information.

Ⓖ You can click **Sign out** to sign out.

Ⓗ You can click **Shut down** (⏻) to shut down your Chromebook.

Ⓘ You can click **Lock** (🔒) to lock the Chromebook's screen.

Ⓙ You can click **Settings** (⚙) to open the Settings app.

❷ Click **Expand menu** (⌃).

The system menu expands to its larger size.

Ⓚ You can click **Collapse menu** (⌄) to collapse the system menu again.

Ⓛ You can click **Toggle volume** (🔊 changes to 🔇) to toggle audio muting on and off.

Ⓜ You can drag the **Volume** slider to adjust the audio volume.

Ⓝ The Brightness slider is located to the right of the Brightness icon (⚙). You can drag the **Brightness** slider to adjust the screen brightness.

3 Click **Audio settings** (🔊).

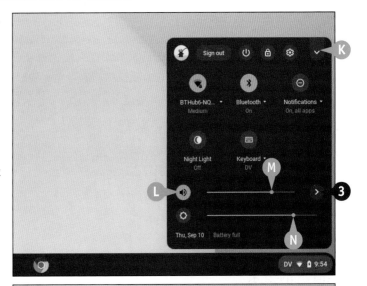

The Audio Settings menu appears, replacing the system menu. From here, you can configure audio devices and settings.

Note: You can also click the text labels below some of the other icons on the system menu to display a related menu. For example, click the Network label — which shows the current Wi-Fi network's name — to display the Network menu, or click the **Notifications** label to display the Notifications menu.

Ⓞ You can click **Previous menu** (⬅) to go back to the previous menu — in this case, the system menu.

4 Click anywhere on the desktop.

The menu closes.

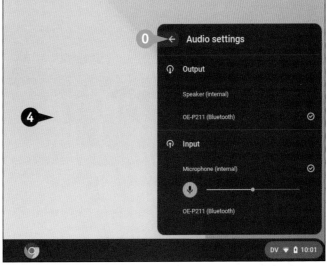

TIP

How can I customize the Chrome OS desktop?
You can customize the Chrome OS desktop in several ways. First, you can apply a wallpaper of your choice; see the section "Change the Wallpaper" in Chapter 2. Second, you can move the shelf to the left side or the right side of the screen, hide the shelf while you are not using it, or change the apps pinned to it; see the section "Configure the Shelf" in Chapter 2. Third, you can change the display scaling, making items look larger or smaller; see the section "Change the Display Scaling" in Chapter 2.

Point, Click, and Scroll with the Touchpad

The touchpad built into your Chromebook enables you to move the cursor around the screen and give commands. Slide your finger across the touchpad to move the cursor over the appropriate object, and then press the bottom section of the touchpad down to click. The number of times you click, and the manner in which you click, determine what happens to the object at which you point.

This section uses the Files app as an example. To open the Files app, press **Shift** while you click **Launcher** (⊙), and then click **Files** (▣).

Point, Click, and Scroll with the Touchpad

Point and Click

1 Slide your finger across the touchpad until the cursor points at the appropriate item.

2 Press the bottom section of the touchpad once to click the touchpad. This is a single click.

Ⓐ The object becomes highlighted, indicating that it is now selected.

Note: To scroll, place two fingers on the touchpad, and then slide them toward the screen to scroll down or toward yourself to scroll up.

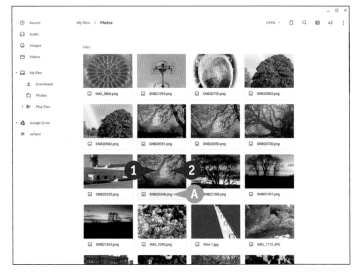

Double-Click

1 Slide your finger across the touchpad until the cursor points at the appropriate item.

2 Click the bottom section of the touchpad twice.

Ⓑ Chrome OS causes the app associated with the file type represented by the item to open and display the file's contents.

In this case, the file is a photo. Chrome OS causes the Gallery app to open and display the photo.

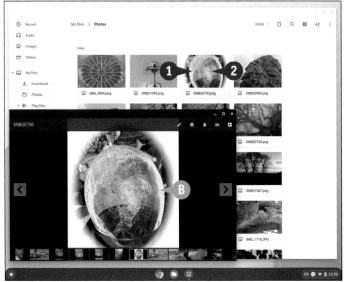

Point, Click, and Drag

1 Slide your finger across the touchpad until the cursor points at the appropriate item.

2 Press down the bottom section of the touchpad and hold it.

The object at which you were pointing becomes attached to the cursor and remains attached until you release the touchpad.

3 Drag your finger on the touchpad to move the object.

4 When you reach the object's destination, lift your finger from the touchpad.

Right-Click

1 Slide your finger across the touchpad until the cursor points at the appropriate item.

Note: To select more than one item at the same time, click the first item, and then press and hold **Ctrl** while you click each of the remaining objects.

2 Using two fingers, click the bottom section of the touchpad. You can also hold down **Alt** and click with one finger.

The contextual menu opens.

3 Point to the appropriate command on the menu, and then click the touchpad once to give the command.

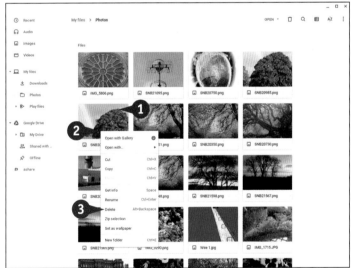

TIP

Can I click by tapping on the touchpad?
Yes, you can click by tapping. You may need to enable the Tap-to-Click feature. Click the status area to open the system menu, and then click **Settings** (⚙) to open the Settings window. Click **Device** (🖥) to display the Device section of the Settings screen, click **Touchpad** to display the Touchpad screen, and then set the **Enable tap-to-click** switch to On (🔘). If you want to be able to tap and then drag, set the **Enable tap dragging** switch to On (🔘) as well. To tap-drag, you tap the object, keep holding the tap, and then drag the object, either with the same finger or with another finger.

Using the Touchscreen

I f your Chromebook has a touchscreen rather than a regular screen, you can give commands via gestures on the screen. You can use the touchscreen at any time to give standard commands, such as tapping an item to select it. But the touchscreen is especially helpful when you have put your Chromebook into Tablet Mode — for example, by folding the keyboard over so that it is hidden underneath the screen. Tablet Mode makes available several extra touchscreen gestures that you cannot use in Laptop Mode.

Click and Right-Click

To click, simply tap the item.

To right-click, tap and hold the item until the contextual menu opens.

Scroll

To scroll, drag your finger in the opposite direction. For example, drag up to scroll down, or drag left to scroll right.

Display the Shelf When Autohide Is On

If you have enabled Autohide for the shelf, swipe toward the middle of the screen from the edge at which the shelf is hiding.

Display the Launcher

To display the Launcher, swipe toward the middle of the screen from the shelf. For example, if the shelf is at the bottom of the screen, swipe up from the bottom of the screen to open the Launcher.

Zoom In or Out

To zoom in, place two fingers close together on the screen, and then move them apart.

To zoom out, place two fingers apart on the screen, and then move them closer together.

Display All Open Windows

In Tablet Mode, tap **Screenshot** (▣) at the right end of the shelf or swipe down from the top of the screen or swipe up from the bottom of the screen to display thumbnails of all the open windows. You can then tap the window you want to display.

Split the Screen Between Two Apps

After displaying all open windows, tap and hold the window you want to position on the left or right side of the screen. When the window expands slightly, drag it to that side of the screen, making it snap to half the screen size. Then tap the window you want on the other half of the screen. You can then adjust the split by dragging the divider bar left or right.

Close a Window

In Tablet Mode, swipe down on a window to close it.

Take a Screenshot

In Tablet Mode, press **Power** and **Volume Up** at the same time. These are the physical buttons, not keys on the keyboard.

Using the Keyboard

Each Chromebook has a physical keyboard for entering text and giving commands. Most of the keys — the letter keys and spacebar, the number and symbol keys, and the modifier keys such as Shift and Ctrl — are in their normal positions. However, to make Chrome OS easier to use, Google has customized the Chromebook's top row of keys — normally the function keys — and replaced the Caps Lock key with the Search key.

Using the Keyboard

A Search Key

Press Q to open the Launcher bar and activate the Search box. Press Alt+Q to toggle Caps Lock on or off.

B Back Key

Press ← to go back to the previous page.

C Forward Key

Press → to go forward to a page from which you have gone back.

D Refresh Key

Press C to refresh the current page.

E Fullscreen Key

Press □ to toggle the active window between full screen and its previous size.

F Switch Windows Key

Press ▭ to display all open windows. Press Ctrl+▭ to capture the full screen. Press Ctrl+Shift+▭ to capture a partial screen.

G Turn Brightness Down Key

Press ○ to reduce the screen brightness by one step.

H Turn Brightness Up Key

Press ○ to increase the screen brightness by one step.

I Mute Key

Press ◁ to toggle muting on or off.

J Volume Down Key

Press ◁ to reduce the volume by one step.

K Volume Up Key

Press ◁ to increase the volume by one step.

L Power Key

Press ⏻ to give a Power command, such as turning the Chromebook on or off. This key appears on non-touchscreen Chromebooks.

Lock Chromebook Key

Press 🔒 to lock the Chromebook. This key appears on touchscreen Chromebooks in place of the Power key. Touchscreen Chromebooks have a separate Power button that is accessible when the keyboard is hidden.

Using Keyboard Shortcuts

You can perform almost any action on the Chromebook by using the touchpad; and, as a visual guide, this book concentrates on taking actions with clicks rather than keyboard shortcuts. But Chrome OS includes a wide variety of keyboard shortcuts that can save you time and effort in your computing.

This section shows you some of the most widely useful keyboard shortcuts — including the keyboard shortcut for opening the Shortcuts app, which gives you details of all the Chrome OS keyboard shortcuts.

Keyboard Shortcuts for Frequent Actions

Keyboard Shortcut	Effect	Keyboard Shortcut	Effect
Ctrl + C	Copies the selected item to the Clipboard	Ctrl + Shift + 0	Resets the screen zoom to 100%
Ctrl + X	Cuts the selected item to the Clipboard	Ctrl + F	Issues a Find command or Search command, depending on the app
Ctrl + V	Pastes in the Clipboard's contents at the cursor's location	Ctrl + G	Issues the Find Next command
Ctrl + Shift + −	Zooms the screen out by one step	Ctrl + Shift + G	Issues the Find Previous command
Ctrl + Shift + +	Zooms the screen in by one step	Ctrl + P	Issues a Print command
		Q + L	Locks the Chromebook

Keyboard Shortcuts for the Chrome Browser

Keyboard Shortcut	Effect	Keyboard Shortcut	Effect
Ctrl + L	Selects the contents of the omnibox	Ctrl + J	Opens a new tab containing the Downloads list
Alt + D	Selects the contents of the omnibox	Ctrl + N	Opens a new window
Ctrl + E	Selects the contents of the omnibox and activates Search	Ctrl + Shift + N	Opens a new Incognito window
Ctrl + K	Selects the contents of the omnibox and activates Search	Ctrl + T	Opens a new tab
Ctrl + Enter	Completes a partial URL by adding *www* before and *.com* after, and then attempts to load the resulting address	Ctrl + ←	Displays the previous tab
		Ctrl + →	Displays the next tab
		Ctrl + 1 through Ctrl + 8	Displays the first tab through the eighth tab in the current window
Ctrl + R	Reloads the current page	Ctrl + 9	Displays the last tab in the current window
Ctrl + D	Adds a bookmark for the current page	Ctrl + Tab	Displays the next tab in the current window
Ctrl + Shift + D	Adds bookmarks for all pages in tabs in the active window	Ctrl + W	Closes the active tab in the current window
Ctrl + H	Displays the History screen	Ctrl + Shift + B	Toggles the display of the Bookmarks bar
		Ctrl + Shift + O	Toggles the display of the Bookmark Manager

Keyboard Shortcuts for Navigation

Keyboard Shortcut	Effect
[Q]+[←]	Gives the Home command
[Q]+[→]	Gives the End command
[Q]+[↑]	Gives the Page Up command
[Q]+[↓]	Gives the Page Down command

Keyboard Shortcuts for Working with Text

Keyboard Shortcut	Effect
Ctrl + Backspace	Deletes the word to the left of the cursor.
[Q] + Backspace	Deletes the character to the right of the cursor.
[Q] + Alt	Toggles Caps Lock on and off.
Ctrl + [←]	Moves the cursor to the start of the previous word. If the cursor is within a word, moves the cursor to the start of that word.
Ctrl + [→]	Moves the cursor to the start of the next word.
Ctrl + Shift + [←]	Selects to the start of the previous word. If the cursor is within a word, selects to the start of that word.
Ctrl + Shift + [→]	Selects to the end of the current word. If the cursor is within a word, selects to the end of that word.
Ctrl + Shift + [V]	Pastes the Clipboard's contents as unformatted text.

Keyboard Shortcuts for Advanced Moves

Keyboard Shortcut	Effect
Ctrl + Alt + [	With multiple users signed in, switches to the previous user
Ctrl + Alt +]	With multiple users signed in, switches to the next user
[Q] + Esc	Opens the Task Manager window
Ctrl + [▭]	Captures a full-screen screenshot
Ctrl + Shift + [▭]	Captures a partial-screen screenshot
Ctrl + [▯]	Switches an external display between mirroring the built-in display and extending the built-in display
Ctrl + Shift + [C]	Rotates the display 90 degrees clockwise
Ctrl + Alt + Shift + [C]	Rotates the active window 360 degrees clockwise
Ctrl + Alt + [?]	Opens the Shortcuts reference window

Connect to a Wi-Fi Network

hromebooks typically connect to the Internet through a wireless connection to a Wi-Fi network. During the setup routine, you connect your Chromebook to one Wi-Fi network. You can add other Wi-Fi networks later, as needed, and switch networks by using the system menu and the Network menu.

Some Chromebook models have built-in Ethernet adapters, allowing you to connect the Chromebook to a network using an Ethernet cable. If you need to use Ethernet with a Chromebook that has no built-in adapter, get a USB Ethernet adapter to add Ethernet capability.

Connect to a Wi-Fi Network

Ⓐ The Wi-Fi icon (🔽) indicates that there is no connection.

① Click the status area.

The system menu opens.

② Click the Network label, which shows either the current network's name or *Not connected: No networks*.

Note: Click the Network label — the text — rather than the icon. Clicking the icon toggles Wi-Fi on or off.

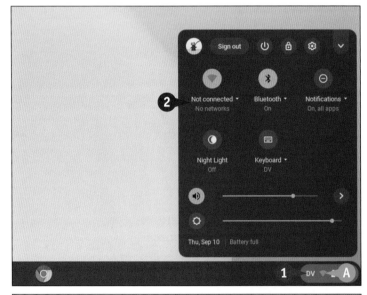

The Network menu opens.

Ⓑ You can click **Network info** (ⓘ) to display the Media Access Control address, or MAC address, of the Wi-Fi adapter. This is a group of hexadecimal pairs, such as 34:CE:F6:59:E1:59. You may need the MAC address for whitelisting your Chromebook on a restricted network.

Note: When the Chromebook is connected to a network, the network information includes the IP address.

③ Click the network to which you want to connect.

Note: If the network does not appear on the Network menu, it may be hidden. See the tip for advice.

The Join Wi-Fi Network dialog box opens.

Ⓒ The SSID box shows the network's name.

Ⓓ The Security drop-down menu shows the security type.

④ Type the password.

Ⓔ You can click **Show Password** (👁) to display the characters you type in the Password field.

⑤ Set the **Allow other users of this device to use this network** switch to On (⬤) or Off ( ), as needed.

⑥ Click **Connect**.

The Join Wi-Fi Network dialog box closes.

Chrome OS connects to the Wi-Fi network.

Ⓕ The Wi-Fi icon (📶) in the status area indicates that there is a connection.

⑦ To see the connected network name, click the status area.

The system menu opens.

Ⓖ The Network label shows the network name and the connection strength, such as *Medium*.

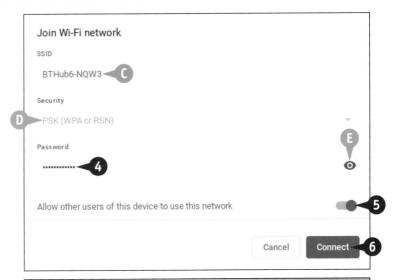

TIP

How do I connect to a Wi-Fi network whose name does not appear on the Network menu?
Click **Join Other Wi-Fi Networks** (🔲) to display the Join Wi-Fi Network dialog box. Type the Wi-Fi network's name, or SSID, in the SSID box. Click **Security** (▼), and then click the appropriate security type, such as **PSK (WPA or RSN)**. Click **Password**, and then type the password; click **Show Password** (👁) if you want to see the characters you type. Set the **Allow other users of this device to use this network** switch to On (⬤) or Off ( ), as needed. Then click **Connect**.

Give Commands

The easiest way to give commands on your Chromebook is by using the cursor. You use the touchpad to move the cursor over the object you want to affect, and then click, double-click, or right-click the object. For example, you can use the cursor to give a command on a menu, on a contextual menu, or on a toolbar.

You can also give commands by using keyboard shortcuts, as discussed in the section "Using Keyboard Shortcuts," earlier in this chapter.

Give Commands

Give a Command from a Menu

1 On the shelf, click the app you want to launch or activate — **Chrome** (🌀) in this example.

Note: If the app is running and you can see its window, you can click the window to activate the app.

The app becomes active.

2 Move the cursor over **Menu** (⋮) and click.

The menu opens.

3 If the command you want to give is on a submenu, click or highlight the submenu.

The submenu opens.

4 Click the command.

The app performs the action associated with the command.

Give a Command from a Contextual Menu

1 On the shelf, click the app you want to launch or activate — **Files** (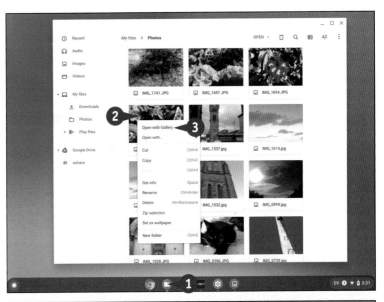) in this example.

The app becomes active.

2 Move the cursor over the object you want to affect, and then click with two fingers.

The contextual menu opens.

3 Click the command.

The app performs the action associated with the command.

Give a Command from a Toolbar

1 On the shelf, click the app you want to launch or activate — **Gallery** () in this example.

The app becomes active.

2 Click the appropriate button on the toolbar.

The app performs the action associated with the command.

A In this example, clicking **Edit** () makes the Gallery app display another toolbar containing editing tools.

Is it better to use the menus or the toolbars — or keyboard shortcuts?

Use whichever means of giving commands you prefer. A toolbar makes it easy to see the available commands, whereas the full menu may provide access to a more extensive range of commands. A contextual menu displays only commands available for the object from which you invoked the menu.

Keyboard shortcuts have more of a learning curve; but once you know the shortcuts you need, they are usually the fastest way of giving commands.

Open, Close, and Manage Windows

ost Chrome OS apps use windows to display information so that you can view it and work with it. Some windows are fixed in size, but you can resize most windows to the size you need or expand a window so that it fills the screen. You can move windows to where you need them or minimize unneeded windows to the shelf.

Chrome OS includes commands for "snapping" a window quickly to one side or other of the screen, enabling you to position two windows side by side quickly and precisely.

Open, Close, and Manage Windows

1 Click **Chrome** (🔵) on the shelf.

Note: If Chrome (🔵) does not appear on the shelf, press **Shift**+click **Launcher** (⭕) to display the Launcher full screen, and then click **Chrome** (🔵).

A Chrome browser window opens.

Ⓐ You can click the window's title bar and drag it to a different location on the screen.

2 Click and drag the lower-right corner of the window down and to the right.

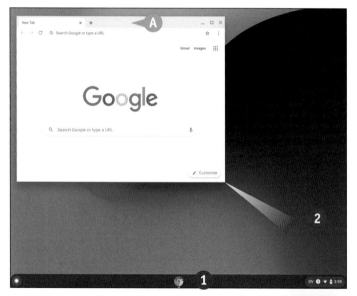

The window's size changes as you drag.

Note: You can drag any corner or border of a window to resize it.

3 Click **Maximize** (◻).

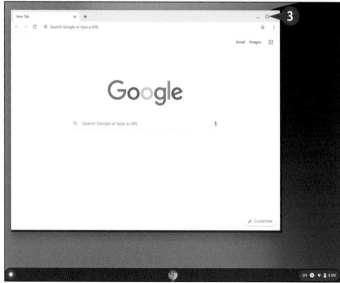

28

Chrome OS maximizes the window, making it take up all the space on the screen — apart from the shelf, if the shelf is not hidden.

4 Click **Restore** (◻).

Chrome OS restores the window to its previous size.

B You can click **Minimize** (▬) to minimize the window, effectively hiding it.

5 When you are ready to close the window, click **Close** (✕).

The window closes.

TIP

How do I split the screen between two windows?
After opening two or more windows, press ▢. Chrome OS displays a thumbnail of each open window. Click the window you want to position on the left, and then drag it toward the left edge of the screen. When Chrome OS displays shading over the left half of the screen, indicating the space the window will occupy, release the window. Chrome OS resizes and repositions the window, moving the remaining thumbnails to the other half of the screen. Then click the thumbnail you want to display in that half of the screen.

Work with Notifications

Chrome OS displays notifications to keep you up to date with what is happening in your apps. When a suitable event occurs, a pop-up panel containing the details of the notification appears briefly above the status area. You can view the notification; take action with the notification, if appropriate; dismiss the notification; or simply wait for Chrome OS to remove the notification automatically after a few seconds.

Work with Notifications

Ⓐ A pop-up panel appears above the status area, notifying you about an event that has occurred.

Depending on what the notification covers, the pop-up panel may contain links for actions.

Ⓑ For example, you can click **Show in folder** to display the screenshot in the folder that contains it.

Ⓒ You can click **COPY TO CLIPBOARD** to copy the screenshot to the Clipboard so that you can paste it into a file.

❶ If Collapse (⌃) appears, click **Collapse** (⌃).

Chrome OS collapses the notification panel to its smaller size, hiding the data area.

Ⓓ You can click **Close** (✕) to close the notification panel and dismiss the notification.

Ⓔ The Notifications readout shows the total number of notifications.

❷ Click **Notifications** (such as ②).

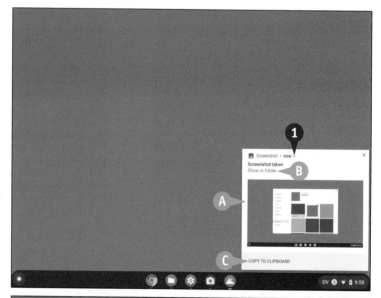

The list of notifications opens above the system menu.

3 Move the cursor over the notification you want to examine or affect.

Controls appear in the upper-right corner of the notification.

F You can click **Snooze** (🚫) to snooze the notification. In the panel that appears, click **Snoozed for** (⌄), and then click the length of time, such as **15 minutes** or **2 hours**.

4 Click **Settings** (⚙).

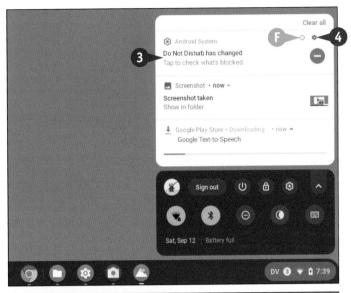

The notification displays the information pane, which shows details of any settings you can change.

G In this example, there are no settings you can change for Do Not Disturb.

5 Click **OK** to close the information pane, returning to the notification pane.

6 When you finish reviewing notifications, click **Clear all**.

Chrome OS clears all the notifications.

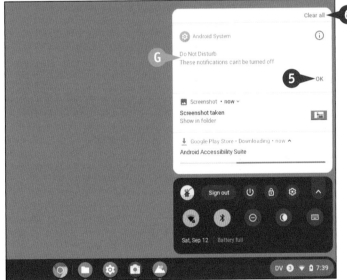

TIP

How can I reduce the number of notifications I receive?
To reduce the number of notifications, you can set Chrome OS to display notifications only from specific apps and services. When you want to see no notifications at all, you can turn on the Do Not Disturb feature. See the section "Configure Notifications and Do Not Disturb" in Chapter 2 for details.

Lock and Unlock Your Chromebook's Screen

When you need to step away from your Chromebook, you can lock the screen, preventing others from seeing your open apps and windows or from using the Chromebook without unlocking the screen.

To save battery power, you can configure Chrome OS to put your Chromebook to sleep when you close the cover. For security, you can set Chrome OS to display the lock screen when your Chromebook wakes from sleep, requiring you to enter your password or PIN. See the section "Set a Screen Lock for Security" in Chapter 2 for details.

Lock and Unlock Your Chromebook's Screen

1 Click the status area.

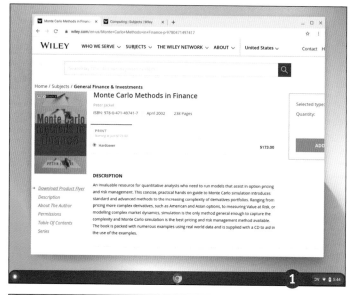

The system menu opens.

2 Click **Lock** (🔒).

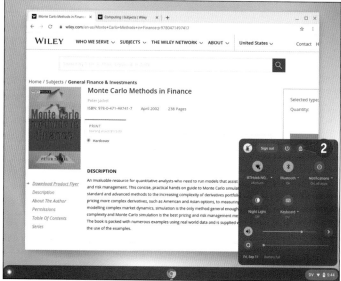

The lock screen appears.

Ⓐ You can click **Sign out** (⬜) to sign out of your Google Account.

Note: Signing out of your Google Account saves any work you had open. Shutting down your Chromebook signs you out of your Google Account first, again saving your work.

Ⓑ You can click **Shut down** (⏻) to shut down your Chromebook.

❸ Type your password.

❹ Click **Sign in** (→) or press Enter.

Chrome OS unlocks the screen.

Ⓒ Your apps appear as you left them.

You can resume your work where you left off.

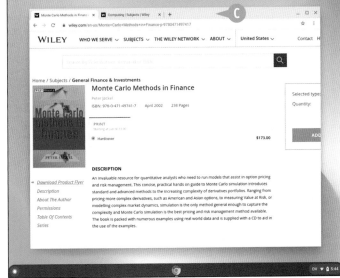

Is there a keyboard shortcut for locking the screen?
Yes: Press 🔍+🔲 to lock the screen.

How do I make the lock screen appear when I wake my Chromebook from sleep?
You need to enable the Show Lock Screen When Waking from Sleep setting. Click the status area to display the system menu, and then click **Settings** (⚙) to open the Settings window. Click **People** (👤) in the left pane to display the People section of the Settings screen, and then click **Security and sign-in** to display the Security and Sign-In screen. Here, set the **Show lock screen when waking from sleep** switch to On (⬤).

Put Your Chromebook to Sleep and Wake It Up

When you are not using your Chromebook, you should put it to sleep to save battery power. Sleep uses only a minimal amount of power but enables you to resume your work in seconds when you wake the Chromebook again.

The standard way of putting a Chromebook to sleep is to close the cover. This method works well as long as the Sleep When Cover Is Closed setting is enabled. See the tip for information on how to enable this setting.

Put Your Chromebook to Sleep and Wake It Up

1 When you are ready to put your Chromebook to sleep, close its cover.

Note: Connecting the Chromebook to an external display disables the Sleep When Cover Is Closed setting. This enables you to use the Chromebook with just an external display rather than having to use the internal display as well.

The Chromebook goes to sleep.

2 When you are ready to wake the Chromebook, open the cover.

The Sign-In screen appears, with your user account selected.

3 Type your password.

4 Click **Sign in** (→) or press Enter.

Chrome OS signs you in.

Ⓐ Your apps and windows appear, as they were when you put the Chromebook to sleep.

You can resume work where you stopped.

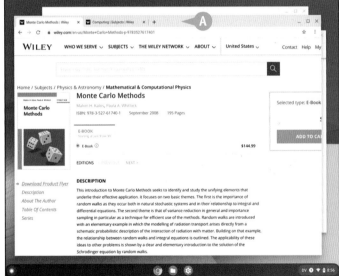

TIP

How do I make my Chromebook go to sleep when I close the cover?

You need to enable the Sleep When Cover Is Closed setting. Click the status area to display the system menu, and then click **Settings** (⚙) to open the Settings window. Click **Device** (🖥) in the left pane to display the Device section of the Settings screen, and then click **Power** to display the Power screen. Here, set the **Sleep when cover is closed** switch to On (⬤).

Sign Out and Sign Back In

When you finish a session using your Chromebook, you can sign out of the Chromebook. When you sign out, Chrome OS automatically saves your work and then signs you out of your Google Account.

When you are ready to resume work, you can quickly sign back in to your account, either on the Chromebook or on another device that uses the same Google Account.

Sign Out and Sign Back In

1 Click the status area.

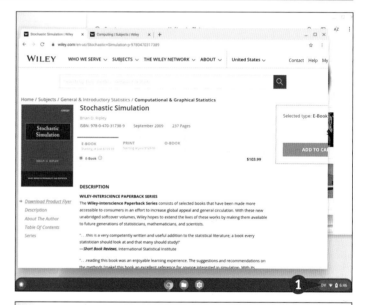

The system menu opens.

2 Click **Sign out**.

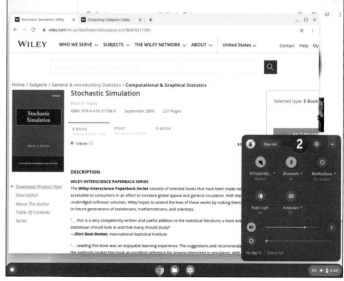

Chrome OS saves any ongoing work and then signs you out of your Google Account.

The Sign-In screen appears.

3 When you are ready to sign in again, click your account if it is not already selected.

4 Type your password.

5 Click **Sign in** (→) or press `Enter`.

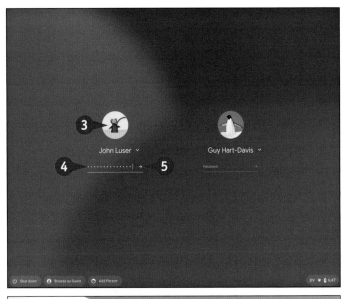

Chrome OS signs you in to your Google Account.

A Chrome OS opens the apps in which it saved work for you.

Note: Chrome OS may not restore all your windows. In this example, Chrome OS restores the Chrome browser window that was open but does not restore the Files app window, which did not contain unsaved work.

You can resume work where you left off.

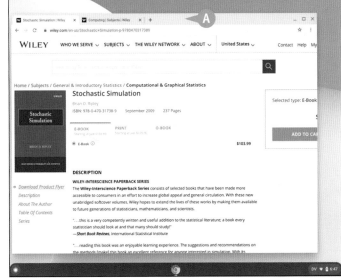

TIPS

Is there a keyboard shortcut for signing out?
Yes. Press `Ctrl`+`Shift`+`Q` twice in immediate succession.

Do any Chromebook models have biometric authentication?
Yes — a few high-end Chromebook models have biometric authentication, typically a fingerprint scanner that enables you to sign in quickly. Google's Pixel Slate device, a tablet that runs Chrome OS, also has a fingerprint scanner.

Shut Down Your Chromebook

When you finish using your Chromebook and you do not plan to use it for a while, you can shut it down using either the system menu or the Power menu. When you give the Shut Down command, Chrome OS saves any unsaved work for you and signs you out of your Google Account before shutting down the Chromebook.

Technically, shutting down your Chromebook is more secure than putting the Chromebook to sleep. But if you plan to use the Chromebook again soon, putting the Chromebook to sleep is usually more practical than shutting it down.

Shut Down Your Chromebook

Shut Down Using the System Menu

1 Click the status area.

The system menu appears.

2 Click **Shut down** (⏻).

Chrome OS saves any unsaved work, logs you out of your Google Account, and shuts down the Chromebook.

Shut Down Using the Power Menu

1 Press **Power** briefly.

Note: On a non-touchscreen Chromebook, press  in the upper-right corner of the keyboard. On a touchscreen Chromebook, press the Power button, which is usually a hardware button on the side of the Chromebook.

The screen dims.

The Power menu appears.

2 Click **Power off** (⏻).

Chrome OS saves any unsaved work, logs you out of your Google Account, and shuts down the Chromebook.

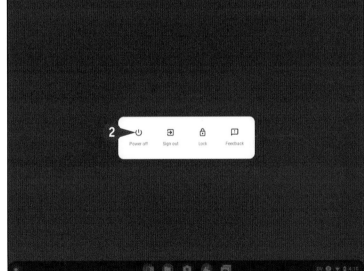

TIP

How do I restart my Chromebook from the user interface?
Unlike many other operating systems, Chrome OS does not have a Restart command in the user interface. The normal way to restart a Chromebook is to shut it down, as explained in the main text of this section, and then power it on again.

CHAPTER 2

Configuring Essential Chrome-book Settings

You can customize many aspects of Chrome OS to make your Chromebook work the way you prefer. You can configure the shelf and the Launcher, change the wallpaper and the display scaling, and adjust a wide range of settings for features from Night Light to Notifications. You can also choose which pages to display when you log in.

Configure the Shelf

The shelf is a control strip that appears on the Chrome OS desktop. By default, the shelf appears at the bottom of the desktop, but you can move it to the left side or right side if you prefer. You can set the shelf to hide itself when you are not using it.

The shelf contains the Launcher icon, which you can click to display the Launcher, plus a row of app icons for launching and switching apps. Some icons are pinned in place for quick access; you can customize the pinned list, as needed.

Configure the Shelf

Configure Autohiding and Shelf Position

1 Right-click anywhere on the desktop.

The context menu appears.

2 To set the shelf to hide itself automatically, click **Autohide shelf**.

The context menu closes.

3 Right-click anywhere on the desktop again.

The context menu appears again.

A The Always Show Shelf command appears in place of the Autohide Shelf command.

4 Click or highlight **Shelf position**.

The Shelf Position submenu opens.

5 Click **Left** (○ changes to ◉).

The context menu closes.

B The shelf appears on the left side of the screen.

6 Right-click anywhere on the desktop once more.

The context menu appears yet again.

7 Click or highlight **Shelf position**.

The Shelf Position submenu opens.

8 Click **Bottom** (○ changes to ◉).

The context menu closes.

The shelf appears at the bottom of the screen.

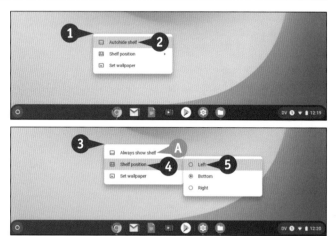

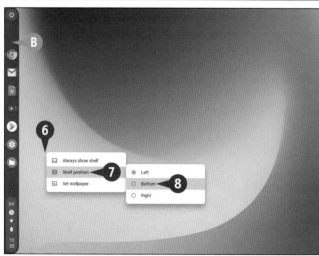

Note: When autohiding is on, the shelf hides automatically when a window is active. To display the shelf, move the pointer to the screen side where the shelf is hiding.

Unpin or Pin an App

1 On the shelf, right-click the app icon you want to unpin.

The context menu opens.

2 Click **Unpin**.

The app icon disappears from the shelf.

3 Click **Launcher** (⊙).

The Launcher bar opens.

4 Click **Full Screen** (ᐱ).

The Launcher expands to full screen.

5 Right-click the app icon you want to pin to the shelf.

The context menu opens.

6 Click **Pin to shelf** (📌).

Chrome pins the app to the shelf.

7 Click **Launcher** (⊙).

The Launcher screen closes.

TIP

How does the shelf behave when I connect an external display to my Chromebook?
When you connect an external display, you can configure the shelf separately for the internal display and the external display. For example, you can set the shelf to autohide on the internal display and appear all the time on the external display.

Configure the Launcher

In Chrome OS, the Launcher is the primary feature for launching apps. To display the Launcher, you click the Launcher button. This button appears at the left end of the shelf when the shelf is at the bottom of the screen; when the shelf is on the left side or right side of the screen, the Launcher button appears at the top of the shelf.

Clicking the Launcher button displays the Launcher bar, which includes a search box and buttons for recent apps. You expand the Launcher to full screen to see all apps and customize the Launcher.

Configure the Launcher

1 Click **Launcher** ( ).

The Launcher bar opens.

2 Click **Full Screen** ( ).

The Launcher appears full screen.

Ⓐ If there are multiple screens of apps, dots appear on the right side of the Launcher screen. The solid white dot represents the current screen. To display another screen, click the appropriate dot or swipe up or down on the touchpad.

3 To rearrange the icons, drag an icon to where you want it to appear.

B The app icon appears in its new position.

4 To create a folder, drag an app icon onto another app icon.

C Chrome OS creates a new folder with the default name *Unnamed*.

5 Click the new folder.

The folder opens.

6 Click the folder's name, and then type a suitable name.

7 Press Return.

The folder takes on the new name.

TIP

What other customizations can I make on the Launcher screen?

You can use drag and drop to customize the pinned items on the shelf. To add an app, drag its icon from the Launcher screen to the shelf, positioning it before the separator line; when the shelf is at the bottom of the screen, drop the icon to the left of the separator line; when the shelf is on the left or right, drop the icon above the separator line.

To remove a pinned app icon, drag it off the shelf.

Change the Wallpaper

You can configure the wallpaper to show the picture you prefer. Chrome OS includes many varied wallpapers, color designs, and solid colors, but you can also use any image file that is in your Chromebook's local file system. For example, you might want to use one of your own photos as wallpaper.

You can also set Chrome OS to change wallpapers for you every day. This feature works only for some categories of wallpapers.

Change the Wallpaper

1 Right-click anywhere on the desktop.

The context menu appears.

2 Click **Set wallpaper** (▣).

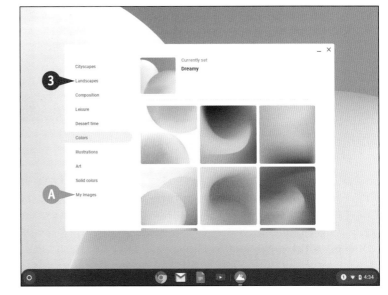

The Wallpaper app window opens.

3 In the left pane, click the wallpaper category you want to browse. For example, click **Landscapes**.

Ⓐ The My Images category contains all the image files that Chrome OS has found in your Chromebook's local file system.

The wallpapers in that category appear.

Ⓑ If the Explore button appears, you can click it to display related wallpapers in a Chrome tab.

④ Click the wallpaper you want to view.

Ⓒ Chrome OS applies the wallpaper.

⑤ Click **Close** (✖).

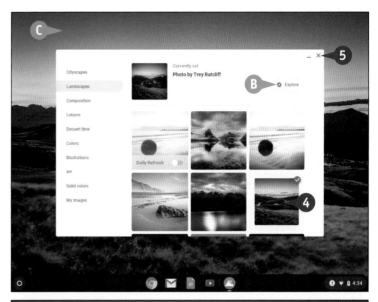

The Wallpaper app window closes.

Ⓓ The wallpaper appears full screen.

TIP

Can I get my Chromebook to change the wallpaper for me?
Yes, you can do this with some categories of wallpapers. Right-click anywhere on the desktop, and then click **Set wallpaper** (🖼) on the context menu to open the Wallpaper app window. In the left pane, click the category of wallpapers you want to use. Then look at the first thumbnail and see whether the Daily Refresh switch appears on it. If so, set the **Daily Refresh** switch to On (⬤). You can then refresh the wallpaper manually by clicking **Refresh** in the upper-right corner of the Wallpaper app window.

Change the Display Scaling

isplay scaling enables you to control the relative size at which items appear on the display or screen. Chrome OS implements display scaling by either stretching the output to make a lower resolution fill the screen or shrinking the output to make a higher resolution fit on the screen.

A Chromebook's screen has a fixed resolution — for example, 1920 x 1080 resolution shows 1920 pixels horizontally by 1080 pixels vertically. This is called the *native resolution*, and the Chromebook normally uses it by default. But if you find items on the screen hard to see, try changing the display scaling.

Set a Suitable Display Resolution

1 Click the status area.

The system menu opens.

2 Click **Settings** (⚙).

The Settings window opens.

3 In the left pane, click **Device** (▢).

The Device category appears.

4 Under the Device heading, click **Displays**.

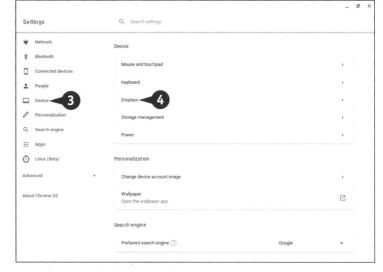

The Displays screen appears.

5 Drag the **Display Size** slider along the Tiny–Huge axis to adjust the size of items on the screen.

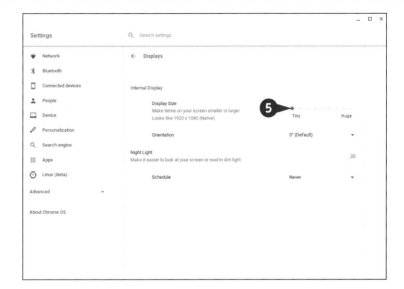

A The display scaling percentage readout appears.

The size of items on screen changes.

6 Click **Close** (✕).

The Settings window closes.

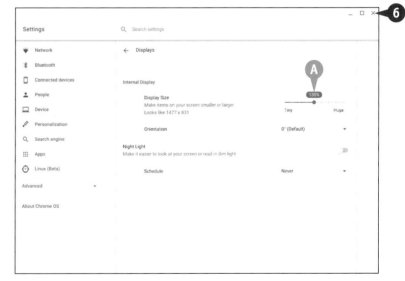

TIP

Which is the best scaling to use?
This depends on your Chromebook and on your eyesight. Start with 100% display scaling, which represents the native resolution. This is theoretically the sharpest, because the displayed pixels align precisely with the physical pixels in the screen rather than being transformed. But if you find that changing the scaling makes the screen look better to you, go with the settings that suit you best.

Configure the Night Light Settings

Blue light from computer screens and other sources can interfere with your body's natural tendency to get sleepy in the evenings. When you are viewing a screen in low light, blue light can also contribute to eyestrain.

Chrome OS provides the Night Light feature to enable you to reduce the amount of blue light your Chromebook's screen emits. You can set Night Light to run on a schedule, automatically reducing blue light for you. You can also enable and disable Night Light manually, as needed.

Configure the Night Light Settings

1 Click the status area.

The system menu opens.

2 Click **Settings** (⚙).

The Settings window opens.

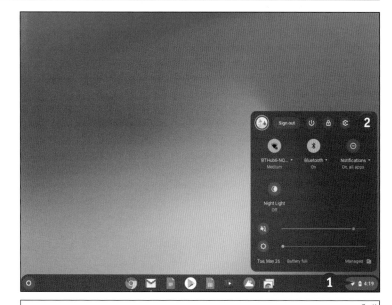

3 In the left pane, click **Device** (🖳).

The Device category appears.

4 Under the Device heading, click **Displays**.

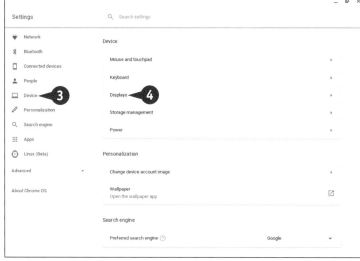

The Displays screen appears.

5 Set the **Night Light** switch to On (⚫).

The Color Temperature control appears.

6 Drag the **Color temperature slider** along the Cooler–Warmer axis to set your preferred color temperature.

Note: A setting toward the Cooler end of the axis has more blue tones. A setting toward the Warmer end of the axis has more yellow tones.

7 Click **Schedule** (▼).

The Schedule drop-down menu opens.

Ⓐ Click **Sunset to Sunrise** if you want your Chromebook to enable Night Light at the predicted times for your location.

8 Click **Custom**.

The Schedule slider appears.

Note: If the current time is outside the scheduled hours, Chrome OS hides the Color Temperature Slider.

9 Drag the blue handles to set the start time and end time for Night Light.

10 Click **Close** (✖).

The Settings window closes.

Choose Power and Sleep Settings

Your Chromebook can run either on battery power or on the charger. To make the most of battery power, you can configure the action Chrome OS takes when you leave your Chromebook idle for several minutes. By default, the Chromebook goes to sleep, but you can set it to turn off the display without going to sleep, or to keep the display on, if you prefer. You can also control whether your Chromebook goes to sleep when you close the lid.

Choose Power and Sleep Settings

1 Click the status area.

The system menu opens.

2 Click **Settings** (⚙).

The Settings window opens.

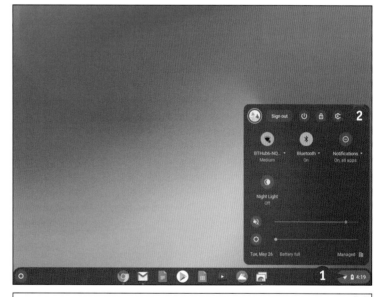

3 In the left pane, click **Device** (🖥).

The Device section appears.

4 In the Device section, click **Power**.

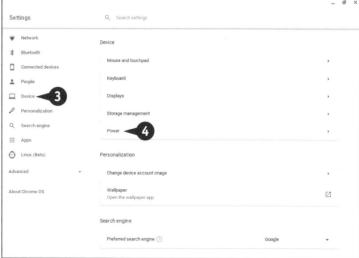

The Power screen appears.

Ⓐ The readout under Power Source shows the estimated runtime on the remaining battery power.

Ⓑ To tell the Chromebook which power source to try to use, click **Power Source** (▼), and then click the appropriate source.

Note: The choices in the Power Source drop-down menu vary by Chromebook model and by what is connected to the USB-C ports.

Note: Most Chromebooks that charge via USB-C designate a USB-C port for charging. For safe charging, use only this port whenever possible.

5 Click **When idle** (▼).

The When Idle drop-down menu opens.

6 Click **Sleep**, **Turn off display**, or **Keep display on**, as needed.

7 Set the **Sleep when cover is closed** switch to On (⚫) if you want the Chromebook to go to sleep automatically when you close the lid.

8 Click **Close** (✕).

The Settings window closes.

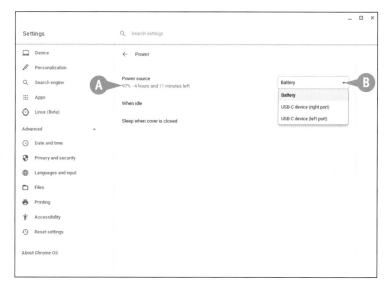

TIP

Why does my Chromebook say "Low-power charger connected" when charging from a different charger?
This message means that the Chromebook has not managed to negotiate a high amount of power from the charger. The problem may be that the charger does not support high-power USB charging or that you are using the wrong port on the charger or on the Chromebook.

Set a Screen Lock for Security

For security, you can set your Chromebook to lock its screen when you wake it from sleep. You must then enter a password or a PIN to unlock the screen before you can use the Chromebook.

If you choose not to have the screen lock when the Chromebook is awakened from sleep, anybody can start using the Chromebook freely using the account that is currently signed in. Leaving the Chromebook accessible like this is seldom a good idea.

Set a Screen Lock for Security

① Click the status area.

The system menu opens.

② Click **Settings** (⚙).

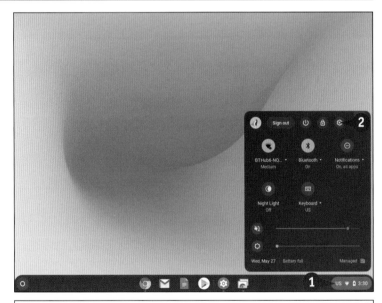

The Settings window opens.

③ Click **People** (👤).

The People category appears.

④ Click **Security and sign-in**.

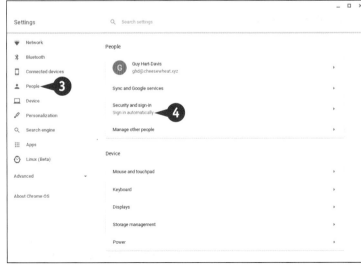

The Confirm Your Password dialog box opens.

5 Type your password.

6 Click **Confirm**.

The Security and Sign-In screen appears.

7 Set the **Show lock screen when waking from sleep** switch to On if you want to lock your Chromebook when it wakes from sleep.

8 In the Lock Screen from Sleep Mode area, click **Password only** (○ changes to ◉) or **PIN or password** (○ changes to ◉), as needed.

Note: Chrome OS supports biometric authentication via fingerprints, but few Chromebooks have fingerprint scanners as of this writing. If your Chromebook does have a scanner, you may find fingerprints a convenient way to sign in and unlock your Chromebook.

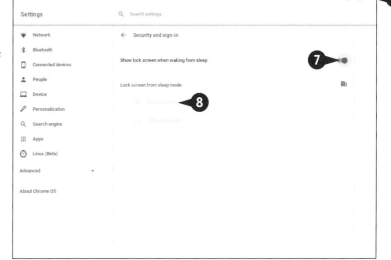

9 Click **Close** (✕).

The Settings window closes.

TIP

Why are the Password Only option button and the PIN or Password option button grayed out?
If the Password Only option button and the PIN or Password option button are grayed out and unavailable, your Chromebook is managed by someone else — for example, by your company, your organization, or your school — rather than by you. The management policy does not allow you to configure these settings.

Configure the Keyboard

To make your Chromebook's keyboard easier to type on, you can adjust the repeat rate and the delay until repeating starts. You can also switch between using the top-row keys for their dedicated functions, such as changing the screen brightness or the volume or as standard function keys — F1, F2, and so on.

Chrome OS also enables you to remap the hardware keys on your Chromebook. For example, you can remap the Search key (🔍) to make it act as a Caps Lock key (Caps lock).

Configure the Keyboard

1 Click the status area.

The system menu opens.

2 Click **Settings** (⚙).

The Settings window opens.

3 Click **Device** (🖵).

The Device category appears.

4 Click **Keyboard.**

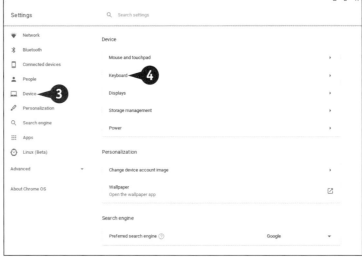

The Keyboard screen appears.

5 Click each drop-down menu, and then click the effect you want the key to have.

For example, click **Search** (▾) to open the Search drop-down menu, and then click the function you want the Search key to have. You can choose **Search**, **Ctrl**, **Alt**, **Caps Lock**, **Escape**, **Backspace**, **Assistant**, or **Disabled**.

6 Set the **Treat top-row keys as function keys** switch to On (⬤) if you want to use the top row keys as F1 through F12.

7 Set the **Enable auto-repeat** switch to On (⬤) if you want keys to repeat when you hold them down.

Note: If you set the **Enable auto-repeat** switch to Off ( ), Chrome OS hides the Delay Before Repeat slider and the Repeat Rate slider.

8 Drag the **Delay before repeat** slider along the Long–Short axis to set the delay.

9 Drag the **Repeat rate** slider along the Slow–Fast axis to set the repeat rate.

10 Click **Close** (✕).

The Settings window closes.

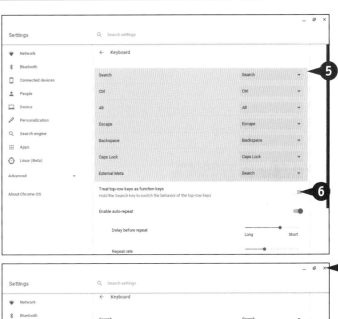

TIPS

What does the External Meta drop-down list control?
The External Meta drop-down list controls the mapping for the meta key on an external keyboard not specifically designed for Chrome OS. On a Windows keyboard, the external meta key is normally the Windows key, ⊞. On a Mac keyboard, the external meta key is normally the Command key, ⌘.

What does the Assistant command do?
This command launches Google Assistant. If Google Assistant is not available for your user account, Chrome OS displays an error message telling you so.

Configure the Touchpad

You can customize the settings for your Chromebook's touchpad to make it work the way you prefer. For example, you can enable or disable the Tap-to-Click feature and the Tap Dragging feature, enable or disable touchpad acceleration, and increase or decrease the speed at which the cursor moves across the screen in response to your finger movements on the touchpad.

You can also change the scrolling direction. With normal scrolling, you move your fingers up the touchpad to scroll the screen down; with Reverse Scrolling enabled, you move your fingers down the touchpad to scroll down.

Configure the Touchpad

1 Click the status area.

The system menu opens.

2 Click **Settings** (⚙).

The Settings window opens.

3 Click **Device** (🖥).

The Device screen appears.

4 Click **Touchpad** or **Mouse and touchpad**.

Note: The name changes from Touchpad to Mouse and Touchpad when a mouse is connected to your Chromebook.

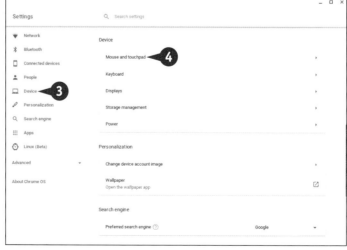

The Touchpad screen or the Mouse and Touchpad screen appears.

Ⓐ The mouse category appears only when a mouse is connected to your Chromebook. You can use these settings to configure the mouse.

⑤ Set the **Enable tap-to-click** switch to On (●) or Off ( ), as needed.

⑥ Set the **Enable tap dragging** switch to On (●) or Off ( ), as needed.

⑦ Set the **Reverse scrolling** switch to On (●) or Off ( ), as needed.

⑧ Set the **Enable touchpad acceleration** switch to On (●) or Off ( ), as needed.

⑨ Drag the **Touchpad speed** slider along the Slow–Fast axis to adjust the speed at which the cursor moves when you use the touchpad.

⑩ Click **Close** (✖).

The Settings window closes.

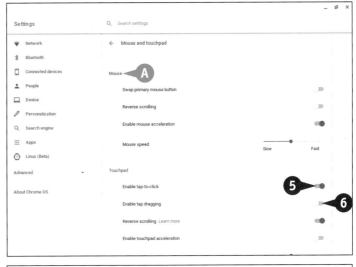

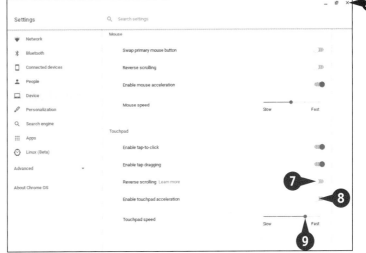

What are touchpad acceleration and mouse acceleration?

Touchpad acceleration controls the rate at which the pointer moves based on the speed at which you move your finger on the touchpad. Set the **Enable touchpad acceleration** switch to Off ( ) if you want the pointer to move exactly proportionally to the distance your finger moves on the touchpad; set this switch to On (●) to have the pointer move farther when your finger moves more quickly, and move less far when your finger moves more slowly.

Mouse acceleration is similar to touchpad acceleration but affects any mouse connected to the Chromebook.

Some people find acceleration helpful for moving the pointer precisely; others find acceleration makes precise movement much more difficult.

Configure Notifications and Do Not Disturb

Chrome OS and apps can raise notifications to alert you when certain events occur. For example, when you start a download, the Download Manager feature displays a notification to monitor the download's progress.

If you do not want to see notifications from a particular app, you can disable notifications from that app. If you want to see no app notifications at all, you can turn on the Do Not Disturb feature. However, Chrome OS also has system notifications, which you cannot disable.

Configure Notifications and Do Not Disturb

1 Click the status area.

The system menu opens.

A The readout shows how Chrome OS is set to treat notifications, such as *On, all apps*.

2 Click **Notifications** (▾). You can click either the text or the drop-down icon (▾).

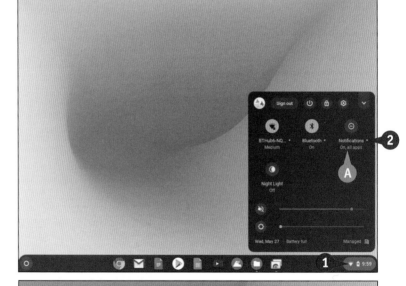

The Notifications system menu appears.

B You can set the **Do not disturb** switch to On (●) to turn on the Do Not Disturb feature. However, it is usually easier to turn on Do Not Disturb from the system menu.

3 Click the check box (☑ changes to ■) for each app you do not want to allow to raise notifications.

4 Click **Back** (⬅).

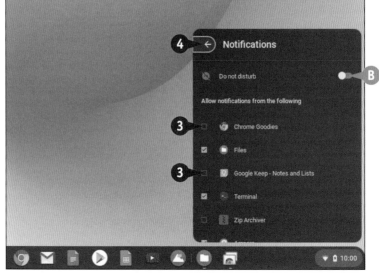

The system menu appears again.

C The readout shows how you have set Chrome OS to treat notifications, such as *Off for 3 apps*.

5 If you want to turn on Do Not Disturb, click **Notifications** (changes to).

D The Do Not Disturb icon ( ) appears in the status area in place of the Notifications icon.

6 Click outside the system menu.

The system menu closes.

TIP

Why can I disable some notifications but not others?
The notifications you can disable come from apps, such as the Play Store app or the Files app. Google categorizes some other notifications as *system notifications* and deems them vital for you to see, so you cannot suppress or disable them. For example, any notifications labeled *Chrome OS* — such as battery and charging status notifications — come directly from the Chromebook's operating system and cannot be disabled.

Configure Sound Settings

A Chromebook contains built-in speakers and one or more microphones, but you can also connect external speakers, headphones, or sound sources. Many Chromebook models include a 3.5mm audio socket — often called a *headphone port* — that you can use to connect analog headphones or speakers. Alternatively, you can connect external audio devices via Bluetooth or USB.

After connecting your audio devices, you can display the Audio Settings system menu, choose which input device and output device to use, and set the playback volume for the output device.

Configure Sound Settings

1 If you want to use an external audio device, connect it to the Chromebook. For example, plug an analog headset into the 3.5mm audio socket, or plug a USB headset into a USB port.

Note: See the section "Connect and Use Bluetooth Devices" in Chapter 4 for instructions on connecting Bluetooth devices.

2 Click the status area.

The system menu opens.

A The Audio Settings icon (⬛⬛) indicates that one or more audio devices are connected.

3 Click **Audio Settings** (⬛⬛).

The Audio Settings system menu opens.

B The Output list shows the available output devices.

C The check mark (☑) appears on the current device.

D The Speaker (Internal) entry is the Chromebook's built-in speaker.

E The Input list shows the available input devices.

F The Front Microphone entry is the Chromebook's front internal microphone.

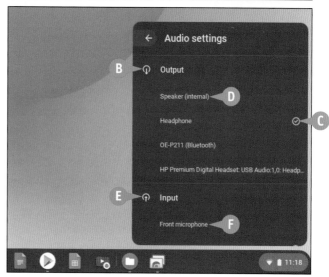

④ Click the input device you want to use.

⑤ Click **Back** (⬅).

The system menu appears again.

⑥ Drag the **Volume slider** left to decrease the volume or right to increase it.

Ⓖ You can click **Sound** (🔊 changes to 🔇) to mute the sound. Click **Sound** again (🔇 changes to 🔊) to unmute the sound.

⑦ Click outside the system menu.

The system menu closes.

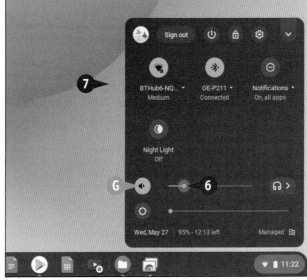

Do I have to open the system menu to change the audio volume?

No. You can adjust the keyboard instead. Press 🔊 to increase the volume, 🔉 to decrease the volume, or 🔇 to mute or unmute the audio.

How do I set the volume for another audio output device?

The Volume slider on the system menu controls the volume for the current audio output device. To set the volume for another device, click **Audio Settings** (🔊) to display the Audio Settings screen, click the appropriate device in the Output list, and then click **Back** (⬅). Back on the system menu, drag the **Volume slider** to set the volume for the device you selected.

Choose Which Pages to Display on Startup

To save time, you can specify which pages Chrome opens when you start it. You have three choices: You can choose to open a new tab for a fresh start; you can have Chrome restore the pages you had open when you last closed Chrome, which is good for continuing what you were doing; or you can have Chrome open a specific page or set of pages.

Choose Which Pages to Display on Startup

1 Click **Chrome** (image).

A Chrome window opens or becomes active.

2 Open each page you want your Chromebook to display on startup.

For example, click **New Tab** (+) to open a new tab, type or paste the page's address in the Omnibox, and then press Enter.

3 Click **Menu** (⋮).

The menu opens.

4 Click **Settings**.

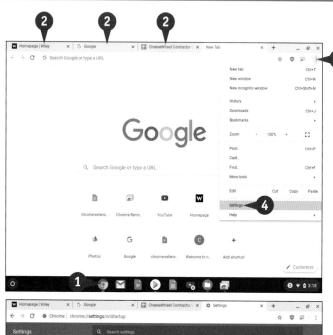

The Settings page appears in a new tab.

5 In the On Startup box, click **Open the New Tab page** (○ changes to ◉), **Continue where you left off** (○ changes to ◉), or **Open a specific page or set of pages** (○ changes to ◉).

To follow this example, click **Open a specific page or set of pages** (○ changes to ◉).

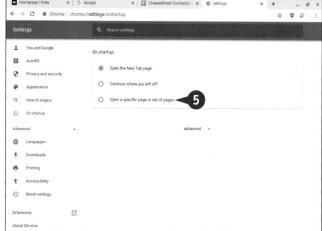

A list of the current pages appears, excluding the Settings page.

Ⓐ If you need to remove a page or edit its URL, click **More** (⋮).

Ⓑ To remove the page, click **Remove**.

Ⓒ To modify the page's URL, click **Edit**, make the changes in the Edit Page dialog box, and then click **Save**.

6 To add a page, click **Add a new page**.

The Add a New Page dialog box opens.

7 Type or paste the page's URL.

8 Click **Add**.

The Add a New Page dialog box closes.

9 When the list is complete, click **Close Tab** (✕).

The tab containing the Settings page closes.

Ⓓ Alternatively, click **Close Window** (✕) to close the Chrome window.

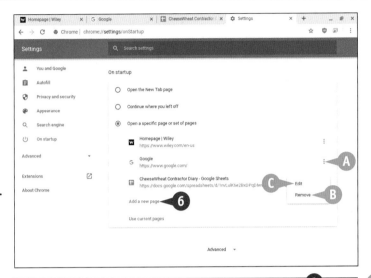

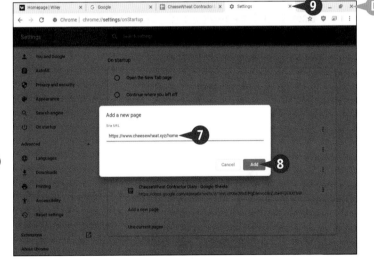

TIP

How can I restore all the open tabs in the last Chrome window I closed?

The short answer is to press `Ctrl`+`Shift`+`T` one or more times and see whether you get what you want.

Chrome keeps a "stack" — a list — of the tabs, windows, and Chrome-based windows you have recently closed. The last item you closed is at the top of the stack, the second-last item you closed is immediately below that top item, and so on.

You can restore items on the stack in top-down order by pressing `Ctrl`+`Shift`+`T`. So if the last Chrome-based item you closed was a window, pressing `Ctrl`+`Shift`+`T` restores every tab that was open in that window. Pressing `Ctrl`+`Shift`+`T` again restores the next item, whether it was a tab, a window of tabs, or another Chrome-based window.

Customize the Default Chrome Theme

Chrome OS uses a *theme* — a collection of settings — to control the overall look of the Chrome browser. The default Chrome theme, which this book uses for most of the screenshots that show Chrome, has a straightforward look based on white backgrounds, gray highlights, and black and blue text.

You can customize the default Chrome theme to make it look the way you prefer. You can change the background, choose which shortcuts to display on the New Tab page, and set primary and secondary colors for the browser's appearance.

Customize the Default Chrome Theme

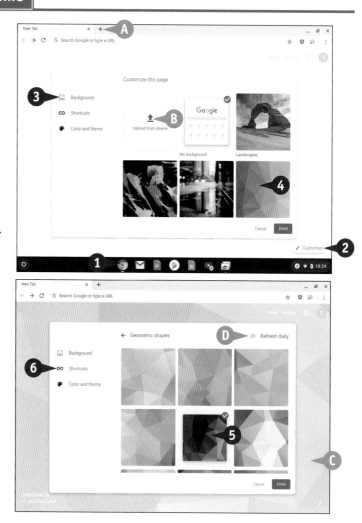

1 Click **Chrome** (🌐) on the shelf.

Note: If Chrome (🌐) does not appear on the shelf, click **Launcher** (⊙), click **Full Screen** (⌃), and then click **Chrome** (🌐).

A Chrome window opens.

Ⓐ If the Chrome window does not show a new tab, click **New Tab** (➕) to display a new tab.

2 Click **Customize** (✏️).

The Customize This Page dialog box opens.

3 Click **Background** (🖼️).

The Background tab appears.

4 Click a category of images.

Ⓑ You can click **Upload from device** (⬆️) to add an image file from your Chromebook.

The images in the category appear.

5 Click the image you want to use.

Ⓒ The selected image appears as the background of the page.

Ⓓ You can set the **Refresh daily** switch to On (⬤) to have Chrome automatically display another image from the category each day.

6 Click **Shortcuts** (🔗).

The Shortcuts tab appears.

7 Click **My shortcuts** or **Most visited sites** to choose which group of shortcuts the New Tab page displays.

E If you prefer to have the New Tab page display no shortcuts, set the **Hide shortcuts** switch to On (⬤).

8 Click **Color and theme** (🎨).

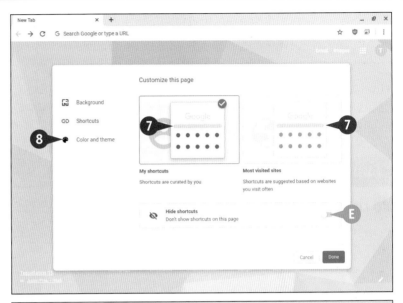

The Color and Theme tab appears.

9 Click the predefined color combination you want to use.

F The default color combination appears here.

10 Click **Done**.

The Customize This Page dialog box closes.

The New Tab page displays the choices you made.

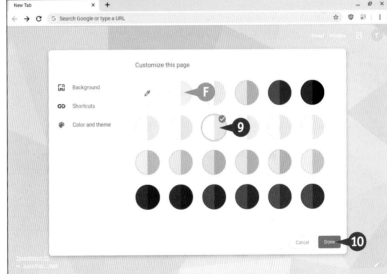

TIP

How do I define a custom primary color for the theme?
On the New Tab page, click **Customize** (✏️) to display the Customize This Page dialog box, and then click **Color and theme** (🎨) to display the Color and Theme tab. Click **Select Color** (✐) to display the Color Picker window, and then click the primary color you want. Chrome automatically generates the secondary color — the lighter color — from the primary color.

Apply a Browser Theme to Chrome

When you want to change Chrome's look, you can install a different browser theme from the Chrome Web Store. The Themes section of the Chrome Web Store contains many themes sorted into various categories. Some themes make subtle changes, whereas others make more dramatic changes.

You can install only a single theme at a time. When you go to install another theme, Chrome uninstalls the current theme, replacing it with the new theme. The default Chrome theme remains available at all times, and you can revert to it easily.

Apply a Browser Theme to Chrome

1 Click **Launcher** (⊙).

The Launcher bar opens.

2 Click **Full Screen** (⌃).

The Launcher expands to full screen.

3 Click **Web Store** (⊙).

The Web Store appears in a Chrome tab.

4 Click **Themes** (🖌).

The Themes list appears.

Ⓐ You can click **Categories** (▼) and click **By Artists**, **By Google**, or **All**.

Ⓑ You can click a rating (○ changes to ◉).

5 Click the theme you want to view.

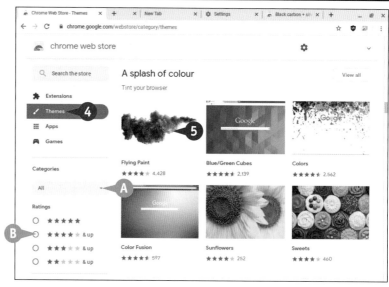

The theme's page appears.

Ⓒ You can browse the theme's overview, reviews, support, and related information.

❻ Click **Add to Chrome**.

Chrome adds the theme.

❼ Click **New Tab** (➕).

The new tab opens.

You can see the effects of the theme.

How do I reapply the default browser theme?
In Chrome, click **Menu** (⋮) to open the menu, and then click **Settings** to open the Settings page in a new tab. In the left pane, click **Appearance** (🎨) to display the Appearance section, and then click **Reset to Default** on the Browser Themes row.

CHAPTER 3

Configuring Accessibility Settings

Chrome OS includes a wide range of accessibility settings that you can configure to make your Chromebook easier to use. In this chapter, you first learn where to find the Accessibility settings. You then meet the features for making the screen easier to see, including zooming with the Magnifier features; explore the accessibility settings for keyboard, mouse and touchpad, and audio; and meet the text-to-speech features.

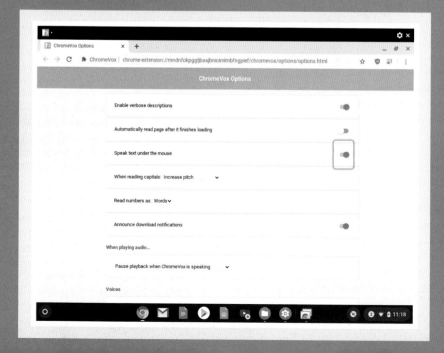

Display the Accessibility Settings

Chrome OS includes a wide range of accessibility settings for making Chromebooks easier to use for anyone who has problems with vision, hearing, or dexterity. For example, you can use text-to-speech features to read on-screen content, use an on-screen keyboard or dictation to input text, and play audio in mono rather than stereo.

To reach the accessibility settings, you open the Settings app and go to the Advanced section. Here, you can choose to add the accessibility options to the system menu for quicker access.

Display the Accessibility Settings

1 Click the status area.

The system menu opens.

2 Click **Settings** (⚙).

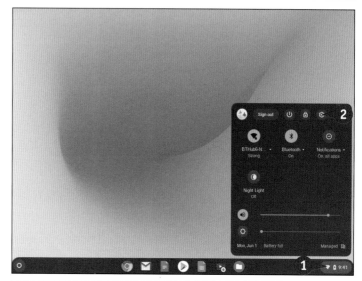

The Settings window opens.

3 If the Advanced section is collapsed, click **Advanced** (▼ changes to ▲).

The Advanced section expands.

4 Click **Accessibility** (🕴).

The Accessibility section of the Settings screen appears.

⑤ Set the **Always show accessibility options in the system menu** switch to On (⬤) if you want to be able to configure accessibility options from the system menu.

⑥ Click **Manage accessibility features**.

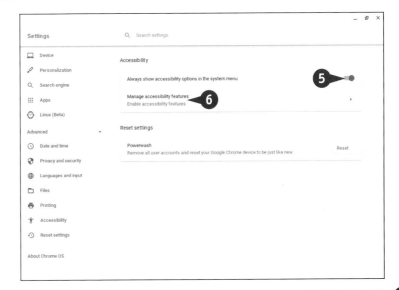

The Manage Accessibility Features screen appears.

From this screen, you can configure accessibility settings, as explained in the following sections.

⑦ When you finish configuring accessibility settings, click **Close** (✕).

The Settings window closes.

TIP

Is there a quicker way to reach the accessibility settings?
Yes. In the Accessibility section of the Settings screen, set the **Always show accessibility options in the system menu** switch to On (⬤). You can then click the status area to open the system menu, and then click **Accessibility** (⊞) to display the Accessibility menu, which enables you to turn on or off accessibility features quickly.

Make the Screen Easier to See

Chrome OS's Accessibility feature includes several settings that enable you to make the screen easier to see. You can enable High Contrast Mode, which inverts the colors of the screen and can help with some lighting conditions. You can also change the display resolution or simply increase the text size.

You can also use the Magnifier features to zoom in on either the entire screen or just part of it. See the next section, "Zoom the Screen with the Magnifier Features," for details.

Make the Screen Easier to See

1 Display the Manage Accessibility Features screen in the Settings app by following steps **1** to **6** in the previous section, "Display the Accessibility Settings."

A You can click **Open display device settings** to go to the Displays screen, where you can change the resolution. See the section "Set a Suitable Display Resolution" in Chapter 2 for details.

2 In the Display section, set the **Use high contrast mode** switch to On (●).

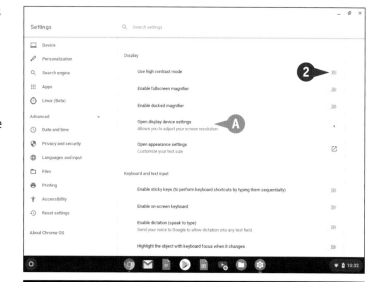

The display output appears with inverted colors.

B Set the **Use high contrast mode** switch to Off ( ) if you want to turn high contrast mode off again.

C See the next section, "Zoom the Screen with the Magnifier Features," for coverage of the Enable Fullscreen Magnifier feature and the Enable Docked Magnifier feature.

3 Click **Open appearance settings**.

The Appearance section of Chrome's Settings page appears in a new tab in the Chrome browser.

Note: When you click **Open appearance settings** in the Settings window, Chrome OS switches you to a Chrome browser window, because the Appearance settings are part of the Chrome browser.

④ Click **Font size** (▼).

The Font Size drop-down list opens.

⑤ Click the size you want, such as **Very large**.

Chrome displays the text at the size you chose.

⑥ When you are satisfied with the font size, click **Close** (✖).

The Chrome window closes.

TIP

Why does only some text in Chrome OS get bigger when I change the font size?
While most of the Accessibility settings affect the entire system, the Appearance settings are in Chrome, the browser, and only affect applications whose pages are rendered using Chrome. The Open Appearance Settings item appears in the Accessibility section of the Settings app, but it is a link that takes you to the Settings screen in Chrome.

This means that system apps and any apps you install from the Play Store are not affected by the font size you set in the Chrome browser. Similarly, changing Chrome's page zoom or fonts affects only pages rendered using the Chrome browser.

Zoom the Screen with the Magnifier Features

If you have difficulty seeing text or other items on the screen, try using the Magnifier features to make the displayed items larger. Chrome OS provides two Magnifier features, the full-screen magnifier and the docked magnifier.

As its name suggests, the full-screen magnifier zooms the entire screen to the magnification you specify. The area around the pointer appears on the display, so you move the pointer around to navigate. The docked magnifier uses a fixed area at the top of the screen to display the zoomed content.

Zoom the Screen with the Magnifier Features

1 Display the Manage Accessibility Features screen in the Settings app by following steps **1** to **6** in the section "Display the Accessibility Settings," earlier in this chapter.

2 In the Display section, set the **Enable fullscreen magnifier** switch to On (⬤).

The Fullscreen Zoom Level row appears.

3 Click **Fullscreen zoom level** (▼).

The Fullscreen Zoom Level drop-down list opens.

4 Click the zoom level you want to use, such as **8x.**

Chrome OS applies the zoom level you chose.

The Chromebook's screen displays only a portion of the full display output.

Move the pointer to control which portion of the display output appears on screen.

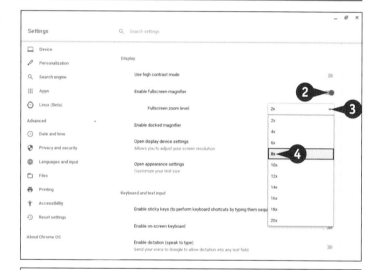

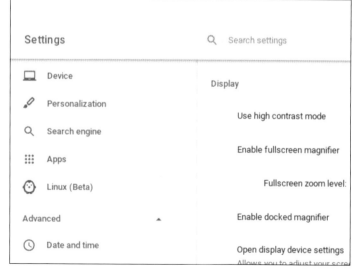

5 Set the **Enable fullscreen magnifier**
switch to Off (   ).

Chrome OS reduces the zoom level to
normal.

6 Set the **Enable docked magnifier** switch
to On ( ).

A The docked magnifier appears in the top
third of the screen, showing the area
where the pointer is.

The Docked Zoom Level row appears.

7 Click **Docked zoom level** ( ).

The Docked Zoom Level drop-down list
opens.

8 Click the zoom level you want to use in
the docked magnifier.

The docked magnifier shows the current
area zoomed to that level.

Move the pointer to control which portion
of the display output appears in the
docked magnifier.

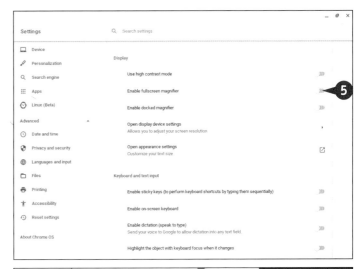

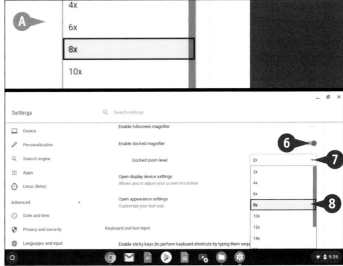

TIP

In the full-screen magnifier, why do some elements appear sharp when zoomed in, when most elements do not?

The full-screen magnifier renders output for the screen as though it were operating the zoom level's multiple of the resolution — for example, if you choose 4x zoom, it will render 16 times the pixels, 4 times the width multiplied by 4 times the height. Most of the elements on the screen are not scalable and will appear blocky when zoomed large. But some elements, such as the Launcher button, are scalable and will look sharp however far they are zoomed.

By contrast, the docked magnifier simply copies pixels from the area where the pointer is and enlarges them, so all elements appear blocky to the same degree.

Configure Keyboard Accessibility Settings

If you find your Chromebook's keyboard hard to use, see whether configuring keyboard accessibility settings helps. The Sticky Keys feature enables you to give keyboard shortcuts in sequence rather than pressing all the keys together. The on-screen keyboard lets you input characters via the Chromebook's screen. And the Dictation feature enables you to enter text by speaking.

Beyond these, Chrome OS includes a feature to highlight the object that has received the keyboard focus and will receive input when you type. You can also have Chrome OS highlight the text caret — the insertion point — when it appears or moves.

Configure Keyboard Accessibility Settings

Configure Keyboard Accessibility Settings

1 Display the Manage Accessibility Features screen in the Settings app by following steps **1** to **6** in the section "Display the Accessibility Settings," earlier in this chapter.

2 Set the **Enable sticky keys** switch to On (⬤) if you want to use Sticky Keys.

3 Set the **Enable on-screen keyboard** switch to On (⬤) to enable the on-screen keyboard.

A The On-Screen Keyboard button (⌨) appears.

4 Click **On-Screen Keyboard** (⌨ changes to ⌨).

B The on-screen keyboard appears.

5 You can click a key to type the associated character.

6 When you finish using the on-screen keyboard, click **Hide On-Screen Keyboard** (⌨ changes to ⌨) to hide the on-screen keyboard.

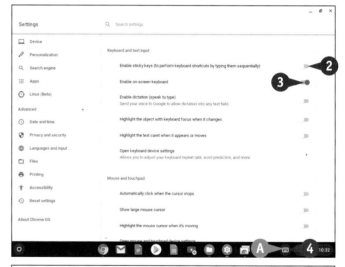

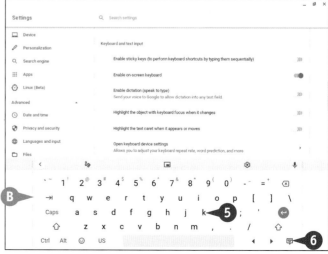

7 Set the **Enable dictation (speak to type)** switch to On (●) if you want to use dictation. See the following subsection for an example.

8 Set the **Highlight the object with keyboard focus when it changes** switch to On (●) if you want Chrome OS to highlight the object that will receive keyboard input.

9 Set the **Highlight the text caret when it appears or moves** switch to On (●) if you want Chrome OS to highlight the text caret.

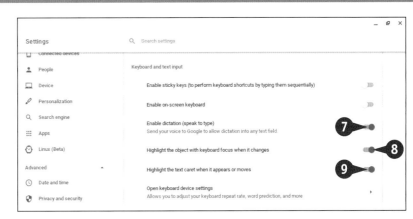

Dictate Text

1 Open an app that accepts text input. This example uses **Google Keep** (🖊️).

2 Position the insertion point where you want to add text.

3 Click **Dictation** (🎤 changes to 🎤).

4 Dictate the text.

C The text appears in the app.

Why does dictation require an Internet connection?

As of this writing, Chrome OS requires an Internet connection for dictation because it sends your audio input across the Internet to Google's servers for audio processing and then receives the text back from them.

It seems likely that Google will release a dictation feature that enables language processing directly within Chrome OS. If so, dictation would not require an Internet connection — but it might require a powerful Chromebook.

Configure Mouse and Touchpad Accessibility Settings

Chrome OS includes accessibility settings you can configure to make the touchpad — and the mouse, if you connect one — easier to use. To make the pointer easier to see, you can increase its size; and you can have Chrome OS display a highlight circle around the pointer when it is moving.

If you have trouble clicking — for example, if you find the pointer moves off the target when you try to click — you can set Chrome OS to click automatically when the pointer stops moving.

Configure Mouse and Touchpad Accessibility Settings

1 Display the Manage Accessibility Features screen in the Settings app by following steps **1** to **6** in the section "Display the Accessibility Settings," earlier in this chapter.

2 Set the **Automatically click when the cursor stops** switch to On (⬤).

A The Automatic Click menu appears. See the tip for details.

3 Click **Delay before click** (▼).

The Delay Before Click drop-down menu opens.

B The countdown circle around the pointer demonstrates the current delay.

4 Click the delay you want to set.

Note: Alternatively, point to the delay you want to set, and then wait for Chrome OS to click it.

5 Set the **Stabilize click location** switch to On (⬤) if you want Chrome OS to anchor on an exact position to click even if the pointer moves during the delay before click.

6 Set the **Revert to left click after action** switch to On (⬤) if you want Chrome OS to revert to left-clicking after you take an action from the Action bar.

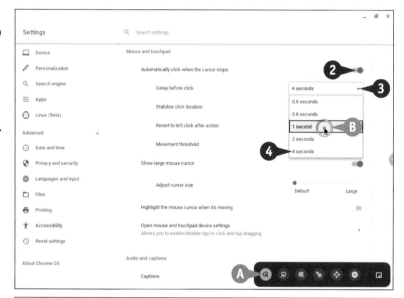

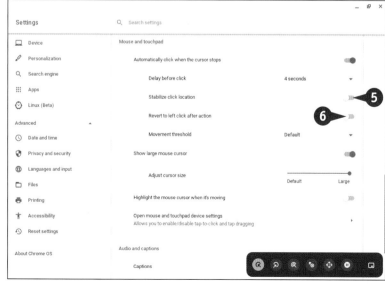

7 Click **Movement threshold** (▼).

The Movement Threshold drop-down menu opens.

8 Click **Extra small**, **Small**, **Default**, **Large**, or **Extra large** to set the movement threshold.

Note: The *movement threshold* is the size of the circle within which the automated click occurs.

9 Set the **Show large mouse cursor** switch to On (●) if you want to use a large pointer.

10 Drag the **Adjust cursor size** slider along the Default–Large axis to set the cursor size.

11 Set the **Highlight the mouse cursor when it's moving** switch to On (●) if you want Chrome OS to highlight the cursor when you move it.

C A red circle appears around the cursor's point.

D You can click **Open mouse and touchpad device settings** to go to the Mouse and Touchpad Settings screen, where you can configure more general settings for the touchpad and mouse.

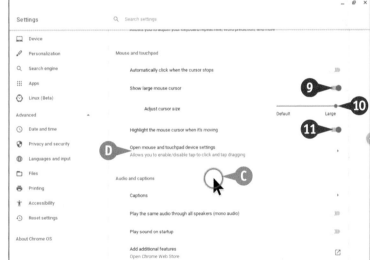

TIP

How do I use the Automatic Click menu?

Select the action you want to take by clicking **Left Click** (🅡 changes to 🅡), **Right Click** (🅡 changes to 🅡), **Double Click** (🅡 changes to 🅡), **Click and Drag** (🖐 changes to 🖐), or **Scroll** (⊕ changes to ⊕); then point to the item you want to affect, and wait for Chrome OS to click automatically.

Click **No Action (Pause)** (⏸ changes to ⏸) to pause automatic clicking; click again (⏸ changes to ⏸) to resume automatic clicking. To move the Automatic Click menu to a different corner, click **Toggle Menu Position** (◰, ◱, ◲, or ◳) until the menu appears where you want it.

Configure Audio Accessibility Settings

hrome OS includes several audio accessibility settings that you can configure to make your Chromebook easier to use. You can configure on-screen captions with exactly the text size, font, and opacity you find easiest to see. You can make your Chromebook play back audio in mono rather than stereo. And you can have Chrome OS play a sound when the sign-in screen appears, to let you know you can sign in.

Configure Audio Accessibility Settings

1 Display the Manage Accessibility Features screen in the Settings app by following steps **1** to **6** in the section "Display the Accessibility Settings," earlier in this chapter.

2 In the Audio and Captions section, click **Captions**.

The Captions screen appears.

3 Click **Text size** (▼), and then click **Very small**, **Small**, **Medium (Recommended)**, **Large**, or **Very large** to set the text size.

4 Click **Text font** (▼), and then click the font you want.

5 Click **Text color**, and then click the color you want.

6 Click **Text opacity**, and then click **Opaque**, **Semi-transparent**, or **Transparent**, as needed.

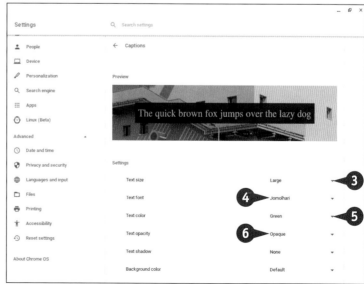

7 Click **Text shadow** (▼), and then click **None**, **Raised**, **Depressed**, **Uniform**, or **Drop shadow**, as you prefer.

8 Click **Background color**, and then click the color you want.

9 Click **Background opacity**, and then click **Opaque**, **Semi-transparent**, or **Transparent**, as needed.

10 Click **Back** (←).

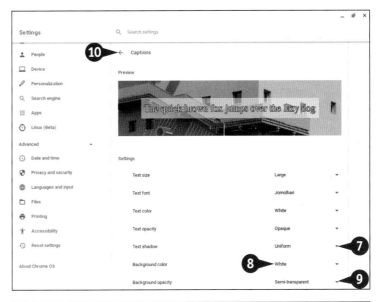

The Accessibility screen appears again.

11 Set the **Play the same audio through all speakers (mono audio)** switch to On (━●).

12 Set the **Play sound on startup** switch to On (━●) if you want your Chromebook to play a sound when the sign-in screen appears.

13 Click **Close** (✖).

The Settings window closes.

TIP

How does mono audio help with audio accessibility?

Stereo uses separate channels for left and right, so some sounds play only — or play more loudly — in one channel. If you have hearing problems, you may find it difficult to follow content in one channel or the other. Mono audio plays all the sounds in the same channel, so you have a better chance of following the content. However, mono audio does not convey the positional information — where a speaker or a sound source is positioned — that stereo audio conveys.

Configure Text-to-Speech Features

Chrome OS includes two text-to-speech features, the ChromeVox spoken-feedback feature and the Select-to-Speak feature, which reads selected text to you. You can enable these features on the Manage Accessibility Features screen. From this screen, you can also access the configuration pages for ChromeVox and for Select-to-Speak, which enable you to customize the way these accessibility features work.

Enable ChromeVox or Select-to-Speak

Click the status area to open the system menu, and then click **Settings** (⚙) to open the Settings window. Click **Advanced** if the Advanced section is collapsed, and then click **Accessibility** (♿) to display the Accessibility section of the Settings screen. Click Manage Accessibility Features to display the Manage Accessibility Features screen.

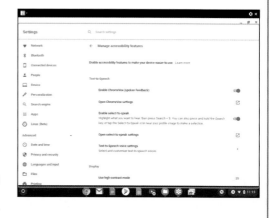

In the Text-to-Speech section, set the **Enable ChromeVox (spoken feedback)** switch to On (●) if you want to use ChromeVox. You can then click **Open ChromeVox Settings** to open the ChromeVox Settings screen in a Chrome tab; see the following subsection for details. Set the **Enable select-to-speak** switch to On (●) if you want to use Select-to-Speak. You can then click **Open select-to-speak settings** to open the Select-to-Speak Settings screen in a Chrome tab; see the "Configure Select-to-Speak Settings" subsection for details. You can click **Text-to-Speech voice settings** to display the Text-to-Speech Voice Settings screen, where you can adjust the speech rate, pitch, and volume; listen to available voices; and set your preferred voices.

Configure ChromeVox Settings

The ChromeVox Settings page contains a large number of settings that you will likely want to explore; this section covers only some of the key settings.

At the top of the page, set the **Enable verbose descriptions** switch to On (●) if you want ChromeVox to speak detailed descriptions. Set the **Automatically read page after it finishes loading** switch to On (●) if you want ChromeVox to start reading pages automatically. Set the **Speak text under the mouse** switch to On (●) to have ChromeVox speak text you point at.

In the When Playing Audio section, click **Pause playback when ChromeVox is speaking** (⌄), and then select **Pause playback when ChromeVox is speaking**, **Play at normal volume even if ChromeVox is speaking**, or **Play at lower volume when ChromeVox is speaking**, as needed.

Configure ChromeVox Settings (continued)

In the Voices section of the ChromeVox Settings page, click **Select current voice** (∨), and then click the voice you want to use.

In the Braille section, you can configure a Braille device for either eight-dot braille or six-dot braille. You can set the **Show braille commands in the ChromeVox menus** switch to On (⬤) if you want to display braille commands.

Toward the bottom of the page, the Bluetooth Braille Display section enables you to connect a physical braille display via Bluetooth. The Virtual Braille Display section provides settings for configuring a virtually braille display in the ChromeVox panel at the top of the screen.

When you finish configuring ChromeVox settings, click **Close** (✖) to close the Chrome tab.

Configure Select-to-Speak Settings

The Select-to-Speak page contains two sections, Speech and Highlighting. In the Speech section, click **Select a voice** (∨), and then click the voice you want to use. If you want to personalize the Text-to-Speech settings, click **Text-to-Speech settings**, and then work on the Text-to-Speech Voice Settings screen.

In the Highlighting section, set the **Highlight each word as it is spoken** switch to On (⬤) if you want Select-to-Speak to highlight each word as it speaks it. You can then click **Color for word highlights** (∨), and then click the highlight color to use.

When you finish configuring Select-to-Speak settings, click **Close** (✖) to close the Chrome tab.

CHAPTER 4

Connecting External Devices

Your Chromebook is a complete portable computer with its screen, keyboard, touchpad, speakers, and microphones; but you can connect external devices to make it easier to use or to add functionality. This chapter shows you how to connect Bluetooth devices, an external keyboard and mouse, or a second display; how to print; how to use SD cards and memory sticks; how to use Chromecast devices; and how to connect and use your Android phone.

Connect and Use Bluetooth Devices

Bluetooth is a convenient way to connect external devices to your Chromebook. For example, you may want to connect a mouse or other pointing device via Bluetooth if you find the Chromebook's touchpad hard to use. Or you can connect Bluetooth headphones or a Bluetooth speaker to enable yourself to enjoy audio at higher quality — or volume or both — than the Chromebook's built-in speakers can deliver.

Before using a Bluetooth device, you must pair it with the Chromebook. Once the two are paired, you can quickly connect and disconnect the Bluetooth device.

Connect and Use Bluetooth Devices

1 Power on the Bluetooth device and put it into pairing mode.

Note: Read the Bluetooth device's instructions to find out how to turn the device on and put it into pairing mode.

2 Click the status area.

The system menu opens.

3 Click **Bluetooth**.

Click the readout that says *Bluetooth On* or *Bluetooth Off*, not the icon.

The Bluetooth system menu opens.

A The Paired Devices list shows devices already paired with your Chromebook.

B The Unpaired Devices list shows devices that have not been paired.

4 Click the device you want to pair.

The Connect to Bluetooth Device dialog box opens and displays details of the connection that Chrome OS is establishing.

C You can click **Cancel** to cancel the connection.

When Chrome OS establishes the connection, the Connect to Bluetooth Device dialog box closes.

Chrome OS displays a notification telling you that the device is paired.

D You can click the notification to display the Bluetooth section of the Settings screen in the Settings app.

Connect and Disconnect a Paired Bluetooth Device

1 Turn on the Bluetooth device.

2 Click the status area.

The system menu opens.

3 Click **Bluetooth**.

Click the readout that says *Bluetooth On* or *Bluetooth Off*, not the icon.

The Bluetooth system menu opens.

E If the *Connected* readout appears, the Chromebook and the device have established the connection automatically. You can start using the device.

4 If the *Connected* readout does not appear, click the device to attempt to establish the connection manually.

5 When you are ready to disconnect a Bluetooth device, click **Settings** (⚙) on the Bluetooth system menu.

The Bluetooth screen in the Settings app appears.

6 Click **Menu** (⋮) for the device.

The menu opens.

7 Click **Disconnect**.

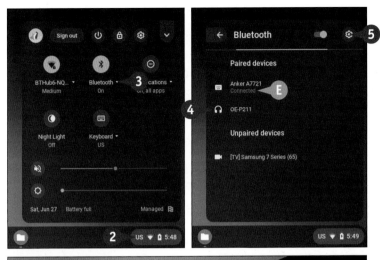

TIP

How do I unpair a Bluetooth device?
Chrome OS uses the term *remove* rather than *unpair* for ending the pairing relationship between devices. Click the status area to open the system menu, and then click **Settings** (⚙) to open the Settings app. Click **Bluetooth** (✳) in the left pane to display the Bluetooth screen. Click **Menu** (⋮) for the device, and then click **Remove from list**.

Connect and Configure an External Mouse

Each Chromebook has a built-in touchpad, and some Chromebook models include touchscreens. But you may want to connect an external mouse — or another pointing device, such as a trackball — to your Chromebook for comfort and accurate pointing during long computing sessions. You can connect a mouse via either USB or Bluetooth.

After connecting a mouse, you can configure it by adjusting the settings in the Mouse and Touchpad section of the Settings screen.

Connect and Configure an External Mouse

1 Connect the mouse to the Chromebook.

For example, plug in a USB mouse.

Note: Depending on your Chromebook's ports, you may need to use a dongle to connect a USB mouse.

2 Click the status area.

The system menu opens.

3 Click **Settings** (⚙).

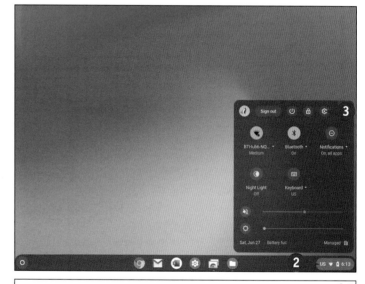

The Settings window opens.

4 Click **Device** (🖥).

The Device section of the Settings screen appears.

5 Click **Mouse and touchpad**.

Note: The name changes from *Touchpad* to *Mouse and Touchpad* when a mouse is connected to your Chromebook.

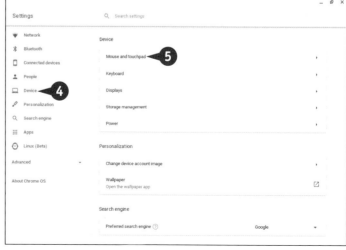

The Mouse and Touchpad screen appears.

6 Set the **Swap primary mouse button** switch to On (●) if you want to swap the left and right mouse buttons.

7 Set the **Enable mouse acceleration** switch to On (●) or Off ( ), as needed.

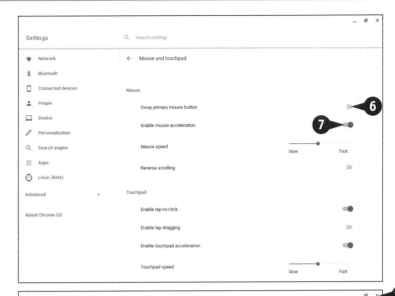

8 Drag the **Mouse speed** slider along the Slow–Fast axis to adjust the speed at which the cursor moves when you move the mouse.

9 Set the **Reverse scrolling** switch to On (●) if you want the screen to scroll in the opposite direction to your rotation of the mouse's scroll wheel.

10 Click **Close** (✖).

The Settings window closes.

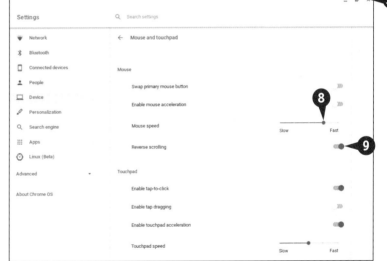

TIP

Can I disable the touchpad on my Chromebook when I am using an external mouse?
It is possible to disable the touchpad — for example, so it does not register unwanted input while you are typing. But Chrome OS does not provide an easy way to disable it, and you must use a *flag* — an advanced setting in Chrome OS — to enable the developer command that allows you to disable the touchpad. If you must disable the touchpad, search for instructions using terms such as *Chromebook disable touchpad flags*. Alternatively, consider using an external keyboard along with your external mouse.

Connect and Configure a Second Display

Y ou can connect one or more external displays to your Chromebook to give yourself more space for your apps. Some Chromebooks have dedicated display ports, such as HDMI, mini-HDMI, micro-HDMI, or mini DisplayPort; but recent Chromebook models may have only USB-C connections that include display output capability. If the Chromebook and the display have matching ports, you need only a cable to connect them; if not, you need to use an adapter.

After connecting the external display, you use the Displays pane in the Settings app to set the resolution and specify the arrangement of the displays.

Connect and Configure a Second Display

1. Connect the display to your Chromebook using a suitable cable or adapter.

2. Click the status area.

   The system menu opens.

3. Click **Settings** (⚙).

Note: If you are planning to use one or more external displays consistently, you may want to look into getting a USB-C docking station, which can simplify the connection process.

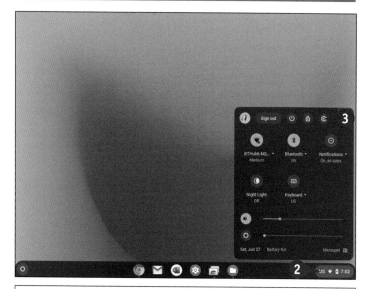

The Settings window opens.

4. Click **Device** (⊡).

   The Device section of the Settings screen appears.

5. Click **Displays**.

Note: You can configure the external display to either mirror the built-in display — making it show the same information — or extend the desktop. Mirroring is mostly useful for presentations or teaching. This example shows extending the desktop.

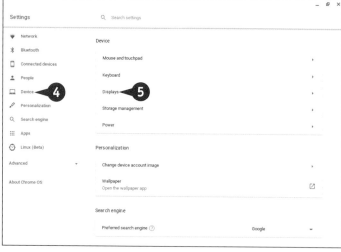

The Displays screen appears.

6 In the Arrangement area, drag the display thumbnails to match the physical placement of the displays.

7 Deselect **Mirror Built-in display** (☐).

8 Click the tab for the external display.

9 Click **Screen** (▼), and then click **Extended display** or **Primary display**, as needed.

Note: Click **Primary display** if you want to make the external display the main display instead of the built-in display.

10 Drag the **Display Size** slider along the Tiny–Huge axis to adjust the size of items on screen.

11 Click **Resolution** (▼), and then click the resolution you want to use.

12 If you need to specify the rotation for the external display, click **Orientation** (▼), and then click **0° (Default)**, **90°**, **180°**, or **270°**, as needed.

Ⓐ You can click **Overscan** (▶) to open the Overscan dialog box, which enables you to adjust where the picture appears on the external display.

13 Click **Close** (✕).

The Settings window closes.

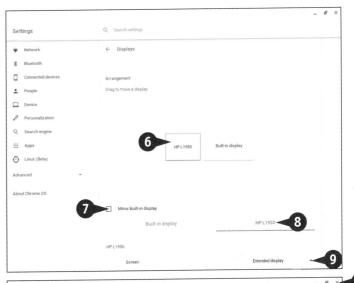

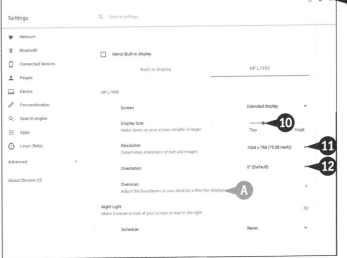

TIPS

Can I connect multiple external displays to my Chromebook?
Yes, but the specifics vary depending on the Chromebook, so you may need to do some research or experimentation.

What is overscan, and should I adjust it?
Overscan adjustment enables you to control where the boundaries of the display output appear on an external display. Normally, you need adjust overscan only if the picture extends beyond the boundaries of the screen.

Connect a Printer and Print

The entirely paperless office remains a future prospect, and Chrome OS makes it easy to print documents from your Chromebook. You can quickly start using many USB printers by simply connecting them to your Chromebook with a USB cable. For other printers, you may need to specify configuration details manually.

After connecting a printer, you can save it to your profile for future use. You can then print documents to the printer.

Connect a Printer and Print

Connect a Printer to Your Chromebook

1 Connect the printer to your Chromebook.

A If the printer is a USB model, and Chrome OS can locate a suitable driver, a notification appears, telling you that the printer is connected and ready.

2 Click **Settings** (⚙) on the shelf.

Note: If Settings (⚙) does not appear on the shelf, click the status area to display the system menu, and then click **Settings** (⚙).

The Settings window opens.

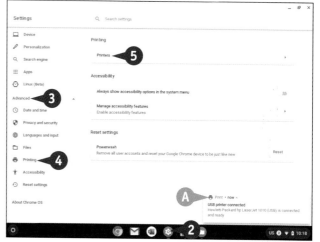

3 Click **Advanced**.

The Advanced section of the sidebar expands.

4 Click **Printing** (🖨).

The Printing section of the Settings screen appears.

5 Click **Printers**.

The Printers screen appears.

6 Click **Save**.

Chrome OS saves the printer to your profile.

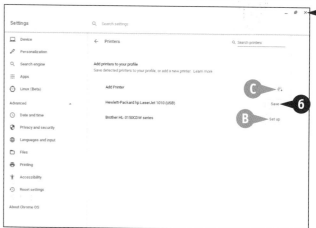

B You can click **Set up** to configure a printer that Chrome OS has detected but not immediately configured.

C You can click **Add printer** (🖶) to manually enter details of a printer or a print server.

7 Click **Close** (✕).

The Settings window closes.

Print a Document

1 Open the document you want to print.

This example uses a Word document in Google Docs.

2 Click **Print** (🖶).

The Print dialog box opens.

3 Click **Destination** (▼), and then click the appropriate printer.

Note: If the printer does not appear in the Destination list, try clicking **See more**. If the printer appears in the Select a Destination dialog box, click it.

4 Click **Pages** (▼), and then click **All** to click all pages or click **Custom** to specify a range of pages.

5 Click **Copies**, and then adjust the number of copies, if needed.

6 Click **Color** (▼), and then click **Black and white** or **Color**, as needed.

Ⓓ You can click **More settings** (❯) to display other settings, such as paper size and pages per sheet.

7 Click **Print**.

The Print dialog box closes.

Chrome OS prints the document.

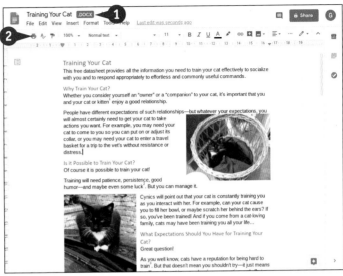

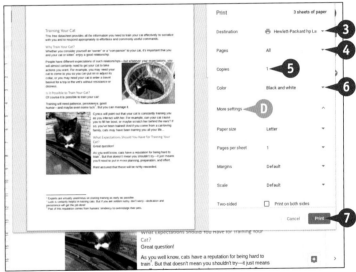

Can I use Google Cloud Print to print to remote printers from my Chromebook?
As of this writing, you can still use the Google Cloud Print service. However, Google has announced that it will shut down Google Cloud Print in December 2020.

How can I make a copy of a document to print later?
Use the Save as PDF feature. Open the document, and then click **Print** (🖶) to open the Print dialog box. Click **Destination** (▼), and then click **Save as PDF** instead of a printer. Choose other settings, as needed, and then click **Save**. In the Save File As dialog box, click the folder in which to save the PDF, and then click **Save**.

Using microSD Cards and USB Memory Sticks

Your Chromebook has some internal storage, which contains Chrome OS, your local data, any files you save, and any apps you install. Most Chromebooks have relatively modest amounts of storage, such as 32GB or 64GB. Even though Chrome OS is a relatively compact operating system, you may find your Chromebook does not have enough storage space left.

You can expand your Chromebook's local storage by using a microSD card or a USB storage device. You may also want to use microSD cards or USB storage devices for transferring files to or from your Chromebook.

Determine Your Choices for Expanding Storage

Start by looking to see whether your Chromebook has a microSD slot — a narrow slot about the width of your fingernail. If so, you may want to use a microSD card, because it normally fits flush to the body of the Chromebook, so you can leave it in place. Be aware that most microSD cards typically give slower performance than USB memory sticks.

Next, check how many USB ports your Chromebook has and what type they are. Most USB sticks have a USB Type A connector — the flat, rectangular connector — but some newer models have the USB Type C connector, the smaller, flat connector with rounded ends. You can use a USB Type C dongle to connect a USB Type A device to a USB Type C port.

Connect a microSD Card or USB Memory Stick

When you insert a microSD card in your Chromebook's microSD slot or connect a USB memory stick to a USB port, Chrome OS may display a Removable Device Detected notification. Click **Open Files App** to open a Files app window showing the contents of the card or memory stick.

Depending on the contents of the microSD card or USB memory stick, Chrome OS may not display a notification but simply open a Files app window showing the contents.

If Chrome OS displays a Removable Device Detected notification with the message *Sorry, your external storage device is not supported at this time*, you need to format the microSD card before you can use it with your Chromebook. See the following subsection, "Format a microSD Card or USB Memory Stick," for instructions.

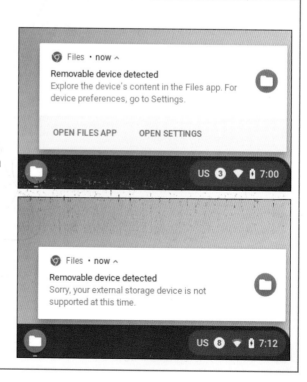

Format a microSD Card or USB Memory Stick

If a microSD card or USB memory stick is formatted with a file system that Chrome OS cannot use or if the card or stick is not formatted at all, you need to format it before your Chromebook can use it.

Click **Files** (🗔) on the shelf or on the Launcher screen to open a Files window, right-click the device's icon in the left pane, and then click **Format device**.

In the Format dialog box that opens, type a name in the Drivename box; click **Format** (▼), and then click FAT32, exFAT, or NTFS, as needed; and then click **Erase and Format**.

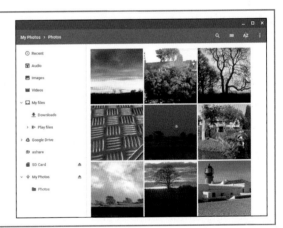

Work with a microSD Card or USB Memory Stick

When you have connected a microSD card or USB memory stick, you can access the files on it by using the Files app. Click **Files** (🗔) on the shelf or on the Launcher screen to open a Files window, and then click the entry for the microSD card or USB memory stick in the left pane. A microSD card appears with the 🗂 icon, whereas a USB device appears with the Ψ icon.

Eject and Remove a microSD Card or a USB Memory Stick

When you finish using a microSD card or USB memory stick, you should eject it from the Chrome OS file system before physically removing it. To eject the device, click **Eject** (⏏) next to its entry in the left pane in the Files app. Once the device's entry has disappeared from the left pane, you can safely remove the device.

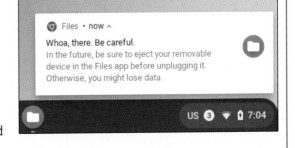

If you remove a device without ejecting it, Chrome OS displays a notification saying *Whoa, there. Be careful.* and reminding you to eject the device in the future.

Cast Content to a Chromecast Device

As well as Chromebooks, Chrome OS, and the Chrome browser, Google makes a line of devices called Chromecast for streaming video content and audio content. The Chromecast device and the Chromecast Ultra device stream video — or just audio, if you prefer — to a connected monitor or TV, whereas the Chromecast Audio device streams audio to connected speakers.

Your Chromebook enables you to *cast* — send — multimedia content to Chromecast devices. You can cast your desktop, an app, or video content to a Chromecast or a Chromecast Ultra, or simply cast audio to a Chromecast Audio.

Cast Content to a Chromecast Device

Cast Your Screen to a Chromecast Device

1 Click the status area.

The system menu opens.

2 Click **Cast** (⛶).

The Cast Screen menu opens.

Ⓐ The Chromecast icon (◉) denotes a Chromecast device to which you can cast the screen.

3 Click the Chromecast device you want to use.

The Share Your Entire Screen dialog box opens.

Note: If your Chromebook has one or more external screens connected, the Share Your Entire Screen dialog box enables you to choose which screen to cast.

4 Click the thumbnail for the screen you want to share.

The Share button becomes enabled.

5 Click **Share**.

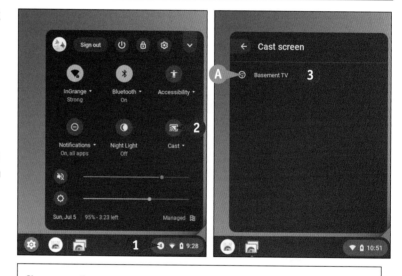

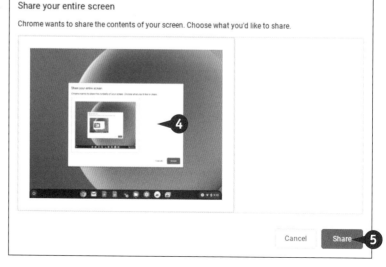

The Share Your Entire Screen dialog box closes.

Ⓑ A Casting notification appears, telling you that you are currently casting your screen.

Ⓒ You can click **STOP** to stop casting.

You can now perform the actions you want to share via casting. For example, you might demonstrate how to use an app.

Stop Casting Your Screen

❶ When you are ready to stop casting your screen, click the status area.

The system menu opens.

Ⓓ The Casting notification appears above the system menu.

Note: To see the Casting notification, you may need to dismiss notifications that have appeared since the Casting notification appeared.

❷ Click **STOP**.

Chrome OS stops casting your screen.

TIP

How do I put the Cast icon on the Chrome toolbar?
In Chrome, click **Menu** (⋮) to display the menu, and then click **Cast** to open the Cast Tab dialog box. While the Cast Tab dialog box is open, the Cast button (⟋) appears on the Chrome toolbar. Right-click **Cast** (⟋), and then click **Always Show Icon**, putting a check mark next to it. You can then click **Cancel** to close the Cast Tab dialog box.

continued ▶

Whenever you cast your desktop or an app, your Chromebook sends data to the Chromecast device, as you might expect. But when you cast video from YouTube or audio that is available on Google Music, your Chromebook tells the Chromecast device to connect to the appropriate service and start streaming the video or audio from that service. Once the Chromecast starts streaming the content, your Chromebook is no longer directly involved, but you can control playback of the video or audio from the Chromebook.

Cast Content to a Chromecast Device (continued)

Cast a YouTube Video to a Chromecast Device

1 Press **Shift** + click **Launcher** (⊙).

The Launcher appears full screen.

2 Click **YouTube** (▶).

The YouTube web app opens in a Chrome tab.

3 Navigate to the video you want to cast.

For example, you can browse or search to find the video.

4 Click **Play on TV** (▣).

The Cast Site dialog box opens.

Ⓔ The TV icon (▢) indicates a video-capable Chromecast device.

5 Click the Chromecast device to which you want to cast the video.

Chrome OS tells the Chromecast device to start streaming the video from YouTube.

6 Once the Chromecast has loaded the video, click **Play** (▶).

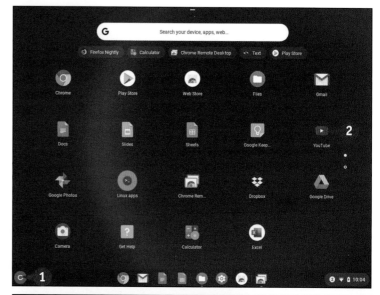

The Chromecast starts playing the video on the screen connected to it.

 The *Playing on* readout shows the Chromecast device that is playing the video.

Rural Properties: The Exciting New Market

Rural Properties
An Exciting New Market

Playing on Basement TV

0:08 / 0:00   Scroll for details

⑦ When you are ready to stop casting the video, click **Play on TV** (⬛).

The Cast Site dialog box opens.

⑧ Move the cursor over the name of the Chromecast device.

The Stop Casting text appears below the device's name.

⑨ Click the button for the Chromecast device.

The Chromecast device stops playing the video.

Rural Properties: The Exciting New Market

Cast www.youtube.com

Basement TV
Stop casting

Sources ▼

Rural Properties
An Exciting New Market

0:03 / 0:50   Scroll for details

TIP

How do I cast music to a Chromecast Audio or Google Home device?
Open a music site that supports casting, such as Google Play Music or SoundCloud, in a Chrome tab. Locate the song you want to play, and then click **Cast** (⬛) to open the Cast Site dialog box. Click the Chromecast Audio device or Google Home device (⬛) to which you want to cast the audio. Chrome OS starts casting the audio from that Chrome tab to the device. To stop casting, click **Cast** (⬛) to open the Cast Site dialog box, move the cursor over the device so that the Stop Casting text appears, and then click the device's button.

Connect Your Android Phone to Your Chromebook

If you have an Android phone, you can connect it to your Chromebook to take advantage of interoperability features that Google has built into Chrome OS. Here, *connect* means not using a cable to make a wired connection between the phone and the Chromebook, but rather setting up permissions for the two devices to work together.

After connecting your Android phone to your Chromebook, you can enable the Smart Lock feature, use Instant Tethering to connect your Chromebook to the Internet through your phone, or set up the Messages feature.

Connect Your Android Phone to Your Chromebook

When your Chromebook detects your Android phone, which is logged into the same Google Account, nearby, it may display a Set Up a Connection notification. You can click this notification to open a Settings app window that shows the Connected Devices section of the Settings screen. Here, click **Set up**.

If no notification appears, click the status area to display the system menu, and then click **Settings** (⚙) to open a Settings app window. Click **Connected devices** (▢) to display the Connected Devices section. Click **Set up**.

In the Connect to Your Phone dialog box that opens, verify that the Select a Device pop-up menu shows the correct phone; if not, click **Select a device** (▼) to open the menu, and then click the correct phone. Read through the information and the disclaimers, and then click **Accept & continue**. In the Enter Your Password dialog box, type your Google Account password, and then click **Done**. Finally, in the Ready! dialog box, click **Done**.

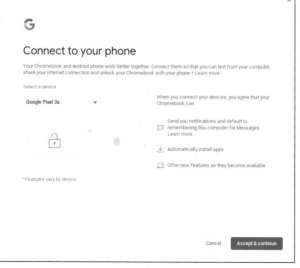

Choose Which Features to Enable

If the Settings window you used to start the connection process is still open, activate that window now. If not, click the status area to display the system menu, click **Settings** (⚙) to open a Settings app window, and then click **Connected devices** (☐) to display the Connected Devices section. Verify that the switch for your Android phone is set to On (⚫), and then tap the main part of the button to display the configuration screen for the phone.

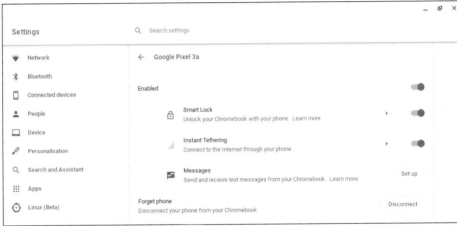

Set the **Smart Lock** switch to On (⚫) if you want to unlock your Chromebook using your phone. Click **Smart Lock** to display the Smart Lock screen, go to the Screen Lock

Options area, and then click **Unlock device only** (○ changes to ◉) or **Unlock device and sign in to Google Account** (○ changes to ◉), as needed.

Set the **Instant Tethering** switch to On (⚫) if you want to connect your Chromebook to the Internet via your phone's cellular connection. Tap **Instant Tethering** to display another screen whose title is your phone's name, and then tap **Connect**.

If you want to send messages from your Chromebook via your phone, tap **Set up** on the Messages line, and then follow the prompts.

Connect to the Internet via Your Android Phone

After connecting your Android phone to your Chromebook, you can use the Instant Tethering feature to give your Chromebook access to the Internet via your phone's cellular connection. Instant Tethering uses Wi-Fi to connect your Chromebook to your phone. Alternatively, you can use USB tethering to let your Chromebook use a phone's Internet connection — either the phone you made a "connected device" or any other phone.

You can connect your Chrome to any Wi-Fi hotspot, including hotspots run by phones. See the section "Connect to a Wi-Fi Network" in Chapter 1 for details.

Connect to the Internet via Your Android Phone

1 Make sure the Android phone is powered on and unlocked.

2 Click the status area.

The system menu opens.

3 Click **Settings** (⚙).

The Settings window opens.

4 Click **Connected devices** (▢).

The Connected Devices section of the Settings window appears.

5 Click the entry for your Android phone.

Note: If the Confirm Password dialog box opens, type your password, and then click **Confirm**.

6 Set the **Enabled** switch to On (⬤).

7 Make sure the **Instant Tethering** switch is set to On (⬤).

8 Click **Instant Tethering** (▲).

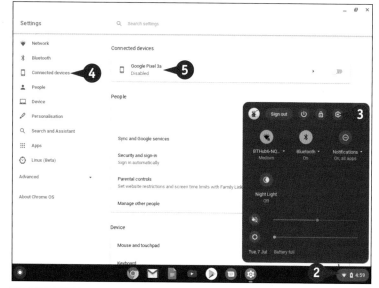

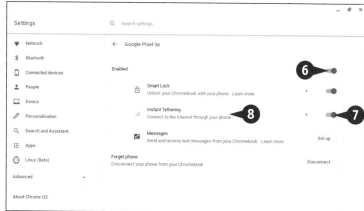

The first time you use Instant Tethering for a phone, the Connect to New Hotspot? dialog box opens.

9 Verify that the Available Device readout shows the correct phone.

10 Click **Connect**.

11 When your phone prompts you for permission to ask the carrier to allow hotspot functionality, give your permission.

The Mobile Data screen appears.

12 Set the master switch to On (⬤).

Note: It may take 30 seconds or a minute for your phone to appear on the Mobile Data screen.

13 Click the button for your phone.

The Settings screen for the phone appears.

A You can see the phone's battery status.

B You can see the phone's signal strength.

14 When you want to stop using the phone via Instant Tethering, click **Disconnect**.

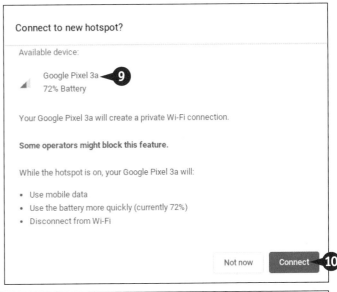

TIP

Is Instant Tethering better than USB tethering?

Instant Tethering uses your phone's cellular data connection, so using Instant Tethering always depletes your cellular data plan. By contrast, USB tethering uses whatever Internet connection your phone currently has — so if the phone has a Wi-Fi connection, USB tethering uses Wi-Fi rather than consuming your mobile data allowance. Unless you have an unlimited or generous mobile data allowance, USB tethering may be a better choice than Instant Tethering.

Connect to the Internet via USB Tethering

As well as connecting your Chromebook to the Internet via Instant Tethering with the Android phone you have made a "connected device," you can connect your Chromebook to the Internet via most recent Android phones using USB tethering.

When connected via USB, your Chromebook sees the Android phone as an Ethernet connection rather than identifying it as a smartphone. Ethernet is a family of standards for wired networking. If necessary, you can configure the Ethernet connection manually, choosing settings such as the IP address and proxy server details. You will not normally need to do this.

Connect to the Internet via USB Tethering

1 Make sure the Android phone is powered on and unlocked.

2 Connect the Chromebook to the USB phone via a suitable USB cable.

3 Click the status area.

The system menu opens.

4 Click **Ethernet** (⟨·⟩).

The Network menu appears.

5 Click **Ethernet** (⟨·⟩).

A Settings window opens, showing the Ethernet screen in the Network section.

A You can click **Configure** to open the Configure Ethernet dialog box, which enables you to change the security and authentication methods used for the connection. You will not normally need to change these.

B The IP Address readout shows the IP address the phone has assigned to the Chromebook.

6 If you need to see more details or to configure network settings manually, click **Network** (⌄).

C You can click **Proxy** (⌄) to configure proxy settings for the connection.

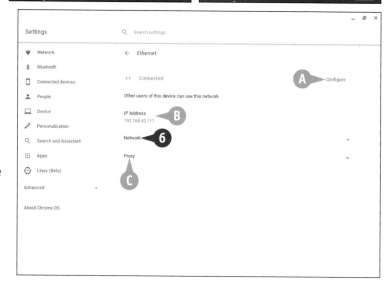

Note: Normally, you need to configure proxy settings only if a network administrator advises you to do so.

7 If you need to specify a static IP address, a routing prefix, or the gateway, set the **Configure IP address automatically** switch to Off (　), and then enter the data in the appropriate field.

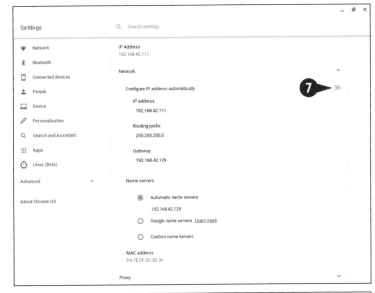

8 If you need to change the name servers, go to the Name Servers section. Then either click **Google name servers** (○ changes to ◉) to use Google's name servers or click **Custom name servers** (○ changes to ◉), and then enter the servers' details in the fields that appear.

D The *MAC Address* readout shows the Media Access Control address for the network connection.

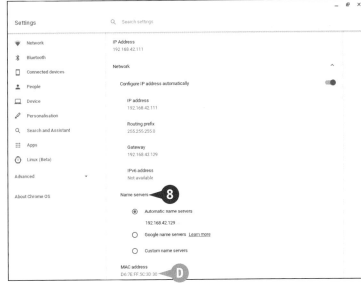

TIP

Can I use an iPhone for USB tethering?
As of this writing, you cannot use USB tethering to give your Chromebook access to your iPhone's Internet connection — but it seems likely that Google will add this functionality soon. In the meantime, use the iPhone's Personal Hotspot feature instead. You will need to set the **Allow Others to Join** switch on the Personal Hotspot screen to On (◉).

CHAPTER 5

Sharing Your Chromebook with Others

Chrome OS makes it easy to share your Chromebook with others without compromising your account security. You can enable the Guest Mode feature, which lets a temporary user browse easily. You can configure the sign-in screen, choose which users can sign in to the Chromebook, and implement parental controls to protect vulnerable users. You can even sign in multiple user accounts at once and switch quickly among them.

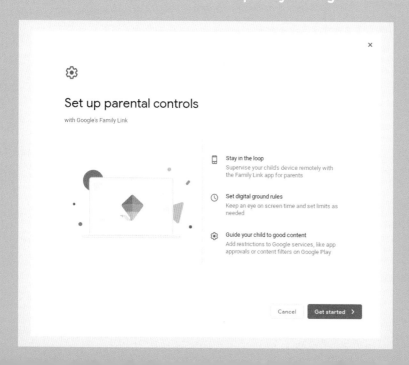

Enable Guest Browsing

Chrome OS includes a Guest account that you can enable when you want to allow someone else to use your Chromebook temporarily. The Guest account has no password, so a guest can quickly log in and start using the account. The guest can use the account much as normal, although there are some restrictions.

Chrome OS resets the Guest account at the end of each use, so any files the guest creates or downloads are deleted when the guest session ends.

Enable Guest Browsing

1 Click the status area.

The system menu opens.

2 Click **Settings** (⚙).

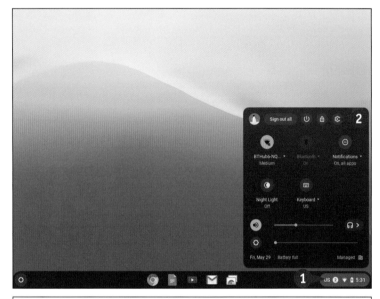

The Settings window opens.

3 Click **People** (👤).

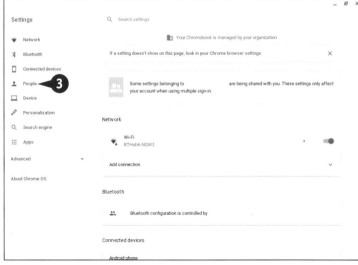

The People screen appears.

④ Click **Manage other people**.

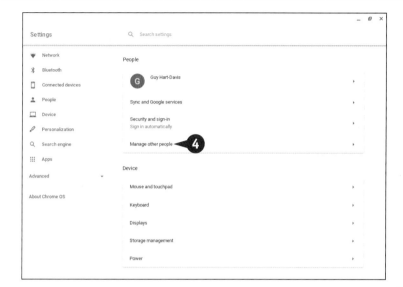

The Manage Other People
screen appears.

⑤ Set the **Enable Guest browsing**
switch to On (●).

⑥ Click **Close** (✖).

The Settings window closes.

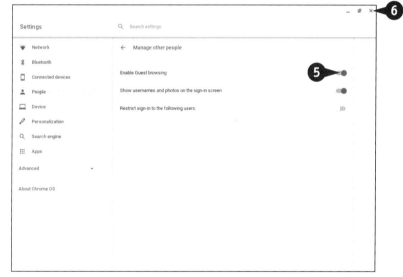

When should I enable Guest browsing on my Chromebook?

Enable Guest browsing when someone needs to use your Chromebook a single time. If someone will need to use the Chromebook regularly, having them sign in with their own account usually makes more sense.

How does Guest browsing compare to letting someone browse in Incognito Mode on my account?

Guest browsing cordons off the guest user in a temporary account, preventing them from accessing any other user's information. By contrast, letting someone use your account to browse in Incognito Mode risks them accessing apps and information available to your account.

Using a Chromebook in Guest Mode

To use a Chromebook in Guest Mode, you simply sign in as Guest from the Sign-In screen. You can then browse using Chrome and download and manage files using the Files app. You can also open the Settings app and take actions such as connecting to Wi-Fi networks or Bluetooth devices.

When you finish using the Chromebook, you exit the Guest session, and the Sign-In screen appears again. Chrome OS removes all data generated during the Guest session, including any files you downloaded or created.

Using a Chromebook in Guest Mode

1 On the Sign-In screen, click **Browse as Guest** ().

Note: If Browse as Guest () does not appear on the Sign-In screen, you need to enable the Guest Browsing feature. See the previous section, "Enable Guest Browsing," for details.

A Chrome window opens, showing a new tab.

A The message *You're browsing as a Guest* appears, warning you that files you download and bookmarks you create won't be preserved.

B The Guest button appears to the right of the omnibox.

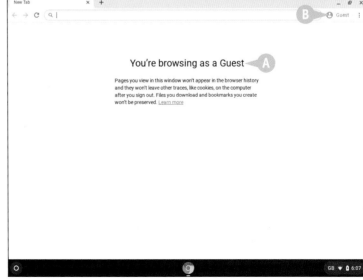

You can now use the Chromebook much as usual.

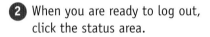 You can open the launcher and run apps. The selection of apps is much more limited.

2 When you are ready to log out, click the status area.

The system menu opens.

3 Click **Exit guest**.

The Sign-In screen appears.

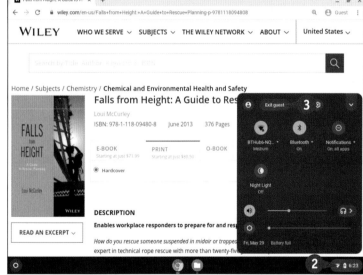

How can I keep files I create while working in Guest mode on someone else's Chromebook?
Usually, the best choice is to copy the files to online storage so that you can access them later from any computer or device. Alternatively, you can email the files to yourself or save them to a storage device, such as a USB stick, that you connect to the Chromebook.

When using Guest Mode, is it safe for me to log into my online accounts?
Yes, it is safe to log in to your online accounts — but make sure you sign out of the accounts before you end the Guest session to invalidate any session data that may persist on the Chromebook.

Configure the Sign-In Screen

By default, the Chrome OS sign-in screen shows the usernames and photos of the users who have signed in so far. A user can start signing in by clicking their username or photo.

Having the usernames and photos is convenient for a Chromebook you share with family or people close to you, but for a wider group, you may prefer to turn off the display of the usernames and photos. Then, a user must enter their username and password to sign in; if their account uses two-factor authentication, the user must go through that too.

Configure the Sign-In Screen

1 Click the status area.

The system menu opens.

2 Click **Settings** (⚙).

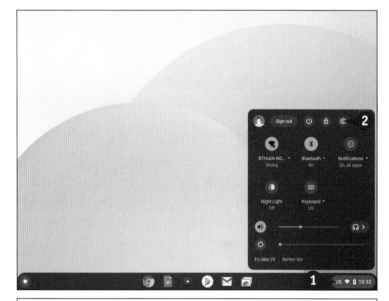

The Settings window opens.

3 Click **People** (👤).

The People section of the Settings screen appears.

4 Click **Manage other people**.

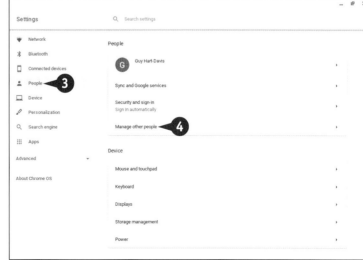

The Manage Other People screen appears.

5 Set the **Show usernames and photos on the sign-in screen** switch to Off ( ).

6 Click the status area.

The system menu opens.

7 Click **Sign out**.

The sign-in screen appears, with the Sign In to Your Chromebook dialog box displayed.

8 Type the email address or phone number for your Google Account.

9 Click **Next**, and then follow the prompts to enter your password and, if required, to verify your identity via two-factor authentication.

What is two-factor authentication?
Two-factor authentication is a security mechanism that adds an extra layer of protection required to access an account. For example, without two-factor authentication, you can log in to a Chromebook by providing your Google Account email address and the associated password. With two-factor authentication, you must provide extra security information, such as entering on your Chromebook a single-use code sent via text message to the verified phone number you have linked to your Google Account.

Restrict the Users Who Can Sign In

Chrome OS enables you to restrict sign-in to your Chromebook to only the Google Accounts you specify. This type of list is sometimes called a *whitelist*. For example, if you want to let only some of your family members sign in to your Chromebook, you can add those members' Google Accounts to the list.

Restrict the Users Who Can Sign In

1 Click the status area.

The system menu opens.

2 Click **Settings** (⚙).

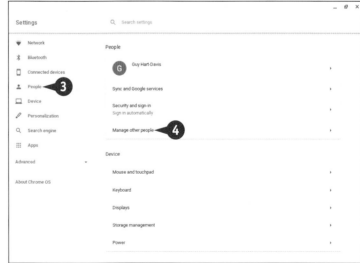

The Settings window opens.

3 Click **People** (👤).

The People screen appears.

4 Click **Manage other people**.

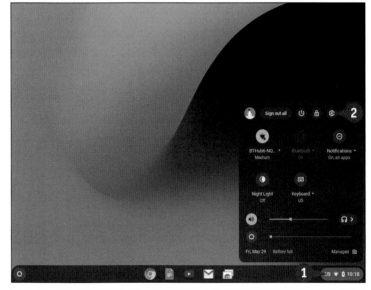

The Manage Other People screen appears.

5 Set the **Restrict sign-in to the following users** switch to On (⬤).

The list of users appears.

Ⓐ You can click **Remove** (✖) to remove a user from the list.

6 If you need to add a user to the list, click **Add user**.

The Add User dialog box opens.

7 Type the email address of the Google Account you want to add.

8 Click **Add**.

The Add User dialog box closes.

The email address appears on the list.

9 Click **Close** (✖).

The Settings window closes.

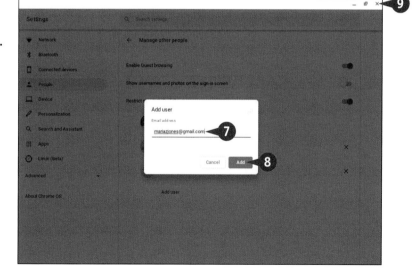

Why does the Restrict Sign-In to the Following Users list show only an email address for a user I added?

When you add a user, the email address you entered appears in the Restrict Sign-In to the Following Users list as a placeholder for the user's information. The user's information appears in the list once the user has signed in to the Chromebook successfully.

Implement Parental Controls

Chrome OS includes parental controls to help you supervise and protect children and other vulnerable users. The parental controls enable you to set restrictions on the content that a child can access online. For example, you can block adult websites and sexually explicit search results, and you can restrict movies and TV shows on the Google Play service. The parental controls also enable you to set screen time limits for a user.

The parental controls work both on Chrome OS — in other words, on the Chromebook — and on Android phones and tablets.

Start the Parental Controls Wizard

Sign in to the Chromebook using the account to which you want to apply parental controls. For example, sign in to your child's account; if you do not know the account password, have your child sign in.

Next, click the status area to open the system menu, and then click

Settings (⚙) to open the Settings window. Click **People** (👤) in the left pane to display the People section of the Settings screen, and then click **Set Up** on the Parental Controls row to start the Parental Controls wizard.

If the Parental Controls row does not appear on the People screen, the account under which you are signed in does not support parental controls. For example, if you are using a corporate account, parental controls are not available.

Learn About the Parental Controls Features and How You Set Them Up

The Parental Controls wizard first displays the Set Up Parental Controls screen. Read the summary of the features, and then click **Get started** to display the How to Set Up Parental Controls screen, which outlines the main steps. Click **Next** to proceed.

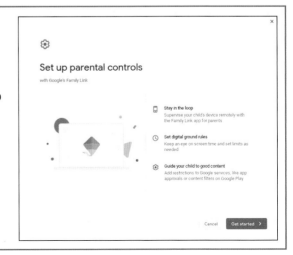

Specify the Child to Supervise

Next, the Parental Controls wizard displays the Is This the Child You Want to Supervise? screen. Verify that the correct name and email address appear, as they will if you started by having the child sign in to the Chromebook. If so, click **Yes** to proceed; if not, click **No**, follow the prompts to have the right child sign in, and then restart the Parental Controls wizard.

Learn Which Devices Can and Cannot Be Supervised

After you specify the child to supervise, the Parental Controls wizard displays the How Parental Controls Work on [Child's] Devices screen. Look through the Devices That Can Be Supervised list to make sure it mentions all the Chrome OS devices and Android devices you want to supervise. The list shows technical descriptions, such as "Google Intel Kaby Lake U Chromebook," rather than model names, so you may need to do some interpretation.

Look also at the Devices That Can't Be Supervised list, which explains devices that cannot be supervised — for example, iPads and iPhones.

Click **Next** when you are ready to proceed.

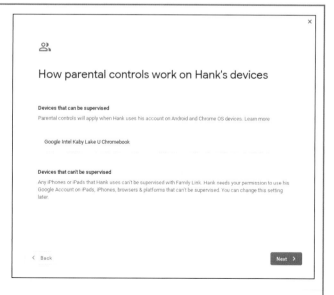

continued ▶

To be able to implement parental controls, you must link your child's Google Account to your own Google Account in a Google family group. Google's Family Link feature walks you through this process, if necessary, when you go to set up parental controls. The process is straightforward, provided that your Google Account and the child's Google Account are registered in the same country.

It is a good idea to discuss parental controls in general with your child before implementing them and then to go through the About Supervision information in the Parental Controls wizard together.

Specify the Parent Account

Next, the Parental Controls wizard displays the Parent Account screen. In the Email or Phone box, type the email address or phone number of the Google Account you will use to supervise your child — for example, your personal Google Account. Click **Next** to display the next screen, enter the password for your Google Account, and then click **Next** again. If you have Two-Step Verification enabled for your Google Account — as you should have — respond to the prompt on the 2-Step Verification screen that follows. For example, open the Gmail app on your phone, open the *Is It You Trying to Sign In?* message, and then tap **Yes**.

Review the Information About Supervision

After you specify the parent account, the Parental Controls wizard displays the About Supervision screen, which explains the supervision feature and the Google family group that you are about to create with your child.

Ideally, you and your child should review the About Supervision information together to make sure you both understand the process. Click **More** to progress through the What Parents Can See and Do section, the What Parents Can't See or Do section, and the How to Start and Stop Supervision section.

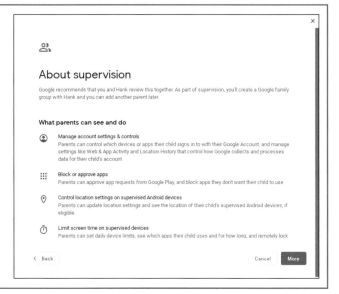

Have Your Child Agree to Supervision

When you reach the end of the About Supervision screen, the [Child], Enter Your Password to Agree to Supervision section appears. Have your child type their password in the box, and then click **Agree** to proceed.

The Parental Controls wizard then displays the Your Accounts Are Linked screen to confirm that you have linked the accounts. Click **Next** to proceed to the next stage, in which you review the child's apps and manage their settings and filters.

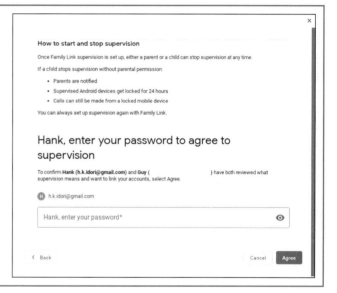

Review Your Child's Apps

On the Review [Child]'s Apps screen of the Parental Controls wizard, look through the Android apps installed on the Chromebook. Set the switch to Off ( ) for any app that you do not want your child to be able to use.

If there are more apps than fit on the Review [Child]'s Apps screen, click **More** to display the next section. When you reach the end of the list of apps, the Next button appears. Click **Next** to proceed to the Manage Filters & Settings screen.

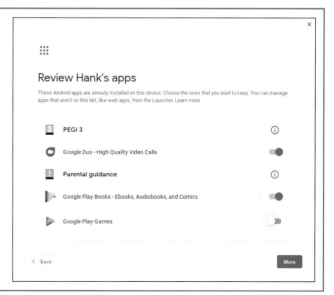

continued ▶

G oogle's parental controls include a feature for controlling whether your child can sign in to iOS devices — such as iPhones and iPads — and browsers that parental controls cannot supervise. By using the Controls for Signing In feature, you can choose between letting your child sign in freely or requiring parental permission.

After you finish setting up parental controls, you must sign your child's account out of the Chromebook. The child then signs back in to the Chromebook, and the parental controls take effect.

Configure Filters and Settings for the Child's Account

The Manage Filters & Settings screen of the Parental Controls wizard shows a list of the different categories of filters and settings you can apply to the account, including Filters on Google Chrome, Filters on Google Search, Google Play Movies, Google Play Purchase & Download Approvals, and Controls for Signing In.

Click the button for the category you want to set, and then click to select the appropriate setting (○ changes to ◉) in the dialog box that opens. For example, you might click **Filters on Google Chrome** to open the Filters on Google Chrome dialog box; click **Helps block mature sites** (○ changes to ◉) or **Approval required for all sites** (○ changes to ◉), as needed; and then click **OK**.

Click **More** on the Manage Filters & Settings screen to display items further down the list. When you reach the end of the list, click **Next**.

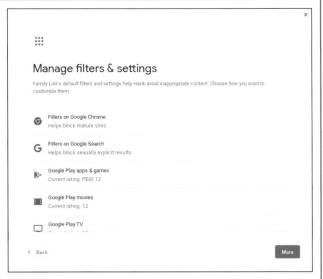

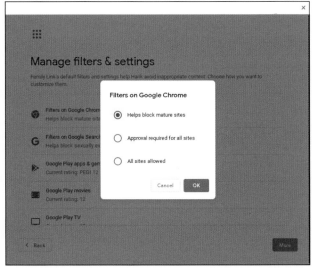

Install the Family Link App on Your Devices

On the Automatically Install Family Link on Your Devices screen of the Parental Controls wizard, select (☑) the check box for each Android device on which you want to install the Family Link app, which enables you to set screen time limits for your child and view their activity in apps.

To install the Family Link app on an iOS device, such as an iPhone or an iPad, open the App Store app and search for **google family link**.

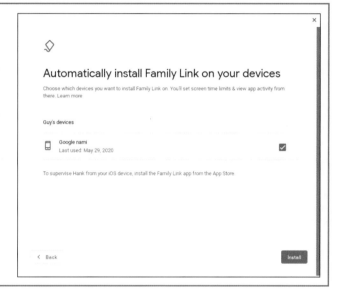

Sign Your Child Out, and Then Have Them Sign In Again

When you reach the Sign Out to Finish screen of the Parental Controls wizard, click **Sign Out**. Chrome OS signs your child's account out of the Chromebook and applies the restrictions to the account.

When the Sign In screen appears, your child's account is marked *Sign-In Required*. Have your child sign in to the account. The parental controls are then in place on the account.

Sign In Multiple Users and Switch Among Them

If you have two or more Google Accounts, you may want to enable the Multiple Sign-In feature. This feature lets you sign in multiple accounts at once and then switch quickly among them, rather than having to sign out of one account before you can use another account.

Multiple Sign-In is convenient, but you should use it only for Google Accounts, or for other people, that you fully trust.

Sign In Multiple Users and Switch Among Them

1 Click the status area.

The system menu appears.

2 Click the icon for the current account.

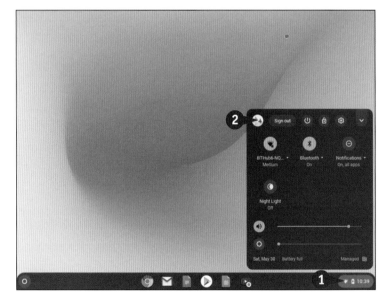

The User Account system menu appears.

3 Click **Sign in another user** (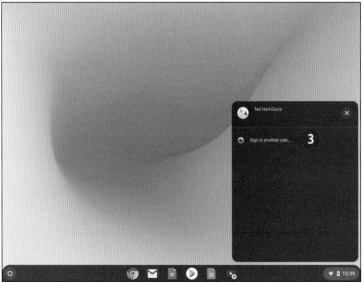).

The sign-in screen appears.

Ⓐ Chrome OS selects one user account.

Ⓑ If you want to use a different account, click it.

Ⓒ Chrome OS warns you that all signed-in accounts can be accessed without a password, so you should use Multiple Sign-In only with accounts and people you trust.

④ Type the password for the account.

⑤ Click **Continue** (➔) or press **Enter**.

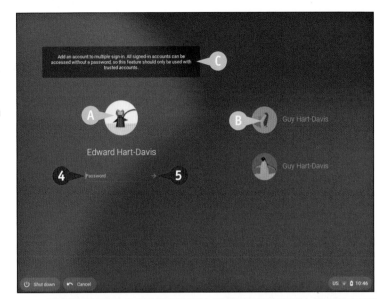

Chrome OS signs you in to the account.

You can then work as normal in the account.

⑥ When you need to switch accounts, click the status area.

The system menu appears.

⑦ Click the icon for the current account.

The User Account system menu appears.

⑧ Click the account to which you want to switch.

Ⓓ You can click **Sign in another user** (🔘) to add another user account to Multiple Sign-In.

TIP

How can I switch quickly between the accounts in Multiple Sign-In?
Press **Ctrl**+**Alt**+**.** to switch to the previous user. Press **Ctrl**+**Alt**+**.** to switch to the next user.
If you are using two accounts, pressing these two key combinations has the same effect.

CHAPTER 6

Running and Managing Apps and Extensions

This chapter shows you how to use apps on your Chromebook to perform tasks. You learn the difference between Chrome OS native apps, Chrome web apps, and extensions, and how to install and use all three. You also learn how to install and run Android apps and how to configure preferences for them.

Understanding Apps and Extensions

Most computers and devices have various "apps," applications or programs that enable you to take actions — for example, a spreadsheet app that enables you to create spreadsheets and crunch data. Similarly, your Chromebook can run a wide variety of programs for browsing, email, word processing, and so on. But the Chromebook's programs are not only apps. Instead, they come in three different types: apps, web apps, and extensions. On many Chromebooks, you can also install and run Android apps.

This section explains the differences among these types of programs and tells you what you need to know about how they work.

Understanding What Apps Are

In Chrome OS, an *app* is a stand-alone program that runs in its own window rather than in the Chrome browser. For example, Chrome OS includes the Files app for managing files and the Settings app for configuring Chrome OS and system settings. When you open the Launcher and then click **Files** (□), the Files app opens in its own window. Similarly, when you open the Launcher and then click **Settings** (⚙), the Settings app opens in its own window. The figure shows a Settings window open in front of a Files window.

Apps of this type are sometimes described as "Chrome OS native apps."

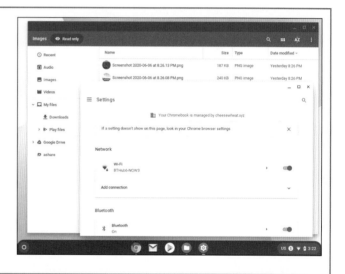

Understanding What Web Apps Are

In Chrome OS, a *web app* is a website that runs on a tab in the Chrome browser rather than running as a stand-alone program. The figure shows a document in the Google Docs app running in a Chrome tab.

You can open multiple tabs in the same Chrome window and then switch from tab to tab to access the apps you want to work in. You can also open multiple Chrome windows and switch from window to window. The advantage of having multiple windows is that you can position them side by side when you need to work in two or more apps at once. For example, you can view a Sheets spreadsheet while writing a report in a Docs document.

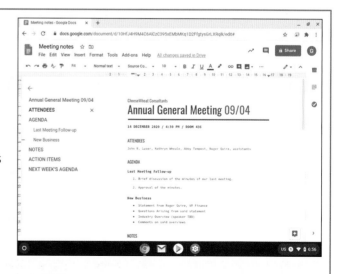

Understanding What Extensions Are

An *extension* is a piece of add-on software that adds extra capabilities to the Chrome browser. For example, the Grammarly for Chrome extension adds features for checking spelling, grammar, style, and tone in text documents you create; the Zoom Scheduler extension enables you to schedule video-conferencing meetings on the Zoom service directly from Google Calendar.

You can browse a wide variety of extensions on the Chrome Web Store. When you find an extension that offers functionality you need, you can add that extension to Chrome to make the functionality available.

Understanding What Android Apps Are

Apart from Chrome OS native apps and Chrome web apps, Chromebooks released in 2017 or thereafter can also run some apps built for Android, Google's smartphone operating system. Far more apps are available for Android than for Chrome OS devices, so this capability greatly increases your choice of apps. For example, Microsoft provides versions of its Office apps — including Word; Excel, shown here; and PowerPoint — for Android but not for Chrome OS.

You can browse a vast number of Android apps on the Google Play Store. Only some of the apps are suitable for running on the Chromebook, and the Play Store app tries to display only apps that will run. As a result, you may sometimes go to install on your Chromebook an app that you use on your Android phone or tablet, only to find yourself unable to locate it on the Play Store.

Run an App

When you need to start using an app on your Chromebook, you run the app by displaying the Launcher screen and then clicking the app's icon. An app or an Android app opens in its own window, whereas a web app opens in a tab in a Chrome browser window.

You can also open an app or a web app by double-clicking a file associated with that app. For example, if you open a Files window and double-click a document in the Google Docs format, the document normally opens in Docs in a Chrome tab.

Run an App

1 Click **Launcher** (⊙).

Note: You can press 🔍 to display the Launcher bar.

The Launcher bar opens.

Ⓐ If the app you want to run appears in the Recent Apps list in the Launcher bar, click its button there.

2 Click **Full Screen** (⌃).

Note: You can press Shift + 🔍 to display the Launcher full screen in a single move.

The Launcher appears full screen.

Ⓑ If the apps appear on multiple screens, a dot appears for each screen. The solid dot represents the current screen. Click another dot to display its screen.

Ⓒ You can click **Search** (**G**) and type a search term or multiple keywords to search.

3 Click the icon for the app you want to open. This example uses **Docs** (▤).

The app opens.

Note: Depending on the app type, it may open in a Chrome tab or in its own window. In this example, Docs opens in a Chrome tab.

④ You can take actions in the app. For example, in Docs, you might click a template to create a new document based on it.

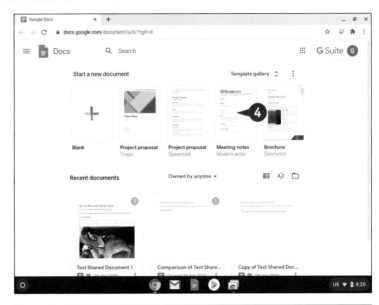

Following this example, the new document opens.

You can then work in the document.

⑤ When you are ready to close the document, click **Close** (✕).

The window closes.

The app closes with the window.

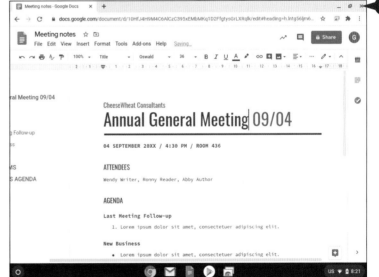

Can I run multiple apps at once?
Yes. To run another app, click **Launcher** (○), and then launch the next app as explained in this section. Some apps allow you to run multiple instances of themselves, but other apps limit you to a single instance. For example, you can open only one instance of the Settings app.

How many apps can I run at the same time?
This depends on the apps you are using and the configuration of your Chromebook. There is no hard limit on the number of apps you can run, but your Chromebook has a finite amount of memory and processing power with which to run them.

Switch Among Open Windows

After you open various windows containing apps, you can switch among them quickly by using the window switcher. The window switcher displays a thumbnail of each open window, enabling you to visually identify the window you want. You can also switch windows by using the icons on the shelf.

Chrome OS lets you quickly dock a window to the left side or right side of the screen, making the window take up half of the screen. Docking is handy for viewing two windows side by side.

Switch Among Open Windows

Switch Apps Using the Window Switcher

1 Open the apps you want to use.

2 Hold down **Alt**, and then press **Tab**.

A The window switcher opens.

B The window that was active appears first in the list.

C Chrome OS selects the next window by default.

3 Still holding down **Alt**, press **Tab** to move the highlight to the window you want to display and make active.

Note: While holding down **Alt**, you can press **Shift** + **Tab** to move backward through the windows in the window switcher.

4 Release **Alt**.

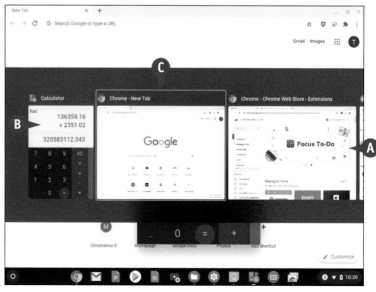

The window switcher closes.

D The window you selected appears at the front and becomes active.

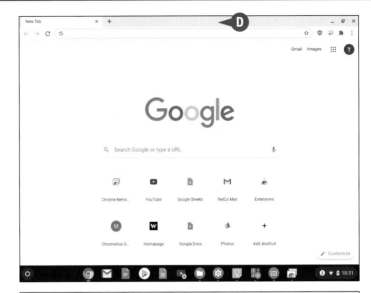

Switch Windows Using the Shelf

1 Click the app icon on the shelf.

E The app's window appears.

F If the app has multiple windows open, the pop-up menu opens showing the list of windows. Click the window you want to display.

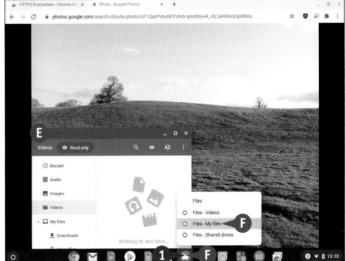

TIP

How can I make a window take up half the screen?

You can dock a non-maximized window by clicking its title bar and dragging it left or right until the cursor hits the side of the screen. When Chrome OS displays an outline of the window taking up half the screen, release the window.

You can also dock a window to the left by pressing Alt + [or to the right by pressing Alt +]. These keyboard shortcuts work even for maximized windows.

However, Chrome OS does not allow certain windows to be docked. Chrome OS also will not dock a window that cannot be scaled down far enough to fit in half the screen's width.

Organize Your Windows with Desks

Chrome OS enables you to create multiple desks — virtual workspaces — to organize your windows. Chrome OS starts you off with a single desk, but you can create up to four desks. Once you have multiple desks, you can drag your open windows to the appropriate desks, and then display the desk you want to use.

You can manipulate desks and windows quickly using keyboard shortcuts. See the tips for details.

Organize Your Windows with Desks

1 Open the apps you want to use.

2 Press ▭.

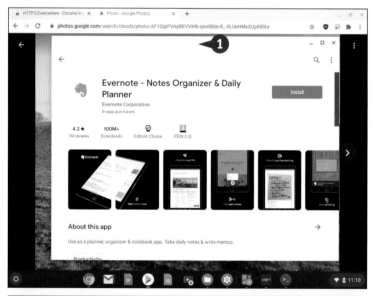

The Desks screen appears.

At first, there is only a single desk.

3 Click **New desk**.

A The Desk 1 thumbnail appears, representing the desk you were using. All the windows are assigned to this desk.

B A Desk 2 thumbnail appears, representing the new desk.

4 Drag a window to the Desk 2 thumbnail to move that window to the new desk.

Note: Drag other windows to the new desk, as needed.

5 When you finish moving windows, click the thumbnail for the desk you want to display.

In this example, you would click **Desk 2**.

The Desks screen closes.

The desk you clicked appears, showing the windows you moved to it.

6 Click the window you want to work in.

The window becomes active, and you can work in it.

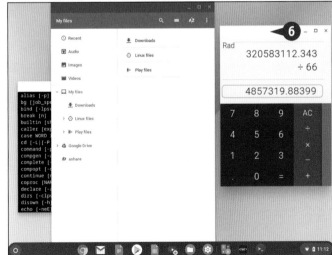

How do I switch desks using the keyboard?
Press Shift + Q + — to create a new desk. Press Q + [to activate the desk to the left, or press Q +] to activate the desk to the right. Press Shift + Q + [to move the active window to the desk to the left, or press Shift + Q +] to move the active window to the desk to the right.

How do I get rid of a desk?
Press ⊡ to display the Desks screen, move the cursor over the desk you want to delete, and then click **Delete** (⊗). From the keyboard, you can press Shift + Q + — to remove the current desk. Any windows on the desk you delete move to the first remaining desk.

Install an App from the Web Store

You can increase the functionality of your Chromebook by installing other apps on it from the Web Store. The Web Store includes a wide variety of both Chrome OS native apps and web apps that Google has approved as being properly designed for Chrome OS. You can find apps by browsing the various categories, such as Education or Productivity, or by searching using keywords.

After identifying a suitable app and installing it, you can run the app immediately from the Launcher screen.

Install an App from the Web Store

Install an App from the Web Store

1 Hold down **Shift** while you click **Launcher** ( ).

The Launcher opens full screen.

A If you cannot see Web Store ( ), click **Search** (**G**), and then start typing *web store* until the Web Store icon ( ) appears.

2 Click **Web Store** ( ).

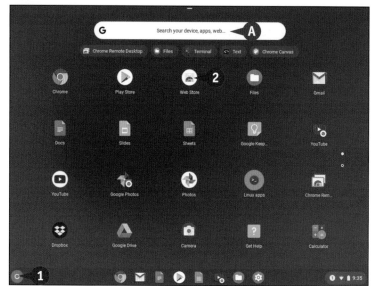

The Chrome Web Store opens in a new Chrome tab

3 Click **Apps** ( ).

The Apps section of the Web Store appears.

B In the Types area, you can click **Chrome Apps** (○ changes to ◉) to display only apps, or you can click **Websites** (○ changes to ◉) to display only web apps.

4 Click the app or web app you want to install.

This example uses an app.

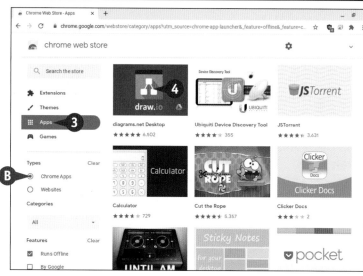

The screen for the app or web app appears.

C You can browse the Overview section, the Reviews section, the Support section, and the Related section to learn about the app.

5 Click **Add to Chrome**.

The Add dialog box opens.

6 Click **Add app**.

Chrome OS installs the app.

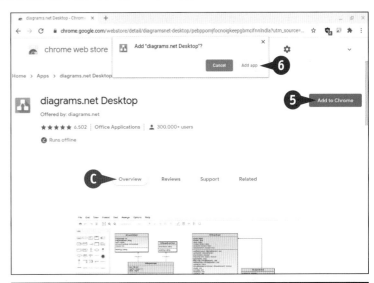

Run the App You Installed

1 Hold down Shift while you click **Launcher** (○).

The Launcher opens full screen.

2 Locate the icon for the app you installed.

D If you want to pin the app to the shelf for quick access, right-click the icon, and then click **Pin to shelf** (📌).

3 Click the app icon.

The app opens, and you can start using it.

TIP

When I have the choice of a Chrome OS app, a web app, or an Android app, which should I pick?
This will depend on the specific apps involved — but in general, either a Chrome OS app or a web app is preferable to an Android app on a Chromebook. This is because Chrome OS apps and web apps are designed to be displayed on a Chromebook's landscape-format screen and used with a keyboard and touchpad for input, whereas most Android apps are designed to be displayed on portrait-format phone screens and used with a touchscreen for input.

Install an Extension

As you have seen earlier in this chapter, you can add functionality to your Chromebook by installing apps or web apps on it. But you can also add functionality to the Chrome browser itself by installing extensions from the Chrome Web Store.

The Chrome Web Store provides a wide variety of extensions. For example, you can find extensions that add enhancements to Gmail in Chrome; extensions for blocking advertisements on YouTube; and extensions for clipping notes to the Evernote service.

Install an Extension

Install an Extension from the Web Store

① Hold down **Shift** while you click **Launcher** (○).

The Launcher opens full screen.

Ⓐ If you cannot see Web Store (◉), click **Search** (**G**), and then start typing *web store* until the Web Store icon (◉) appears.

② Click **Web Store** (◉).

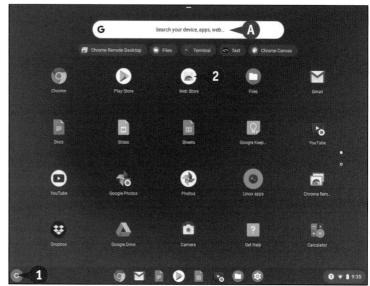

The Chrome Web Store opens in a new Chrome tab.

③ Click **Extensions** (✖).

The Extensions section of the Web Store appears.

Ⓑ In the Categories area, you can click ▼ to open the pop-up menu, and then click a category, such as **By Google**.

④ Click the extension you want to install.

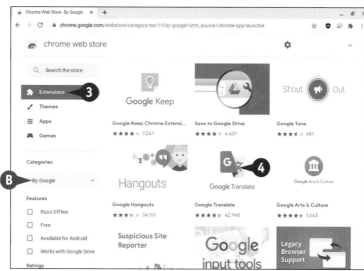

The screen for the extension appears.

C You can browse the Overview section, the Reviews section, and the Related section to learn about the extension.

5 Click **Add to Chrome**.

The Add dialog box opens.

D The It Can list tells you which actions the extension can perform on your Chromebook. See the tip for advice.

6 Click **Add extension**.

Chrome installs the extension.

Using the Extension You Installed

1 Open a Chrome tab to a suitable web page.

This example illustrates opening a foreign-language page and using Google Translate to translate it.

2 Click the icon for the extension.

E The extension's control panel appears.

3 Use the controls, as needed.

For example, in Google Translate, you can click **English** to translate a foreign-language page to English.

4 When you finish using the extension, click **Close** (✖).

The extension's control panel closes.

TIP

Which actions should I allow for an extension?
Which actions you should allow depends on what the extension does and who offers it. Read the It Can list carefully and make sure that the actions the extension is allowed to perform match what the extension is supposed to do and do not reach beyond its functionality. You should also consider the reputation of the developer and their financial motivation for offering the extension.

Pin and Unpin Extensions

For quick access, you can pin one or more extensions to the toolbar near the top of the Chrome window. Each pinned extension appears as an icon between the right side of the omnibox and the Menu button. You can then click an icon to execute the extension's action or display information about the extension — the effect varies depending on the extension — or right-click an icon to display Chrome's context menu for that extension.

Because only a limited amount of space is available on the toolbar, it is best to pin only those extensions you will use frequently.

Pin and Unpin Extensions

1 Click **Chrome** (🔵) on the shelf.

Note: If Chrome (🔵) does not appear on the shelf, press Shift+click **Launcher** (⭕) to open the Launcher full screen, and then click **Chrome** (🔵).

Chrome opens or becomes active.

2 Click **Extensions** (🧩).

The Extensions pop-up panel opens.

3 To pin an extension, click **Pin Extension** (📌 changes to 📍).

4 To unpin an extension, click **Unpin Extension** (📍 changes to 📌).

5 Click **Close** (⚙️).

The Extensions pop-up panel closes.

A The extensions you pinned appear on the toolbar.

6 Right-click an extension's icon.

Chrome's context menu for the extension appears.

B You can change settings for the extension.

C You can remove the extension from Chrome.

D You can give any command that appears for the extension.

Note: To run an extension whose icon does not appear on the toolbar, click **Extensions** (🧩), and then click the extension's name.

Configure Settings for an Extension

After installing an extension to add functionality to the Chrome browser, look to see whether the extension has settings you can configure. Most extensions do have settings, but what the settings enable you to do varies widely, depending on what the extension itself does. You may need to read the documentation for the extension to get a clear picture of what some settings do and how to configure them to best meet your needs.

Configure Settings for an Extension

1 Click **Chrome** (🌐) on the shelf.

Note: If Chrome (🌐) does not appear on the shelf, press Shift +click **Launcher** (○) to open the Launcher full screen, and then click **Chrome** (🌐).

Chrome opens or becomes active.

2 Right-click the extension's icon on the toolbar.

Chrome's context menu for the extension opens.

3 Click **Options**.

The extension's Options page appears.

Note: Some extensions may not have an Options page.

4 Navigate to the category of options you want to set.

In this example, you can click **Settings** to display the Settings category.

5 Choose settings as needed.

6 When you finish choosing settings, click **Close** (✕).

The extension's Options page closes.

Manage and Remove Extensions

The best way to determine whether a Chrome extension is useful to you is to install it and use it — which means you may end up installing many extensions on your Chromebook but using only some of them.

If you find you do not use an extension, you can disable it temporarily or simply remove it from Chrome. Disabling an extension can be a good way to find out how much — if at all — you will miss an extension before you actually remove it.

Manage and Remove Extensions

1 Click **Chrome** () on the shelf.

Note: If Chrome (⚙) does not appear on the shelf, press **Shift**+click **Launcher** (⚪) to open the Launcher full screen, and then click **Chrome** (⚙).

Chrome opens or becomes active.

2 Click **Extensions** (✦).

The Extensions panel opens.

3 Click **Manage extensions** (⚙).

The Extensions screen appears.

4 Set each extension's switch to On (   ) or Off (⬤), as needed.

5 To see detailed information about an extension, click **Details**.

The Details page for the extension appears.

Ⓐ You can read the description.

Ⓑ You can determine the version number.

Ⓒ You can see the extension's size on disk.

Ⓓ You can examine the permissions you have granted the extension.

Ⓔ You can see which websites the extension can interact with.

⑥ Set the **Allow in incognito** switch to On (⬤) or Off ( ), as needed. See the tip for advice.

Ⓕ You can click **View in Chrome Web Store** (☐) to display the extension's page in the Chrome Web Store.

⑦ Click **Back** (⬅).

The Extensions screen appears.

⑧ To remove an extension, click **Remove**.

The Remove dialog box for the extension appears.

⑨ Click **Remove**.

Chrome removes the extension.

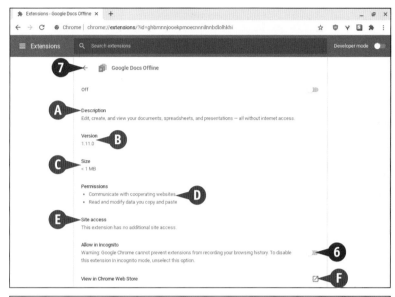

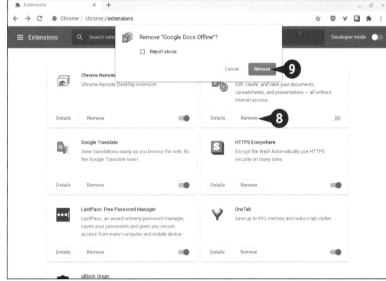

TIP

When should I allow an extension in Incognito Mode?

Generally, you should allow only privacy-focused extensions in Incognito Mode — for example, extensions that block advertisements, tracking cookies and tokens, and malicious scripts.

When you are using Incognito Mode to do work that depends on functionality from specific extensions, you should allow those extensions strictly as needed and on a case-by-case basis.

Install an Android App

A ndroid, as you no doubt know, is Google's smartphone operating system. Chrome OS enables you to install and run Android apps on your Chromebook. As of this writing, around 3 million Android apps are available. Not all those apps will run on Chromebooks — but even so, being able to use Android apps greatly increases your choice of apps.

The capability to install and run Android apps is available on all Chromebooks released in or after 2017. If you have a pre-2017 Chromebook, it will not be able to install or run Android apps.

Install an Android App

1 Hold down **Shift** while you click **Launcher** (⊙).

The Launcher opens full screen.

A If you cannot see Play Store (▶), click **Search** (**G**), and then start typing *play store* until the Play Store icon (▶) appears.

2 Click **Play Store** (▶).

The Play Store app opens in a window.

B You can click **Search for apps & games** and type one or more keywords to search by.

C You can browse the available apps and games by clicking categories, such as **For you** or **Top charts**.

D You can click **Games** (🎮), **Apps** (🔡), **Movies & TV** (🎬), or **Books** (📖) to display those categories of items.

3 When you locate the app or game you want to install, click it.

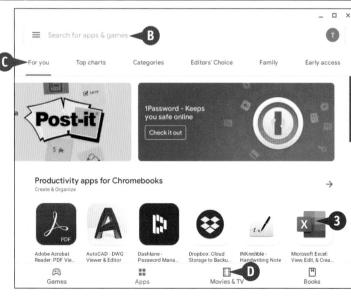

The screen for the app or game appears.

E You can view screenshots and information for the app.

4 Click **Install**.

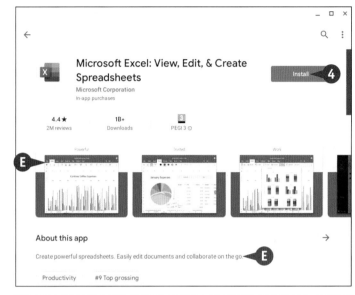

Chrome OS installs the Android app.

F When installation is complete, you can click **Open** to open the app.

G Alternatively, you can click **Back** (←) to return to the previous screen in the Play Store app.

H You can click **Close** (✖) to close the Play Store app.

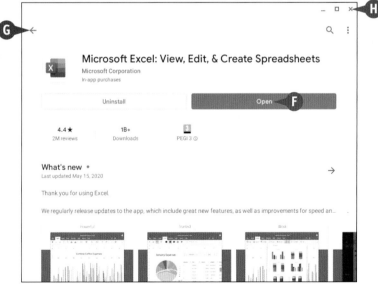

TIP

Why are some Play Store apps available for phones but not for Chromebooks?
Some apps depend on features that Android phones — or some Android phones — have but that Chromebooks do not have. For example, many apps are built to support only processors based on ARM designs, whereas Chromebooks generally use Intel or AMD processors, which have different designs. If you see the message that an app or game "isn't available on Google Play on this device," the app or game will not run on your Chromebook.

Run an Android App

After installing one or more Android apps on your Chromebook, you can run those apps from the Launcher just like Chrome OS apps or web apps. Like Chrome OS native apps, Android apps open in their own windows rather than in Chrome tabs.

If an app becomes unresponsive and will not close, you can force it to stop. See the tip for details.

Run an Android App

1️⃣ Press Shift+click **Launcher** (🔘).

The Launcher appears full screen.

2️⃣ Click the app you want to run.

Note: If you cannot see the app's icon, click **Search** and start typing the app's name.

The app opens.

🅐 The first time you run an app, you may need to perform some setup, such as signing in to an account.

Note: Some Android apps may run in portrait mode on a Chromebook, as if they were running on a phone.

Once the app is running, you can take actions in it.

B For example, you can choose a type of file to create and specify where to save it.

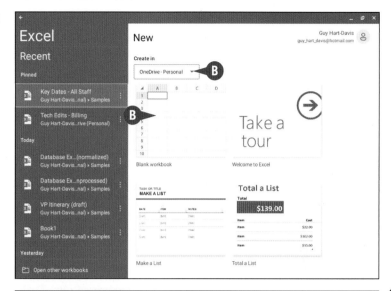

After creating or opening a file, you can work in it.

C For example, you can enter data in an Excel worksheet.

D Many apps save your changes automatically. When using an app that does not save automatically, make sure you save your work frequently.

3 When you finish working in an app, click **Close** (✕).

The app closes.

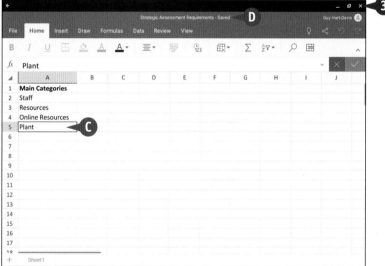

TIP

How do I close an Android app that has crashed?

If an Android app stops responding, try to close it by using normal means. First, try clicking **Close** (✕) in the upper-right corner of the window. If that fails, try right-clicking the app's icon on the shelf and then clicking **Close** (⊗) on the context menu. Failing that, right-click the app's icon on the shelf again, and then click **App info** (ⓘ) to display Chrome OS's Settings screen for the app. Click **More settings and permissions** (☑) to display Android's App Info screen for the app. Click **Force stop**, and then click **OK** in the Force Stop? dialog box that opens.

Configure Preferences for Android Apps

If you install and run Android apps on your Chromebook, it is a good idea to configure preferences for how the Android subsystem in Chrome OS runs apps. The Android subsystem has many preferences, most of them picked up directly from the Android operating system for smartphones and tablets. Only some of the settings are relevant for Chromebooks.

This section shows you how to open the Settings screen for the Android subsystem in Chrome OS and how to adjust some of the settings that you may find helpful.

Open the Settings Screen for the Android Subsystem

Click the status area to open the system menu, and then click **Settings** (⚙) to open the Settings app. Click **Apps** (▦) to display the Apps section, and then click **Google Play Store** to display the Google Play Store screen. Click **Manage Android preferences** (⧉) to open the Settings app for the Android subsystem, shown on the left here.

You can then click a settings category to display its contents. For example, click **System** (⊚) to display the System screen, shown on the right here.

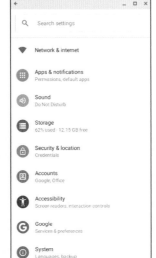

Configure Apps & Notifications Settings

Click **Apps & notifications** (⬤) on the Settings screen to display the Apps & Notifications screen, shown on the left here. The Recently Opened Apps list at the top of these screen shows Android apps you have run recently. You can click **See all apps** to see the full list of Android apps on your Chromebook.

Click the app for which you want to configure settings or notifications. The App Info screen for the app appears, such as the App Info screen for the Dropbox app, shown on the right here. You can then click the category of settings you want to configure. For example, click **Notifications** to configure settings for notifications; or click **Permissions** to examine current permissions settings and change them, if needed.

View and Control an App's Data Usage

The Android subsystem enables you to view an app's data usage. You may find this capability useful when using your Chromebook through a metered connection, such as your cellular connection.

To view an app's data usage, click **Apps & notifications** (⊕) on the Settings screen to display the Apps & Notifications screen, and then click the app whose data usage you want to see. On the App Info screen for the app — such as the App Info screen for the Google Play Store app, shown in the upper screenshot — click **Data usage** to display the App Data Usage screen, shown in the lower screenshot.

If necessary, change the date range by tapping ▼ and then tapping the appropriate date range. Then look at the Total readout, the Foreground readout, and the Background readout. *Foreground* means data usage that occurs when the app is active; *background* means data usage that occurs when the app is not active.

Many apps transfer most of their data when they are in the foreground, but others transfer a lot of data when they are in the background. For example, the Google Play Store app will frequently download updates while it is in the background.

If you want to prevent an app from transferring data in the background, set the **Background data** switch to Off (⬤).

If you want to allow an app unrestricted data usage when the Data Saver feature is on, set the **Unrestricted data usage** switch to On (⬤).

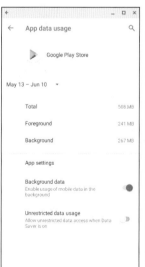

CHAPTER 7

Managing Your Files and Folders

Chrome OS simplifies file storage and management as much as possible, but you still need to know where to store files and how to work with files and folders. This chapter explains your file storage options; shows you around your Chromebook's local storage and your Google Drive online storage; and then walks you through key operations, from copying and moving files to recovering deleted files on Google Drive.

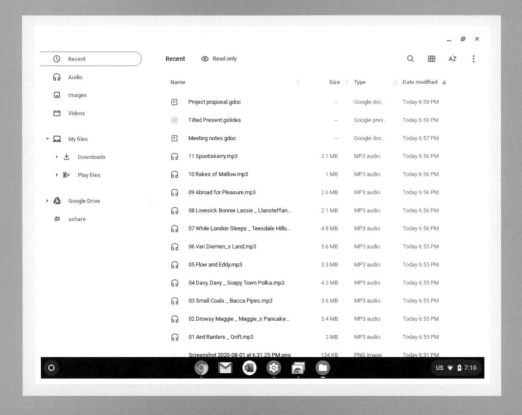

Understanding Your File Storage Options

Before you start working with files on your Chromebook, you should understand your file storage options so that you can store your files in the locations you will find most convenient.

You have four main options for file storage: your Chromebook's internal storage, which may be modest in capacity; your Google Drive, to which your Chromebook connects automatically; other storage services, such as Dropbox or OneDrive; and removable storage devices, such as USB drives and microSD cards, that you can connect to your Chromebook.

Your Chromebook's Internal Storage

Chromebooks are designed to store many files online, but you can also save files to local storage. Most Chromebook models have relatively little local storage, such as 32GB or 64GB, both to keep prices down and to encourage you to store your files online, where they can be backed up automatically.

To see the amount of storage used and the amount of storage available on your Chromebook, click the status area, and then click **Settings** (⚙) on the system menu. In the Settings window that opens, click **Device** (🖥) to display the Device section of the Settings screen, and then click **Storage management** to display the Storage Management screen. The histogram at the top shows the amount of storage in use and the amount that remains available.

Your Google Drive Storage

When you sign in to your Chromebook using your Google Account, the Chromebook connects automatically to your storage on Google Drive, and you can store files there. You can access Google Drive either through the Chrome browser, as shown here, or through the Files app.

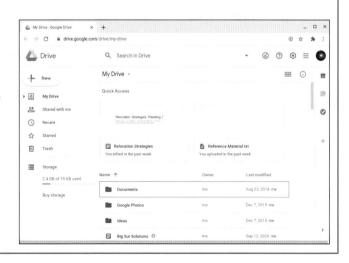

Google Drive gives you a certain amount of storage — as of this writing, 15GB — for free. If you need more storage, click **Buy storage** to explore your options. Current plans are 100GB, 200GB, and a massive 2TB.

Other Cloud Storage Services

Google Drive is so convenient for Chromebook usage that it is hard to turn down, but you can use other cloud storage services as well as, or instead of, Google Drive. For example, if you already store your data on Microsoft's OneDrive service or on the Dropbox service, you can connect your Chromebook to that service, giving it access to your data.

USB Drives and microSD Cards

You can connect a USB drive to your Chromebook to provide additional storage. USB drives come in a wide range of physical sizes and storage capacities, from ultraportable USB thumb drives — also called *USB sticks* — up to brick-size external drives containing one or more hard drives.

Many Chromebook models have a microSD card slot, enabling you to increase storage capacity by inserting a microSD card. If your Chromebook model does not have a microSD card slot, you can use a USB card reader to connect a microSD card.

Both USB drives and microSD cards can also be convenient for transferring files from one device to another.

Open the Files App and Explore Local Storage

Chrome OS provides the Files app to enable you to manage files on your Chromebook and on connected drives.

On the left side of the Files window is the sidebar, which shows key locations in your Chromebook's filesystem. Some locations are views that round up all items of a certain type — for example, the Recent view shows all recently modified files, and the Audio view shows all audio files. Most other locations are either actual folders or locations that function as folders. For example, Downloads is an actual folder, whereas Google Drive appears as a folder for your convenience.

Open the Files App and Explore Local Storage

1 Click **Launcher** (◉).

The Launcher bar opens.

2 Click **Full Screen** (⌃).

The Launcher appears full screen.

3 Click **Files** (▢).

Note: If you cannot see Files (▢), click **Search** (**G**), and then start typing *files*. Click **Files** (▢) when you can locate the icon.

The Files app opens in a window.

Ⓐ In this example, the Files app displays the My Files location at first.

Ⓑ The sidebar enables you to navigate among key categories and locations in the filesystem.

Ⓒ You can click **Audio** (🎧) to display the Audio category, which contains all audio files.

Ⓓ You can click **Images** (🖼) to display the Images category.

Ⓔ You can click **Videos** (🎬) to display the Videos category.

4 Click **Recent** (🕐).

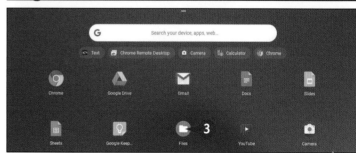

The Recent view appears, showing all the files you have modified recently.

Note: The Recent view shows recently modified files in reverse chronological order — in other words, the most recently modified file first. For technical reasons, the Recent view does not include files you have recently accessed but not modified.

Ⓕ The arrow (↓ or ↑) shows which column is currently used for sorting and the sort's direction.

Ⓖ You can click a column heading to change the sorting. Click again to reverse the sort direction.

❺ Click **Downloads** (⬇).

The contents of your Downloads folder appear.

Ⓗ You can double-click a file to open it in its default app.

❻ When you finish working in the Files window, click **Close** (✖).

The Files window closes.

TIP

How do I delete a file from the Recent view?

You cannot delete a file from the Recent view — nor from the Audio view, the Images view, or the Videos view. Instead, you must locate the file in the folder that actually contains it — for example, in the folder in the My Files folder structure or on Google Drive — and then delete the file from there.

Explore Your Google Drive Storage

Google Drive is Google's online storage service used for personal accounts and G Suite accounts. Your Google Account includes an amount of storage provided using Google Drive.

You can directly access the My Drive section of your Google Drive storage through the Files app built into Chrome OS, through a browser on any modern device, or through Google's mobile apps. Google Drive is closely connected with Google's productivity apps, such as Google Docs and Google Sheets, and these apps can open files directly from Google Drive. You can create new documents in these apps from Google Drive.

Explore Your Google Drive Storage

1 Press **Shift**+click **Launcher** (◎).

The Launcher appears full screen.

2 Click **Google Drive** (▲).

Note: If you cannot see Google Drive (▲), click **Search** (**G**), and then start typing *drive*. Click **Google Drive** (▲) when you can locate the icon.

Note: If you plan to use the Google Drive web app frequently, pin it to the shelf. Right-click **Google Drive** (▲) on the Launcher screen, and then click **Pin to shelf** (📌).

A Chrome tab opens showing your Google Drive.

Ⓐ The My Drive category (△) is selected at first.

Ⓑ The Quick Access section provides links to files you have used recently.

Ⓒ You can click **Shared with me** (👥) to display files that others have shared with you. Google Drive notifies you about newly shared files by default.

Ⓓ The files in the current category appear here.

3 Click **Recent** (🕐).

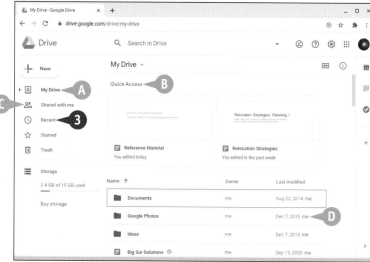

156

The Recent category appears, showing files that you have saved recently.

E You can double-click a file to open it in the default app for that file type.

Note: You can right-click a file to display the contextual menu, which includes other actions you can take with the file — for example, renaming the file, sharing it with others, or downloading it.

4 To create a new document or folder, or to upload an existing file or folder, click **New** (+).

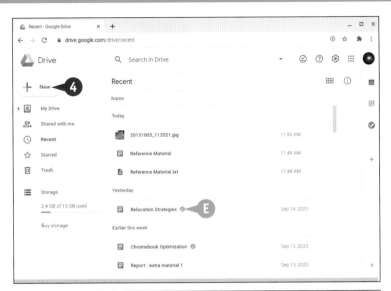

The New menu opens.

F You can click **Folder** (⊞) to create a new folder.

G You can click **File upload** (⬆) to upload a file from your Chromebook.

H You can click **Folder upload** (⬆) to upload a folder from your Chromebook.

I To create a new document, click the appropriate app, and then click the template. For example, to create a spreadsheet, click **Google Sheets** (⊞), and then click **Blank spreadsheet**.

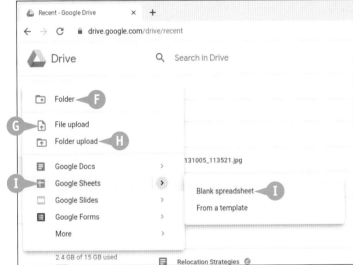

What uses my Google Drive storage space?

Any files you upload to Google Drive will use an amount of storage proportional to their size.

Files you have sent or received as attachments in Gmail also occupy Google Drive storage, even though you cannot access these files directly from Google Drive.

Documents stored in Google apps formats, such as documents in Google Docs format or presentations in Google Slides format, do not count against your storage usage. But if you export such a document to a non-Google format and save the exported document in Google Drive, it will count against your storage.

Any media files you store in Google Photos on the Original Quality setting will also use Google Drive storage.

Enable and Use Google Drive's Offline Mode

As an online storage site, Google Drive requires an Internet connection. But if you will need to work on your Google Docs, Google Sheets, or Google Slides files stored on Google Drive when you do not have an Internet connection, you can enable Google Drive's Offline Mode before going offline.

Chrome OS saves copies of your most recently opened Google Drive files, and other files you specify, to your Chromebook's local storage. You can then work on these files when the Chromebook is offline. Once connected to the Internet again, Google Drive synchronizes the local files with the online files.

Enable and Use Google Drive's Offline Mode

Enable Google Drive's Offline Mode

1 Press **Shift**+click **Launcher** (◯).

The Launcher appears full screen.

2 Click **Google Drive** (▲).

Note: If you cannot see Google Drive (▲), click **Search** (**G**), and then start typing *drive*. Click **Google Drive** (▲) when you can locate the icon.

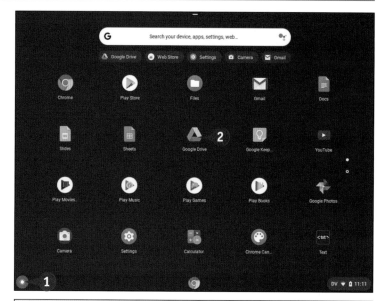

A Chrome tab opens showing your Google Drive.

3 Click **Settings** (⚙).

The Settings panel opens.

4 Click **Settings**.

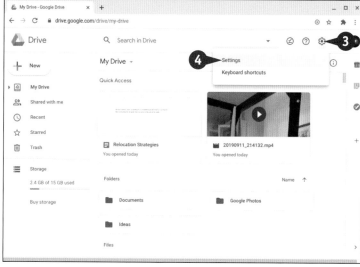

The Settings screen for Google Drive appears.

The General category of settings appears at first.

5 In the Offline area, select **Create, open and edit your recent Google Docs, Sheets, and Slides files on this device while offline** (☑).

6 Click **Done**.

The Settings screen for Google Drive closes.

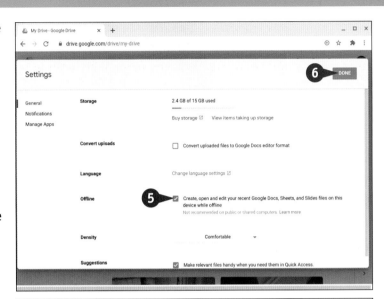

Make a File Available Offline

1 In Google Drive, right-click the file you want to make available offline.

The contextual menu appears.

2 Click **Available offline** (changes to ⬤).

A A confirmation message, such as *Making 1 file available offline*, appears briefly.

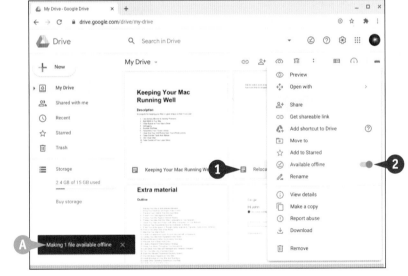

TIP

How do I make a Google Drive file available offline while I am editing it?

When you have a Google Docs, Google Sheets, or Google Slides file open for editing, you can make it available offline by clicking **File** to open the File menu and then clicking **Make available offline**. A readout such as *Document now available offline* appears in the lower-left corner of the window to confirm the change.

If you click **File** again, you will see the File menu displays a check mark next to the Make Available Offline command.

Work with Files on USB Drives or microSD Cards

M ost Chromebook models have only a modest amount of built-in storage, such as 32GB or 64GB, so you will likely want to store some files on external media. USB drives — especially USB memory sticks — and microSD cards are convenient both for storing files and for transferring files between devices.

Once you connect a USB drive or insert a microSD card, it appears in your Chromebook's file system, and you can access it through the Files app. After you finish using the drive, it is important to eject it from the file system before physically disconnecting it from the Chromebook.

Work with Files on USB Drives or microSD Cards

1 Plug the USB drive into a USB port on the Chromebook, or insert the microSD card into the microSD slot.

Note: If your Chromebook has only a USB-C port and the USB drive has a USB-A connector, you will need a USB-C to USB-A dongle to make the connection. USB-C has a small, symmetrical connector, whereas USB-A is the larger, rectangular connector.

A A notification pop-up panel appears with the message *Removable device detected*.

2 Click **Open Files app**.

A Files app window opens, showing the contents of the USB drive or microSD card.

B The drive appears in the left pane.

3 Click **Expand** (▶ changes to ▼).

Note: You can double-click a location or folder to expand or collapse its contents. Double-clicking is often easier than clicking **Expand** (▶) or **Collapse** (▼).

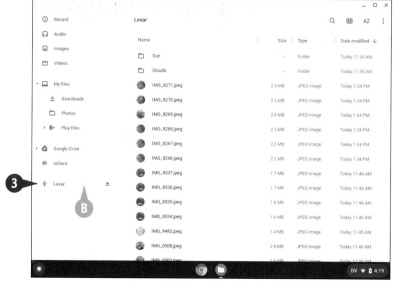

The contents of the folder or location appear.

Ⓒ In this example, you would double-click the Sun folder as well to display its contents.

④ Click the folder whose contents you want to view.

The contents of the folder appear.

⑤ Click **Thumbnail view** (⊞).

The window's contents switch to Thumbnail view.

Ⓓ After switching to Thumbnail view, you can click **List view** (☰) to switch back to List view.

⑥ Take the action or actions needed. For example, click a file and drag it to a folder on your Chromebook to copy it there.

⑦ When you finish working with the USB drive or microSD card, click **Eject** (⏏).

Chrome OS unmounts the drive or card from the filesystem and removes its entry from the sidebar in the Files app.

⑧ Unplug the USB drive or remove the microSD card from your Chromebook.

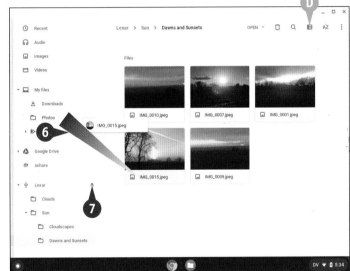

Why does dragging files from a USB drive to my Chromebook's storage copy the files rather than move them?

Dragging causes the Files app to copy files when the destination folder is on a different drive or volume to the source folder. So when you drag a file from a USB drive or microSD card to your Chromebook's storage, the Files app copies the file rather than moving it. If you want to move the file instead of copying it, hold down **Alt** as you drag the file to its destination folder.

Connect Your Chromebook to a Network Drive

You can connect your Chromebook to network drives on your local network so that you can work with files on those drives.

This example shows you how to connect to a network drive that uses the Server Message Block communication protocol. This protocol, usually abbreviated to SMB, is widely used by operating systems, including Windows, macOS, and Linux.

Connect Your Chromebook to a Network Drive

1 Press Shift+click **Launcher** (⚬).

The Launcher appears full screen.

2 Click **Files** (▢).

Note: If you cannot see Files (▢), click **Search** (**G**), and then start typing *files*. Click **Files** (▢) when you can locate the icon.

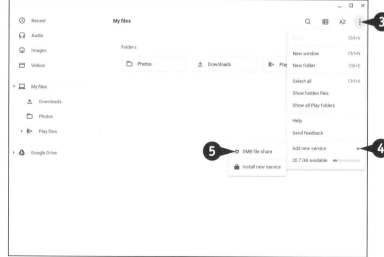

A Files app window opens.

3 Click **Menu** (⋮).

The menu opens.

4 Click or highlight **Add new service** (◡).

The Add New Service submenu opens.

5 Click **SMB file share** (🖳).

The Add File Share dialog box opens.

6 Click **File share URL** (▼), and then click the appropriate file share URL on the drop-down menu.

Note: If the URL you need does not appear, type the URL in the format *server_name**share_name*.

7 In the Display Name box, optionally change the default drive name to something more descriptive.

8 Type your username for the connection, if needed.

9 Type your password, if needed.

10 Select (☑) **Remember sign-in info** if you want Chrome OS to store your credentials.

11 Click **Add**.

The Add File Share dialog box closes.

Chrome OS connects to the drive and displays its contents.

Ⓐ The Network icon (🖳) indicates that this is a network drive.

You can now work with the drive. For example, double-click the drive to expand its list of folders, and then click the folder you want to view.

12 When you want to stop using the drive, right-click it in the left pane.

The pop-up menu opens.

13 Click **Close**.

Chrome OS disconnects the drive.

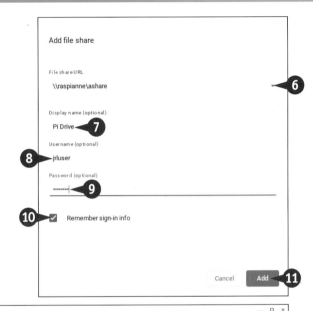

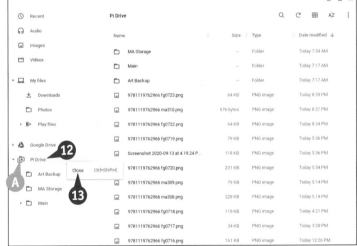

TIP

Should I disconnect a network drive when I finish using it?
It is usually a good idea to disconnect a network drive when you finish using it, because disconnecting makes sure that you no longer have any files open on the network drive — so there is no risk of data loss if you pick up your Chromebook and go elsewhere.

Connect to Another Cloud File Service

Out of the box, your Chromebook is configured to access Google Drive seamlessly — all you need do is provide your Google Account credentials, which you do when you sign in to the Chromebook. But if you store data on other cloud file services, such as the Dropbox service or Microsoft's OneDrive service, you will likely need to connect your Chromebook to those services, too.

To connect to another cloud file service, you will need to install an extension that provides the required connectivity. This section shows you how to do so, using Dropbox as the example service.

Connect to Another Cloud File Service

① Press Shift+click **Launcher** (○).

The Launcher appears full screen.

② Click **Files** (□).

Note: If you cannot see Files (□), click **Search** (G), and then start typing *files*. Click **Files** (□) when you can locate the icon.

A Files app window opens.

③ Click **Menu** (⋮).

The menu opens.

④ Click or highlight **Add new service** (∨).

The Add New Service submenu opens.

⑤ Click **Install new service** (🔒).

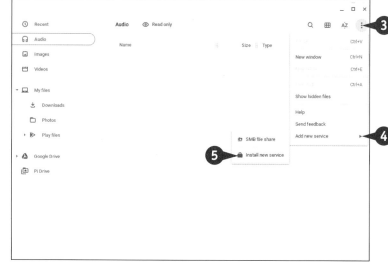

The Available Services dialog box opens.

Ⓐ You can click **Install** to install a service directly from the opening pane of the Available Services dialog box. But often it is a good idea to view the detailed information about the service before installing it.

⑥ Click the service you want to install, such as **File System for Dropbox**.

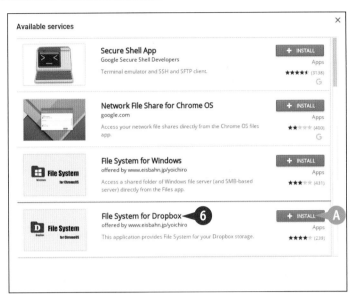

The details pane for the service appears.

⑦ Browse the screenshots and information, scrolling down as needed.

⑧ Assuming you decide to install the service, click **Install**.

Which is the best cloud file service to use with my Chromebook?
Generally speaking, Google Drive is the best cloud file service for a Chromebook, because Google has designed Chrome OS to work seamlessly with Google Drive. But if you prefer not to trust Google with your data or if you have already committed to another cloud file service for other reasons, using another cloud file service may be a better choice for you, even if that service offers poorer integration with Chrome OS.

continued ▶

When connecting to another cloud file service, you must provide login information for the cloud file service so that it can access your account. The cloud file service extension normally stores your login information, so you do not need to enter it each time.

When you no longer need a cloud file service extension, you can either disable it, keeping it for future usage, or remove it altogether.

Connect to Another Cloud File Service (continued)

The Add "File System for Dropbox"? dialog box opens.

⑨ Look through the It Can list to see that the service you are installing does only what you would expect it to. For example, a cloud file service would not normally need access to your contacts.

⑩ Click **Add app**.

The Add "File System for Dropbox"? dialog box closes.

The File System for Dropbox dialog box opens.

⑪ Click **Mount your Dropbox**.

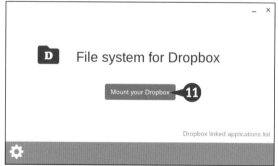

The Sign In to Dropbox to Link with File System for ChromeOS screen appears.

Ⓑ You can click **Sign in with Google** to sign in using your Google Account as your credentials.

⑫ Click **Email** and type your email address.

⑬ Click **Password** and type your password.

⑭ Click **Sign in**.

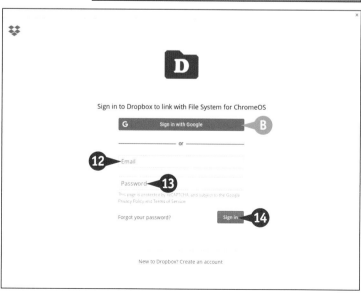

A screen appears prompting you to give File System for ChromeOS permission to access the files and folders in your Dropbox.

⑮ Click **Allow**.

File System for ChromeOS mounts your Dropbox as a location in your Chromebook's file system.

Ⓒ The Files window displays the contents of your Dropbox.

You can now work with the files stored in your Dropbox.

Open a File from Storage

To work with a file in an app, you open the file from the location or folder in which it is stored. The Files app enables you to access locations and folders on your Chromebook, on Google Drive, and on other drives you have connected.

Each file type has a default app associated with it. For example, the Gallery app is the default for the .jpeg image file type. When you double-click a file in the Files app, the default app opens the file. To use a different app than the default, you can use the Open With command.

Open a File from Storage

1 Press **Shift** + click **Launcher** (⚪).

The Launcher appears full screen.

2 Click **Files** (▢).

Note: If you cannot see Files (▢), click **Search** (**G**), and then start typing *files*. Click **Files** (▢) when you can locate the icon.

A Files app window opens.

Ⓐ The Files app normally displays the My Files location at first.

Ⓑ If the Files app opens in Thumbnail view, as in this example, you can click **List view** (▦) to switch to List view.

3 Click the location or folder whose contents you want to view.

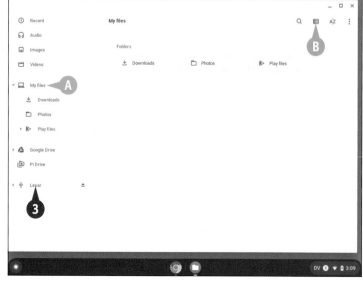

The content of the location or folder appears.

C You can double-click a folder in the Folders list to open that folder so that you can see its contents.

4 Double-click the file you want to open.

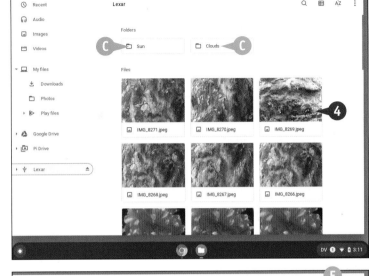

D The file opens in its default app.

Note: If the file is of a type for which your Chromebook has no default app, Chrome OS tries to identify a suitable app available on the Chrome Web Store.

In this example, the file is a photo that opens in the Gallery app.

You can now work with the file in the app.

E You can click **Maximize** (☐) to maximize the window so that you can see as much of the file as possible.

TIP

How do I open a file in a different app from the default app?

Open a Files app window to the folder that contains the file you want to open. Right-click the file you want to open, click or highlight **Open with** on the contextual menu, and then click the app you want to use.

Alternatively, you can start from the app you want to use. Launch the app from the Launcher; if the app is already running, click its icon on the shelf to switch to it. Then give the Open command from the app's interface — for example, press [Ctrl]+[O] — and select the file you want to open.

Change the Default App for a File Type

If you find you frequently need to open a particular file type using an app that is not the default app, you may want to change the default app for that file type. Changing the default app enables you to open the file in your preferred app by double-clicking the file in the Files app.

To change the default app for a file type, you work from the Files app.

Change the Default App for a File Type

1 Press **Shift** + click **Launcher** (⊙).

The Launcher appears full screen.

2 Click **Files** (🗁).

Note: If you cannot see Files (🗁), click **Search** (**G**), and then start typing *files*. Click **Files** (🗁) when you can locate the icon.

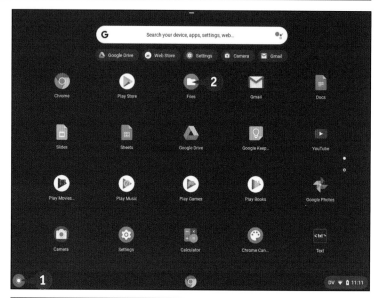

A Files app window open.

3 Navigate to a folder that contains a file of the file type whose default app you want to change.

4 Click a file of that file type.

5 Click **Open** (▼).

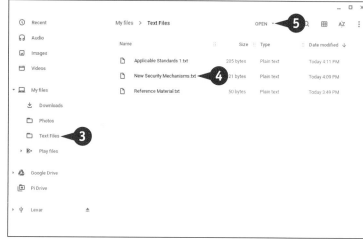

The Open pop-up menu appears.

6 Click **Change default**.

The Change Default dialog box opens.

7 Click the app you want to use.

The Change Default dialog box closes.

Chrome OS changes the default app to the app you clicked.

You can now double-click a file of this file type to verify that it opens in the correct app.

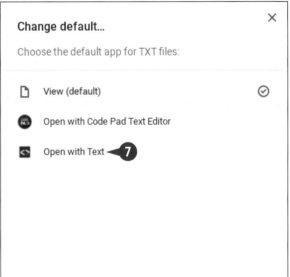

TIP

TIP

How can I reset all the default apps for file types on my Chromebook?
As of this writing, the only way to reset all the default apps for file types is by performing a Powerwash to reset your Chromebook to factory default settings; see the section "Powerwash Your Chromebook" in Chapter 12 for more information. Normally, you would not want to run a Powerwash to make this relatively trivial change. Instead, use the Change Default command, as explained in this section, to reset each default app you want to change.

Copy a File or Folder

The Files app enables you to copy a file from one location or folder to another. Copying is useful when you need to share a file with other people or when you need to keep a copy of the file safe from harm.

You can copy either by clicking and dragging or by using the Copy command and the Paste command. You can copy a single file or folder at a time or copy multiple items.

Copy a File or Folder

1 Press **Shift**+click **Launcher** (**o**).

The Launcher appears full screen.

2 Click **Files** (**🗀**).

Note: If you cannot see Files (**🗀**), click **Search** (**G**), and then start typing *files*. Click **Files** (**🗀**) when you can locate the icon.

A Files app window opens.

3 Click the folder that contains the file you want to copy.

4 Click **Menu** (**⋮**).

The menu opens.

5 Click **New window**.

A new Files app window opens.

6 Resize and position the two Files app windows so you can see them both.

For example, drag one window to the left side of the screen, making Chrome OS fit the window to the left half of the screen. Then drag the other window to the right side.

7 In the second window, click the destination folder.

8 Press and hold Ctrl while you click the file and drag it to the destination folder.

Note: Pressing and holding Ctrl while dragging causes Chrome OS to copy the file rather than move it when the source folder and destination folder are on the same drive. When the folders are on different drives, Chrome OS copies the file automatically, and pressing Ctrl has no effect. So to ensure copying without needing to worry which drives are involved, always press Ctrl when dragging to copy.

Chrome OS copies the file to the destination folder.

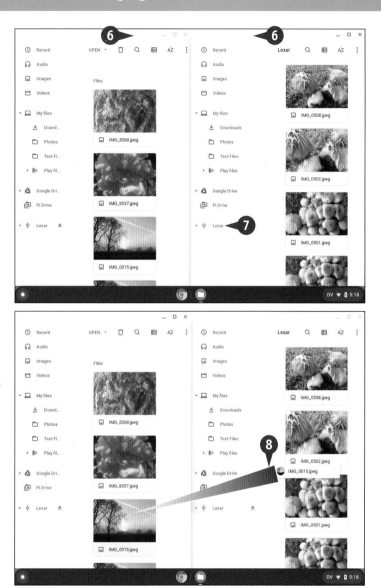

TIP

How do I copy a file using Copy and Paste?

Open a Files window, and then navigate to the folder that contains the file. Right-click the file to display the contextual menu, and then click **Copy**; you can also simply click the file, and then press Ctrl + C.

Now navigate so that you can see the destination folder, either in the same Files window or in a different window. Right-click the folder to display the contextual menu, and then click **Paste into folder**. Alternatively, right-click open space in the folder, and then click **Paste** on the contextual menu; or click the folder, and then press Ctrl + V to paste in the file.

Move a File or Folder

The Files app enables you to easily move a file from one folder to another. You can either use the Cut command and the Paste command, as illustrated in this section, or drag the file quickly from its current folder to the destination folder.

Moving a file by dragging has one complication: When the destination folder is in the same location as the source folder, Chrome OS moves the file; but when the folders are in different locations, Chrome OS copies the file by default, and you must press and hold Alt to move the file instead.

Move a File or Folder

1 Press Shift+click **Launcher** (o).

The Launcher appears full screen.

2 Click **Files** (☐).

Note: If you cannot see Files (☐), click **Search** (**G**), and then start typing *files*. Click **Files** (☐) when you can locate the icon.

A Files app window opens.

3 Navigate to the folder that contains the file you want to move.

4 Right-click the file you want to move.

The contextual menu opens.

5 Click **Cut**.

Chrome OS marks the file as having been cut from the folder.

Note: Chrome does not actually remove the file from the source folder until you specify the destination folder.

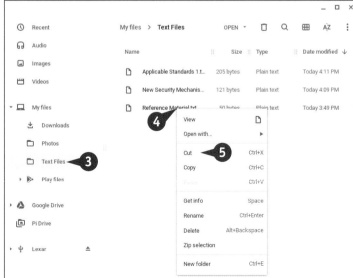

6 Navigate to the destination folder.

Note: You can navigate to the destination folder in either the same Files app window or another window. To open a new window, click **Menu** (⋮), and then click **New window**.

7 Right-click the destination folder.

The contextual menu opens.

8 Click **Paste into folder**.

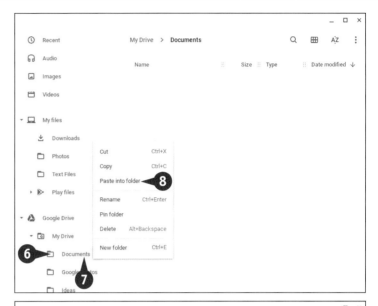

Chrome OS moves the file to the folder, removing it from the source folder.

A The file appears in the folder.

B A pop-up message giving details of the Move operation appears for a few seconds.

C You can click **Dismiss** or simply wait for the pop-up message to disappear.

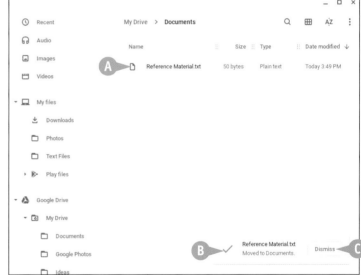

TIP

Is there a command for undoing a Move operation?
Chrome OS does not provide a specific Undo command for actions such as this. Instead, you can undo the Move operation by moving the file back to the source folder.

Rename a File or Folder

The Files app lets you rename any file or folder you have created. It is often helpful to rename files and folders to keep your Chromebook's file system well organized and to enable yourself to find the files and folders you need.

The Files app displays only those files and locations that you are permitted to work with. Chrome OS prevents you from accessing system files through the Files app. This approach is substantially different from other operating systems, such as Windows and macOS, whose file-management apps let you access — and sometimes change — system files.

Rename a File or Folder

1 Open a Files app window.

For example, press **Shift**+click **Launcher** (**○**) to display the Launcher screen, and then click **Files** (**□**).

2 Navigate to the folder that contains the file or folder you want to rename.

3 Right-click the file or folder.

The contextual menu opens.

4 Click **Rename**.

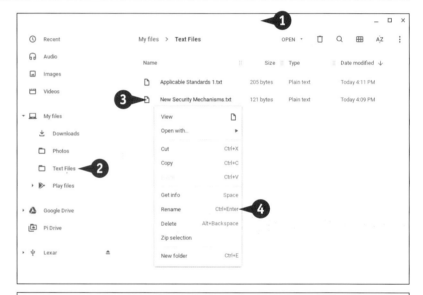

An edit box appears around the current name.

Note: You can also start renaming a file or folder by selecting it and then pressing **Ctrl**+**Enter**.

5 Edit the name as needed.

6 Press **Enter** or click elsewhere.

The Files app applies the new name.

Get Info on a File or Folder

Chrome OS stores a large amount of information about each file or folder. When you view the file or folder in List view in the Files app, you can see the item's name and some basic information about it, such as the file size, the file type, and the date it was last modified. If you switch to Thumbnail view, you can see each item's name and a visual preview.

To see more information, you can open the Info view by invoking the Get Info command.

Rename a File or Folder

1 Open a Files app window.

For example, press **Shift**+click **Launcher** (⊙) to display the Launcher screen, and then click **Files** (🗀).

2 Navigate to the folder that contains the file or folder whose info you want to view.

3 Right-click the file or folder.

The contextual menu opens.

4 Click **Get Info**.

Note: You can also switch to Info view by selecting the file or folder, and then pressing **Spacebar**.

The Files window switches to Info view.

Ⓐ The General Info section includes the file size, date modified, file type, and file location.

Ⓑ The lower section varies depending on the file size. For example, the Image Info section for a photo includes its dimensions, the device used to shoot it, and the photographic settings.

Ⓒ For an image, a preview appears.

Note: Press ⬆ or ⬇ to display info for the previous file or next file.

5 Click **Back** (⬅).

Info view closes.

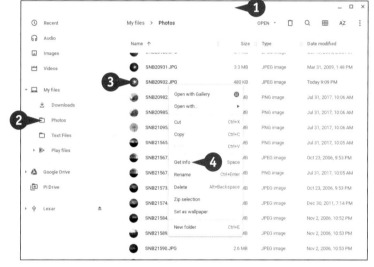

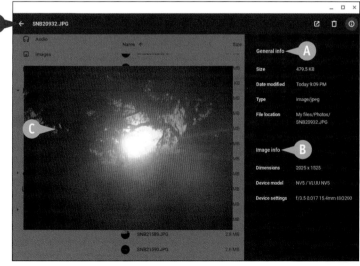

Search for a File or Folder

When you need to locate a file or folder on your Chromebook, you can search for it. To search, you open the Files app, select the location you want to search, activate the Search field, and then type your search terms. The Files app displays a list of matching results, which you can browse to locate the file you want.

You can also perform searches from the Launcher, as explained in the tip.

Search for a File or Folder

1 Press **Shift**+click **Launcher** (o).

The Launcher appears full screen.

2 Click **Files** (▢).

Note: If you cannot see Files (▢), click **Search** (**G**), and then start typing *files*. Click **Files** (▢) when you can locate the icon.

Note: You can open a Files app window showing the My Files location by pressing **Alt**+**Shift**+**M**.

A Files app window opens.

3 Navigate to the location or folder in which you want to search.

For example, click **Photos** (▢) to select the Photos folder.

The contents of that location or folder appear.

4 Click **Search** (Q).

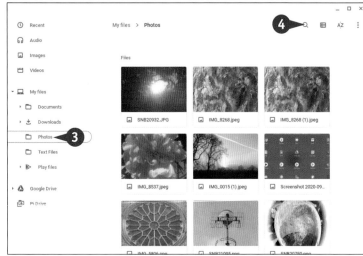

The Search field appears.

5 Type your search term.

Ⓐ Matching results appear.

6 If you want to open a file, double-click it.

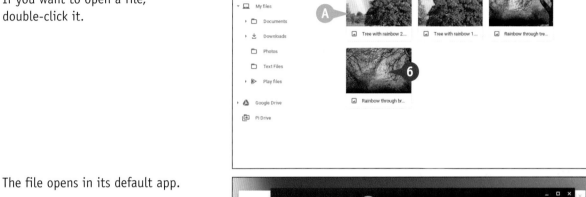

The file opens in its default app.

Ⓑ In this example, the photo opens in the Gallery app.

Compress and Uncompress Files

Chrome OS includes a compression tool called Zip Archiver that enables you to create compressed archive files commonly called Zip files. Zip Archiver can also uncompress Zip files.

A Zip file can contain one or more files or folders. Zip files are especially useful for files you need to transfer across the Internet, place on a limited-capacity medium such as a USB stick or microSD card, or archive for storage. A Zip file contains a copy of the files you chose to compress. The original files remain unchanged.

Compress and Uncompress Files

Compress Files to a Zip File

1 Open a Files app window.

For example, press **Shift**+click **Launcher** (●) to display the Launcher screen, and then click **Files** (▣).

2 Navigate to the folder that contains the files you want to compress.

3 Select the files.

4 Right-click in the selection.

The contextual menu opens.

5 Click **Zip selection**.

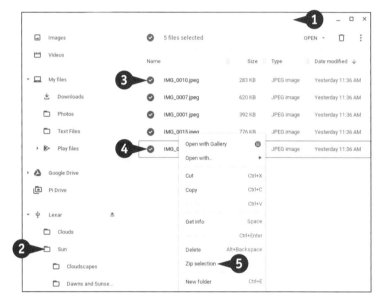

Note: When you compress one file, Zip Archiver gives the Zip file the file's name, but with the .zip file extension. When you compress multiple files, Zip Archiver names the Zip file Archive.zip.

6 Click the Zip file, and then press **Ctrl**+**Enter**.

An edit box appears.

7 Type the new name and press **Enter**.

The file takes on the new name.

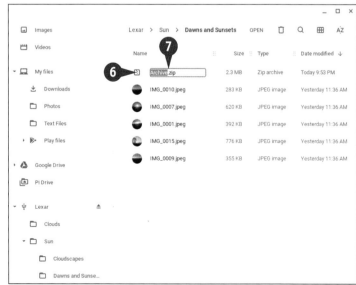

Extract Files from a Zip File

1 Open a Files app window.

For example, press **Shift**+click **Launcher** (○) to display the Launcher screen, and then click **Files** (▢).

2 Navigate to the folder that contains the Zip file.

3 Double-click the Zip file.

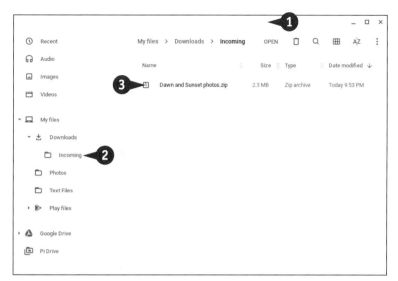

A Chrome OS mounts the Zip file in the Chromebook's file system and selects the file.

B The contents of the Zip file appear.

You can then copy the files to another location in your Chromebook's file system.

C The contents of the Zip file are read-only, so you cannot save changes to them unless you copy them to another location.

TIP

I compressed a music file, but the Zip file is bigger than the original file. What has gone wrong?
Oddly enough, nothing has gone wrong. Compression removes extra space from the file and can squeeze some graphics and text files down by as much as 90 percent. But if you try to compress an already compressed file, such as an MP3 audio file or an MPEG video file, Zip Archiver cannot compress it further, and the Zip file packaging adds a small amount to the file size.

Recover a File from the Trash on Google Drive

When you delete a file stored on Google Drive, Google Drive does not delete the file immediately but instead moves it to the Trash folder, where it remains until you empty the Trash. This process is more obvious in the Chrome browser, as the command for getting rid of a file on Google Drive is called Remove, than in the Files app, which uses the Delete command.

If necessary, you can recover a file from the Trash on Google Drive. To recover a file, you must use a Chrome browser tab rather than a Files app window.

Recover a File from the Trash on Google Drive

1 Press **Shift** + click **Launcher** (**◉**).

The Launcher appears full screen.

2 Click **Google Drive** (**▲**).

Note: If you cannot see Google Drive (**▲**), click **Search** (**G**), and then start typing *drive*. Click **Google Drive** (**▲**) when you can locate the icon.

Note: If you are working in the Files app, you can quickly open a Chrome browser tab to Google Drive by clicking **Menu** (⋮), and then clicking **Go to drive.google.com**.

A Chrome tab opens showing your Google Drive.

3 Click **Trash** (**🗑**).

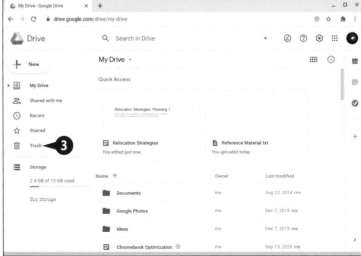

The contents of the Trash appear.

④ Right-click the file you want the recover.

The contextual menu opens.

⑤ Click **Restore** (⟳).

Ⓐ You can click **Delete forever** (🗑) to delete the file permanently.

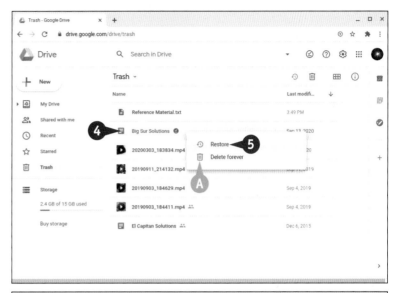

Ⓑ The Restored pop-up panel appears.

Ⓒ You can click **SHOW FILE LOCATION** to go to the file's location.

Ⓓ If you want to delete the remaining files in the Trash permanently, click **Trash** (▼), and then click **Empty trash**.

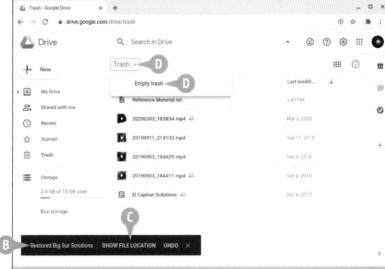

TIP

How long do files stay in the Trash on Google Drive?

In the past, Google Drive permanently deleted files after a period of 30 days; later, the period became 60 days. As of this writing, there is no time limit, so files remain in the Trash until you recover them or delete them permanently.

CHAPTER 8

Surfing the Web

Chrome OS includes the Chrome browser for surfing the web. In this chapter, you learn how to open one or more web pages at a time, navigate among them, and return to pages you have recently visited. You also learn how to set your search engine, set and use bookmarks, download files, and configure Chrome for security and privacy.

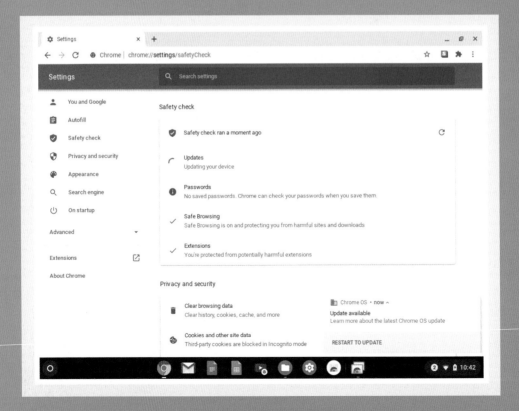

Open a Web Page

The Chrome browser enables you to browse the web in various ways. The most straightforward way to reach a web page is to type or paste its unique address, which is called a *uniform resource locator* or *URL*, into the omnibox in Chrome. The *omnibox* is Chrome's combined address box and search box.

This technique works well for short addresses but is slow and awkward for complex addresses. Instead, you can click a link or click a bookmark for a page you have marked. If you do not have a bookmark, you can use a search engine, such as the Google search engine, to locate the address.

Open a Web Page

1 Click **Chrome** ( ) on the shelf.

A new Chrome window opens, or an existing Chrome window becomes active.

2 Click anywhere in the omnibox or press Ctrl + L.

Chrome selects the current address.

3 Type the URL of the web page you want to visit.

Note: You do not need to type the http:// or https:// part of the address. Chrome adds this automatically for you when you press Enter.

A Chrome displays suggestions based on what you typed. You can click a suggestion to display that page.

4 Press Enter.

Chrome displays the web page.

Note: To search, click the omnibox and start typing your search terms. If the Suggestions list displays a result that is what you want, click that result to go to the page. Otherwise, finish typing your search terms and press Enter to display a page of search results, and then click the result you want to see.

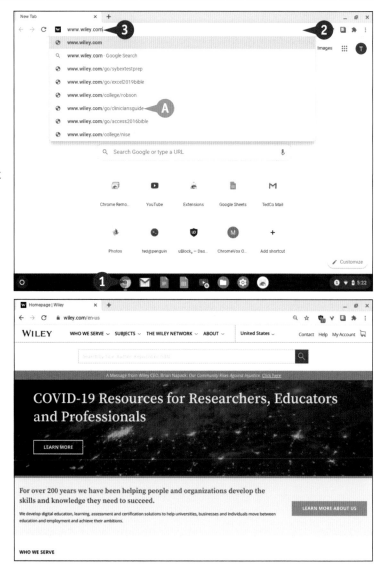

Follow a Link to a Web Page

You can click a link on a web page in Chrome to navigate to another page or another marked location on the same page. Most web pages contain multiple links to other pages, which may be either on the same website or on another website. Some links are underlined, whereas others are attached to graphics or to different-colored text. When you position the pointer over a link, the pointer changes from the standard arrow (➤) to a hand with a pointing finger (👆).

Follow a Link to a Web Page

1 In Chrome, position the pointer over a link (➤ changes to 👆).

A The address for the linked page appears on a pop-up in the lower-left corner of the Chrome tab.

2 Click the link.

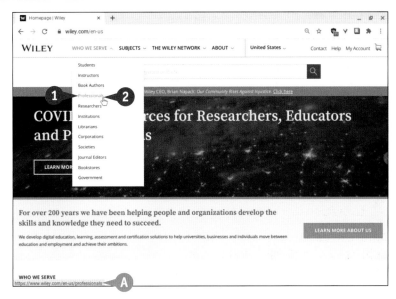

Chrome shows the linked web page.

B The omnibox displays a shortened version of the page's address, omitting the protocol — the http:// or https:// — and the www. prefix, if the site uses it.

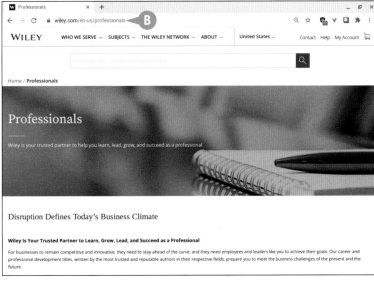

Open Several Web Pages at Once

Chrome enables you to open multiple web pages at the same time, which is useful for browsing quickly and easily. You can open multiple pages either on separate tabs in the same window or in separate windows. You can drag a tab from one window to another.

Use separate tabs when you need to see only one page at a time. Use separate windows when you need to compare two pages side by side.

Open Several Web Pages at Once

Open Several Pages in Tabs in the Same Chrome Window

1 Go to the first page you want to view.

Note: You can also click **New Tab** (**+**) or press **Ctrl**+**T** to open a new tab showing your home page. Type a URL in the omnibox, and then press **Enter** to go to the page.

2 Right-click a link.

The contextual menu opens.

3 Click **Open link in new tab**.

A Chrome opens the linked web page in a new tab.

Note: You can repeat steps **2** and **3** to open additional pages in separate tabs.

4 To change the page Chrome is displaying, click the tab for the page you want to see.

Open Several Pages in Separate Chrome Windows

1 Go to the first page you want to view.

2 Right-click a link.

The contextual menu opens.

3 Click **Open link in new window**.

Note: You can also open a new window by pressing Ctrl+N.

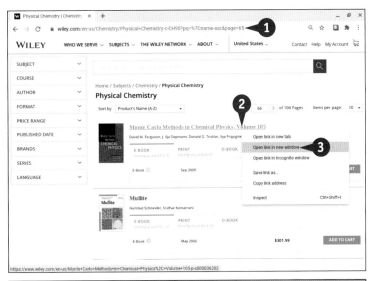

B Chrome opens the linked web page in a new window.

4 To move back to the previous window, click it. If you cannot see the previous window, click **Chrome** ( ) on the shelf, and then click the appropriate window on the pop-up menu.

Note: You can also move back to the previous window by closing the new window you just opened.

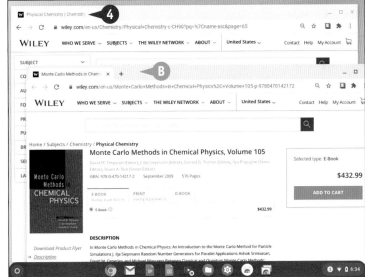

How can I navigate quickly among tabs in a Chrome window?

With the keyboard, press Ctrl+1 through Ctrl+9 to display the first tab through the ninth tab from the left. With the touchpad, swipe left or right with three fingers to navigate quickly between tabs.

How can I organize my Chrome tabs?

Within a window, you can drag tabs into the order you want. You can also drag a tab from one window to another; drag a tab into space to create a new window. To move the active tab to a window you cannot see, right-click the tab, click or highlight **Move tab to another window** on the contextual menu, and then click the appropriate window on the submenu.

Navigate Among Web Pages

Chrome makes it easy to navigate among the web pages you browse. Chrome tracks the pages that you visit so that the pages form a path. You can go back along this path to return to a page you viewed earlier. After going back, you can go forward again, as needed.

Chrome keeps a separate path of pages in each open tab or window, so you can move separately in each tab or window. You can also navigate using the browser history, as explained in the next section, "Return to a Recently Visited Page."

Navigate Among Web Pages

Go Back One Page

1 In Chrome, click **Back** (←).

Note: You can also press ← on the top row of the keyboard to go back.

Chrome displays the previous page you visited in the current tab or window.

Go Forward One Page

1 Click **Forward** (→).

Note: The Forward button is available only when you have gone back. Until then, there is no page for you to go forward to.

Note: You can also press → on the top row of the keyboard to go forward.

Chrome displays the next page for the current tab or window.

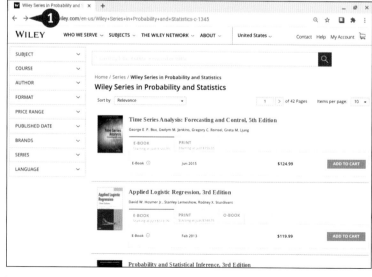

Go Back Multiple Pages

1. In Chrome, click and hold
   Back (←).

   A pop-up menu opens showing
   the pages you have visited in the
   current tab or window.

2. Click the page you want to view.

   Chrome displays the page.

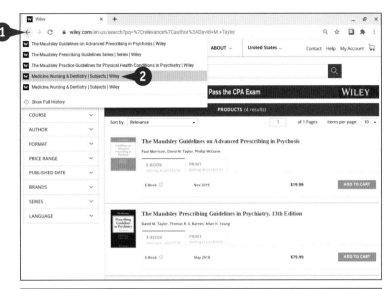

Go Forward Multiple Pages

1. In Chrome, click and hold
   Forward (→).

   A pop-up menu opens showing the
   pages further along the path for the
   current tab or window.

2. Click the page you want to view.

   Chrome displays the page.

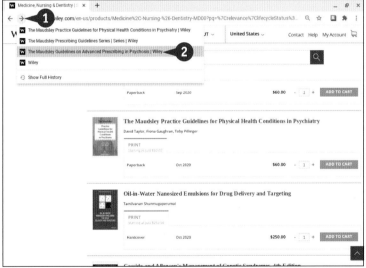

TIP

What other commands does Chrome provide for managing tabs?

If you want to keep a tab available, right-click the tab, and then click **Pin**. Chrome reduces the tab to an icon, so it takes up less space.

If you want to close all tabs in the current window apart from the active tab, right-click the active tab, and then click **Close other tabs**. If you want to close all the tabs to the right of the active tab, right-click the active tab, and then click **Close all tabs to the right**.

Return to a Recently Visited Page

To help you return to web pages you have visited before, Chrome adds each page you visit to the History list. You can browse or search your History to find a page to which you want to return.

Normally, each person who uses your Chromebook has a separate Google account, so each person has their own History. But if you sometimes use a shared account, you can clear the History list to prevent other people from seeing what web pages you have visited. You can also control the length of time for which Chrome stores the list of pages in History.

Return to a Recently Visited Page

Return to a Page on the History List

1 In Chrome, click **Menu** (⋮).

The menu opens.

2 Click or highlight **History**.

The History submenu opens.

Ⓐ Your History includes Settings app screens you have accessed recently; recursively, History even includes History itself.

Ⓑ If the item you want appears on the History submenu, click the item to display it.

3 Click **History**.

The History page appears in a new tab.

Ⓒ At first, Chrome displays the Chrome History category.

Ⓓ You can click **Tabs from other devices** to display tabs you accessed on other devices using the same Google account.

Ⓔ You can click **Search history** and type a search term to make Chrome display matching results.

4 Click the item you want to display.

Chrome opens the page in the same tab.

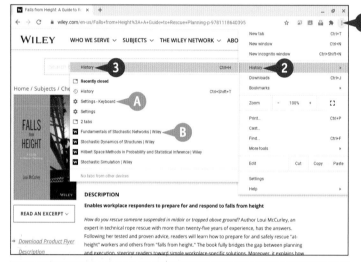

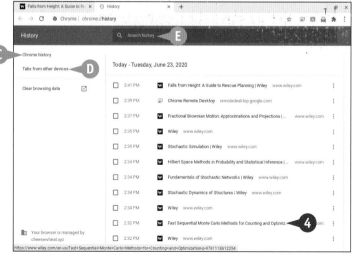

Clear Your Browsing History

1 In Chrome, press Ctrl + H.

The History page appears in a new tab.

2 Click **Clear browsing data** (☑).

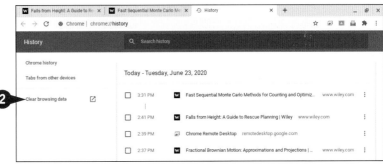

The Settings screen for Chrome opens in a new tab.

The Clear Browsing Data dialog box opens in front of the Settings screen.

3 Click **Advanced**.

The Advanced tab appears.

4 Click **Time range** (▼), and then click **Last hour**, **Last 24 hours**, **Last 7 days**, **Last 4 weeks**, or **All time** to specify the range to clear.

5 Select the check box (☑) for each item you want to clear.

For example, select **Browsing history** (☑) to clear your browsing history.

Note: Scroll down to reach the lower part of the Advanced tab.

6 Click **Clear data**.

Chrome clears the data you specified.

TIP

Which browsing data should I clear?

Clear your browsing history, your download history, and cached images and files if they contain potentially embarrassing items. Clear cookies and other site data if you want to delete identification files and data that websites have stored on your Chromebook.

Clear passwords and other sign-in data if you want to remove stored passwords and the like. You will need to supply your credentials anew for websites that need them. Clear Autofill form data to remove stored data, such as your address details, that Chrome can automatically fill in for you. Clear site settings to remove settings for specific websites. Clear hosted app data to remove from your Chromebook data such as that stored by Gmail Offline.

Play Music and Videos on the Web

Many websites contain music files or video files that you can play directly in the Chrome browser. Chrome can play many widely used types of audio files and video files, and most sites provide easy-to-use buttons — such as a Play/Pause button and a volume slider — to enable you to control playback. This section shows the SoundCloud music website and the YouTube video website as examples.

You can play music and videos either directly on your Chromebook or to an external monitor and speakers you have connected to it.

Play Music and Videos on the Web

1 In Chrome, navigate to a music website and browse to find a song you want to play.

Note: This example uses the SoundCloud site, www.soundcloud.com. There are many other music sites.

2 Click **Play** (such as ▶).

The song starts playing.

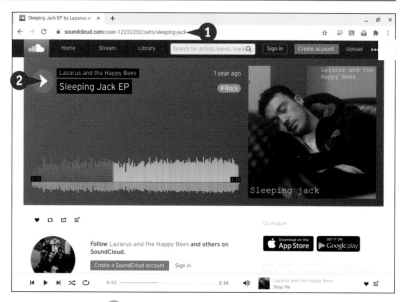

A The progress indicator shows playback progress.

3 Click **Pause** (such as ⏸) if you want to pause the music.

B The Audio icon (🔊) appears on a tab that is playing audio. Click **Audio** (🔊 changes to 🔇) to mute the audio.

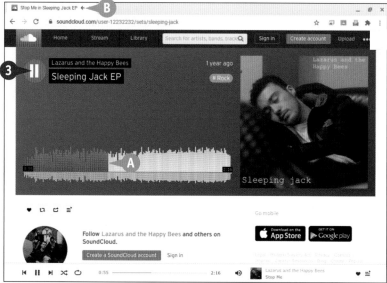

Play Videos

① In Chrome, navigate to a video website and browse to find a video you want to play.

Note: This example uses the YouTube website, www.youtube.com. There are various other video websites; see the tip for information on some.

② Click the video to open it.

The video starts playing automatically.

ⓒ You can click **Settings** (⚙️) to change the playback speed or the quality.

③ Click **Enter Full Screen** (⬜).

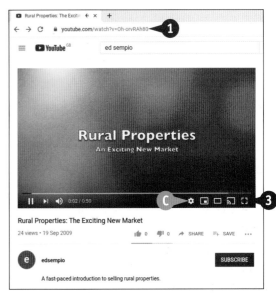

The video appears full screen.

④ Move the cursor over the video.

The playback controls appear, and you can use them to control playback.

ⓓ You can click **Exit Full Screen** (⊞) to return from full screen to a window.

ⓔ You can click **Cast** (📺) to cast the video to a TV or monitor connected to a Chromecast device.

TIP

What are the main video sites on the web?
As of this writing, the most popular video websites include YouTube (www.youtube.com), Netflix (www.netflix.com), Vimeo (www.vimeo.com), and Dailymotion (www.dailymotion.com). Alternatively, search for videos using a search engine, such as Google's Videos search filter.

Set Your Search Engine

Like any browser, the Chrome browser uses a *search engine* — an Internet-based search service — to perform searches and return search results. Chrome is typically configured to use the Google search engine by default, but you can set Chrome to use another search engine if you so choose.

Chrome comes configured to connect to various search engines. The selection varies by country or region. For example, if your Chromebook is configured for usage in the United States, the search engines typically include Google, Bing, Yahoo!, and DuckDuckGo. You can add other search engines manually, if needed.

Set Your Search Engine

1 In Chrome, click **Menu** (⋮).

The menu opens.

2 Click **Settings**.

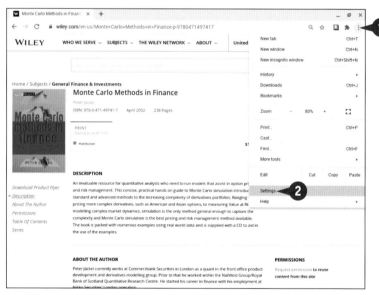

The Settings screen for Chrome opens in a new tab.

3 Click **Search engine** (🔍).

The Search Engine section of the Settings screen appears.

4 Click **Search engine used in the address bar** (▾).

The Search Engine Used in the Address Bar drop-down menu opens.

5 Click the search engine you want to use in the omnibox.

6 Click **Manage search engines**.

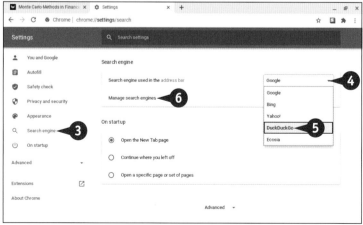

The Manage Search Engines screen appears.

7 To make a search engine the default, click **Menu** (⋮), and then click **Make default**.

Ⓐ You can click **Edit** to edit the entry for a search engine.

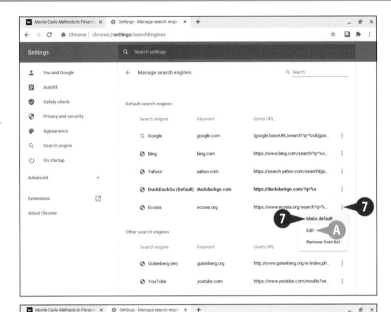

8 To remove a search engine, click **Menu** (⋮), and then click **Remove from list**.

Ⓑ You can click **Add** to add a search engine that does not appear in either the Default Search Engines list or the Other Search Engines list.

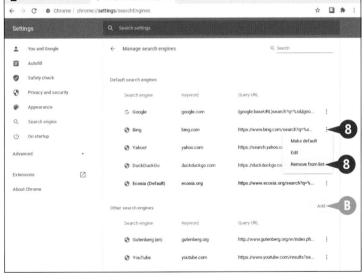

TIP

How do I restrict my search to a particular website?
Use the *site:* operator to specify the site. For example, when searching using Google, you can restrict your search to the Wiley website, wiley.com, by entering *site:wiley.com* followed by your search terms — for example, *site:wiley.com stochastic processes*.

Create Bookmarks for Web Pages

The Chrome browser enables you to create *bookmarks*, markers that contain the addresses of web pages you want to be able to revisit easily. When you have displayed such a web page, you can create a bookmark for its address, assign the bookmark a descriptive name, and store it on the Bookmarks bar or in a Bookmarks folder.

You can then return to the web page's address by clicking the bookmark you created. The content of the web page may have changed by the time you return.

Create Bookmarks for Web Pages

Create a New Bookmark

(A) If the Bookmarks bar is not displayed, display it by pressing `Ctrl`+`Shift`+`B` or clicking **Menu** (⋮), clicking **Bookmarks**, and then clicking **Show bookmarks bar**.

1 In Chrome, navigate to a web page you want to bookmark.

2 Click **Bookmark This Tab** (☆ changes to ★).

The Bookmark Added dialog box opens.

(B) Chrome adds the bookmark to the Bookmarks bar.

3 Edit the bookmark name in the Name box, as needed.

4 Click **Folder** (▼), and then click the folder to use.

5 Click **Done**.

Organize Your Bookmarks

1 Click **Menu** (⋮).

The menu opens.

2 Click or highlight **Bookmarks**.

The Bookmarks submenu opens.

3 Click **Bookmark manager**.

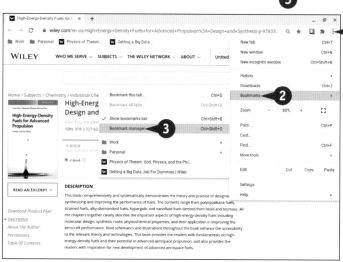

Note: You can also press `Ctrl`+`Shift`+`O` to display the Bookmark Manager.

The Bookmark Manager opens in a new tab.

C The left pane contains the various bookmarks folders.

D The Bookmarks Bar folder contains the subfolders and bookmarks that appear on the Bookmarks bar.

E You can click **Menu** (⋮) for a bookmark to display the menu of actions you can take, such as opening the bookmark in a new tab, editing the bookmark, or deleting it.

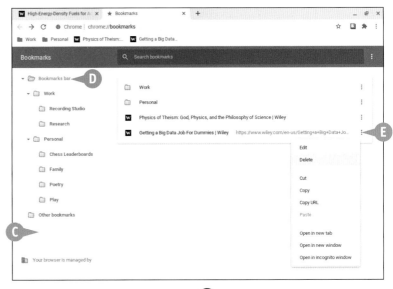

Note: Double-click a collapsed folder to display its contents, or double-click an expanded folder to collapse it to the folder.

4 Drag a bookmark to the folder in which you want to place it.

F To create a new folder, click the folder in which you want to create it. Then click **Organize** (⁞) and click **Add new folder** to open the Add Folder dialog box. Type the name for the folder, and then click **Save**.

5 When you finish organizing bookmarks, click **Close** (✖).

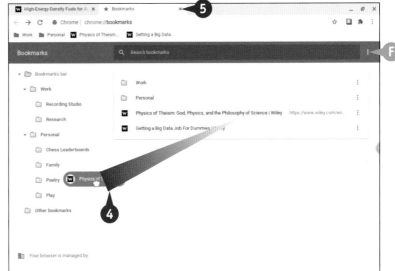

TIP

How do I go to a bookmark I have created?

If you placed the bookmark on the Bookmarks bar, click the bookmark on the Bookmarks bar; if the Bookmarks bar is not displayed, press Ctrl + Shift + B to display it. If the bookmark is in a folder on the Bookmarks bar, click the folder, and then click the bookmark. If the bookmark is in a folder elsewhere, click **Menu** (⋮) to open the menu, click **Bookmarks** to display the Bookmarks submenu, click the folder, and then click the bookmark.

Download Files

Many websites provide files to download, and Chrome makes it easy to download files from websites to your Chromebook's file system. For example, you can download photos and videos you have stored online, download songs to play, or download tax forms that you need to complete.

Your Chromebook can open many types of files, including photos, videos, music, PDFs, and various types of documents. If necessary, you can install other apps or web apps to open files of types your Chromebook cannot open out of the box.

Download Files

1 In Chrome, navigate to the web page that contains or links to the file you want to download.

This example uses a video in Google Photos.

2 Issue the Download command. This varies depending on the website.

For example, in Google Photos, click **Menu** (⋮) in the upper-right corner of the page, and then click **Download**.

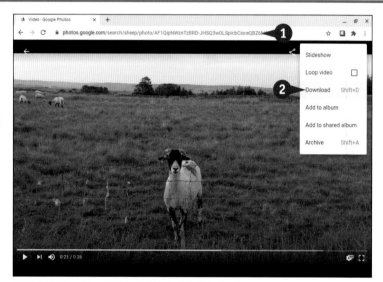

Chrome starts the download.

A The Download Manager displays a notification showing the progress of the download.

3 Click **Menu** (⋮).

The menu opens.

4 Click **Downloads**.

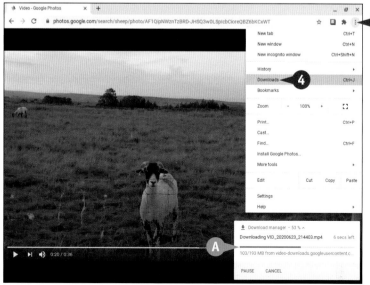

The Downloads page opens in a new tab.

5 Click **Show in folder**.

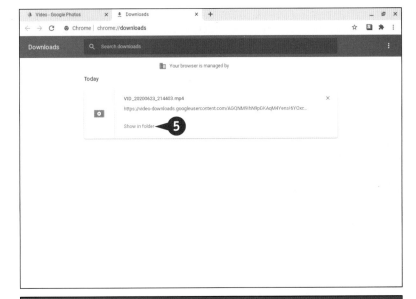

A Files window opens, displaying the contents of the Downloads folder.

6 Right-click the file you downloaded.

The contextual menu opens.

7 Click the appropriate command.

For example, for a video, click **Open with Video Player**.

The file opens, and you can work with it.

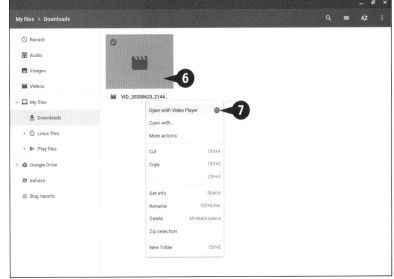

What should I do when clicking a download link opens the file instead of downloading it?
If clicking a download link on a web page opens the file instead of downloading it, right-click the link, and then click **Save link as** to open the Save File As dialog box. You can then select the location in which to save the file; change the filename, if necessary; and then click **Save**.

When you open a file unintentionally in Chrome like this, look for a Download button, such as ⬇. If one appears, click it to open the Save File As dialog box, and then save the file.

Run a Safety Check in Chrome

The Chrome browser includes a feature called Safety Check that gives you an easy way to verify the status of several security features. First, Safety Check makes sure that your Chromebook's operating system is up to date; if an update is available, Safety Check causes Chrome OS to download it. Second, Safety Check scrutinizes your saved passwords for potential problems. Third, Safety Check makes sure that the Safe Browsing feature is enabled. Fourth, Safety Check lets you know whether your Chromebook is protected from potentially harmful extensions.

Run a Safety Check in Chrome

1 Click **Chrome** ( ) on the shelf.

A Chrome window opens.

2 Click **Menu** (⋮).

The menu opens.

3 Click **Settings**.

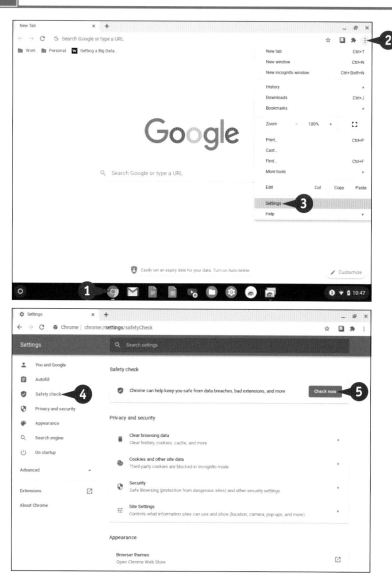

The Settings page appears.

4 Click **Safety check** ( ).

The Safety Check section appears at the top of the Settings page.

5 Click **Check now**.

Safety Check runs.

The Safety Check area shows the results of the check.

Ⓐ The Safety Check line tells you when Safety Check last ran.

Ⓑ You can click **Repeat** (Ⅽ) to run Safety Check again.

Ⓒ The Updates line tells you whether updates are available. If updates are available, Chrome OS downloads them automatically.

Ⓓ The Passwords line tells you about any problems Chrome has identified with your saved passwords.

Ⓔ The Safe Browsing line tells you whether Safe Browsing is on.

Ⓕ The Extensions line tells you the status of Chrome extensions.

Ⓖ If Chrome OS displays a notification saying an update is available, click the notification.

The About Chrome OS screen appears in the Settings app, showing details of the update.

Note: You can click **Restart to Update** on the notification if you do not want to view information about the update.

⑥ Click **Restart**.

Chrome OS restarts your Chromebook and applies the update.

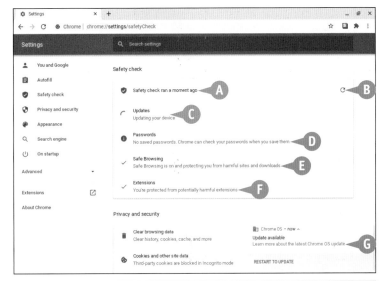

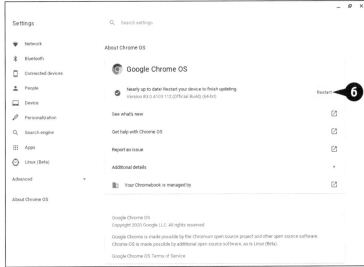

What does the Safe Browsing feature do?
The Safe Browsing feature checks the addresses of web pages against Google's latest list of unsafe pages. When you enter an address or when you click a link on a web page, Chrome checks the address to see whether it is deemed unsafe and warns you if it is. When you attempt to download a file, Safe Browsing checks the file for malicious appearance or contents and warns you of any concerns.

Configure Chrome for Security and Privacy

The web contains many fascinating sites and a lot of useful information. But it is also full of malefactors and criminals who want to attack your Chromebook and steal your valuable data.

To keep your Chromebook safe when browsing, you can configure the Chrome browser for security and privacy. Your options include enabling the Safe Browsing feature, clearing your browsing data, and limiting sites access to your Chromebook's hardware and features. You can also set Chrome to send "Do Not Track" requests to websites you visit, but there is no guarantee any website will honor these requests.

Configure Chrome for Security and Privacy

1 Click **Chrome** () on the shelf.

A Chrome window opens.

2 Click **Menu** (⋮).

The menu opens.

3 Click **Settings**.

The Settings page appears.

4 Click **Privacy and security** (🛡).

The Privacy and Security section of the Settings page appears.

A You can click **Clear browsing data** (🗑) to clear some or all of your browsing data. See the section "Return to a Recently Visited Page," earlier in this chapter, for details.

5 Click **Cookies and other site data** (🍪).

The Cookies and Other Site Data screen appears.

6 In the General Settings area, click **Block third-party cookies in Incognito** (○ changes to ◉) or **Block third-party cookies** (○ changes to ◉). See the tip for advice on which setting to choose.

7 Set the **Clear cookies and site data when you quit Chrome** switch to On (changes to ●) if you want Chrome to forget your actions and identity each time you close it.

8 Set the **Send a "Do Not Track" request with your browsing traffic** switch to On (changes to ●) if you want Chrome to request that websites not track you.

9 Set the **Preload pages for faster browsing and searching** switch to On (changes to ●) to have Chrome predictively fetch content from pages it thinks you likely are to visit from the current page.

B You can click **See all cookies and site data** to display the All Cookies and Site Data page, which lists the websites that have stored cookies and other data on your Chromebook. You can examine the types of data stored and delete items, as needed.

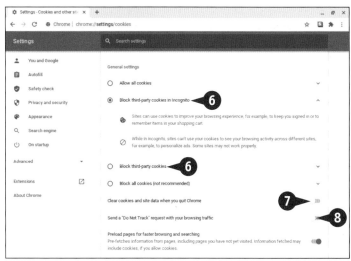
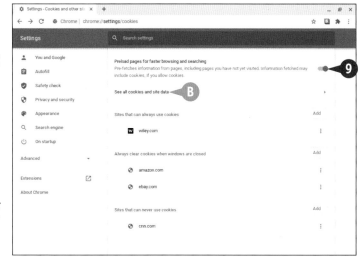

TIP

What are cookies, and should I block them?

A *cookie* is a small text file that a website uses to store information about what you do on the site — for example, what products you have browsed or added to your shopping cart. Cookies from sites you visit are usually helpful to you; these are called *first-party cookies*. Cookies from other sites — called *third-party cookies* — are mostly used to track your visits to sites and your movement between them. These are less useful to you, and you may choose to block them, but doing so may prevent cross-site integration features from working properly. Generally speaking, selecting **Block third-party cookies in incognito** (◉) is a good compromise between functionality and privacy.

continued ▶

At the bottom of the Cookies and Other Site Data screen are three lists for controlling which sites can set and keep cookies on your Chromebook: the Sites That Can Always Use Cookies list, the Always Clear Cookies When Windows Are Closed list, and the Sites That Can Never Use Cookies list. You can customize these lists by adding sites and by moving sites from one list to another.

You can also configure physical security keys and digital certificates for authentication. You may need to do this if you work for a large corporation or a government body.

Configure Chrome for Security and Privacy (continued)

C The Sites That Can Always Use Cookies list contains sites that are always allowed to use cookies.

D The Always Clear Cookies When Windows Are Closed list contains sites allowed to set cookies but not keep them.

E The Sites That Can Never Use Cookies list contains sites not allowed to set cookies.

F Click **Add** to add a site to a list.

G Click **Menu** (⋮) for a site to display actions you can take. See the tip for details.

10 Click **Back** (←) at the top of the Cookies and Other Site Data screen.

The Privacy and Security screen appears.

11 Click **Security** (🛡).

The Security screen appears.

12 Select **Enhanced protection** (◉) to give your Chromebook maximum protection.

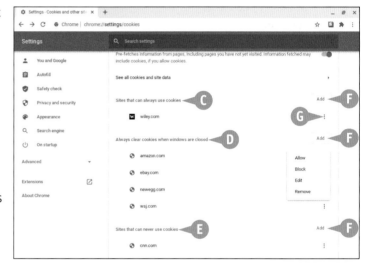

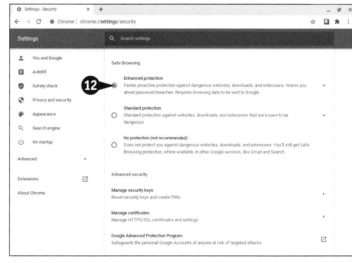

Note: Enhanced Protection includes sharing information about your browsing and about your Chromebook with Google, and receiving warnings if your passwords may be compromised by password breaches. If you do not want to use these features, click **Standard protection** (○ changes to ◉), click **Expand** (⌄), and then set the **Help improve security on the web for everyone** switch and the **Warn you if passwords are exposed in a data breach** switch to Off ( ).

H If you need to use a physical security key, click **Manage security keys**, and then work on the Manage Security Keys screen.

I If you need to manually import digital certificates and configure them for authentication, or explicitly trust or distrust certificate authorities, click **Manage certificates**, and then work on the Manage Certificates screen.

13 Click **Back** (←) at the top of the Security screen.

The Privacy and Security section of the Settings screen appears.

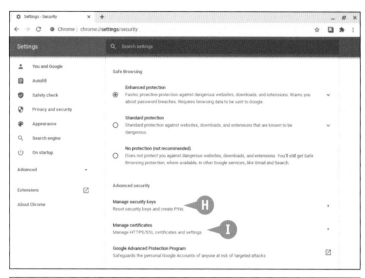

14 Click **Site settings** (⯐).

The Site Settings screen appears.

J The Recent Activity section shows sites for which you have recently changed settings — for example, blocking notifications for a site.

15 To review the permissions set for a site, click the site's name.

Note: The Privacy and Security Settings area gives you various ways to access the permissions for websites. This example uses the Recent Activity list.

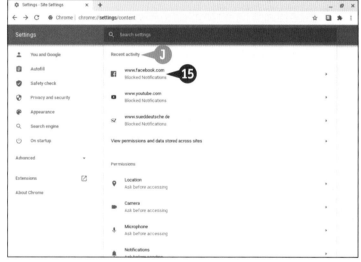

TIP

How do the menu actions on the Cookies and Other Site Data screen work?

When you click **Menu** (⋮) for a website in one of the lists on the Cookies and Other Site Data screen, the menu offers four of the following five actions: Allow, Block, Clear on Exit, Edit, Remove.

Click **Allow** to move the website to the Sites That Can Always Use Cookies list. Click **Block** to move the website to the Sites That Can Never Use Cookies list. Click **Clear on exit** to move the site to the Always Clear Cookies When Windows Are Closed list. Click **Remove** to remove the site from the list. Or click **Edit** to open the Edit Site dialog box, in which you can edit the address for the site.

continued ▶

hrome enables you to control which sites can access particular aspects of your Chromebook, such as the camera and microphone, and your personal data, such as your location and your files. You can choose the default setting for each permission — for example, to always block the camera and microphone. You can then set exceptions for each permission for individual sites — for example, to allow a chat website to use the camera and microphone. You can review each permission, such as using the camera, to see which sites have specific exemptions to the default permission.

Configure Chrome for Security and Privacy (continued)

The details screen for the site appears.

Ⓚ The Usage section shows how much storage the site is using on your Chromebook.

Ⓛ You can click **Clear data** to delete the data.

Ⓜ The Permissions list shows how each permission is set for this site.

Ⓝ You can click **Reset permissions** to reset the site's permissions to your default settings.

⑯ Set permissions, as needed, by clicking ▼ and then clicking the appropriate setting, such as **Ask**, **Allow**, or **Block**.

⑰ Click **Back** (←).

The Site Settings screen appears again.

⑱ In the Permissions list, click the permission you want to review and configure.

To follow this example, click **Notifications** (🔔).

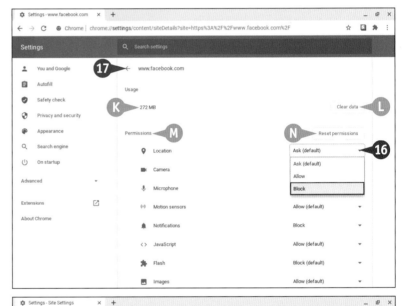

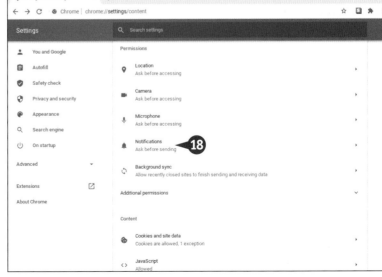

The appropriate screen appears.

In this example, the Notifications screen appears. The following configurations instructions are specific for notifications.

19 Set the **Sites can ask to send notifications** switch to On (⚫) or Off ( ), as needed.

20 If you allow sites to send notifications, you can set the **Use quieter messaging** switch to On (⚫) or Off ( ), as needed.

O The Block list shows sites whose requests to send notifications you have denied.

P The Allow list shows sites allowed to send notifications.

Q Some allowed sites are web apps.

R The Extension icon (🧩) indicates that the Allow setting is enforced by an extension.

S You can click **Menu** (⋮) to display the menu. You can then click **Allow** to move a site to the Allow list, click **Block** to move a site to the Block list, click **Edit** to edit the site's URL, or click **Remove** to remove the site.

21 Click **Back** (←).

The Site Settings screen appears.

You can then configure other site permissions.

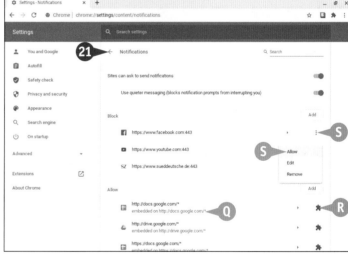

TIP

What is JavaScript, and should I disable it?
JavaScript is a scripting language used by many websites to provide interactive features. While it is possible for malefactors to perform some unwelcome actions with JavaScript, such as borrowing your computer's processing power to "mine" cryptocurrency, the language is widely used for positive purposes and is required for many websites to be usable. What is more of a threat to your Chromebook's security is Java, a full-featured programming language that can run on many computer platforms and is often used by web-delivered services. JavaScript is completely different from Java but is sometimes tainted by association with Java.

CHAPTER 9

Sending and Receiving Email

Chrome OS and your Chromebook make it easy to send and receive email messages. Your Chromebook connects to your Google email account automatically, but you can use other email accounts as well.

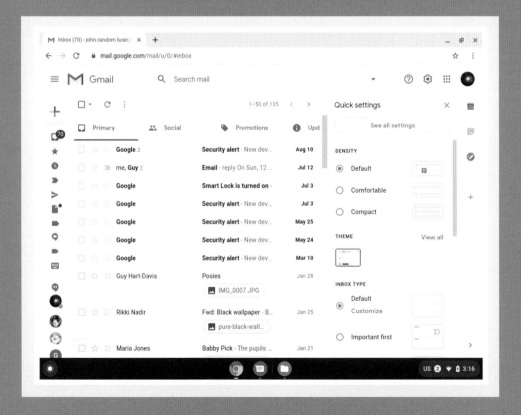

Add External Email Accounts to Gmail

After you sign in to your Chromebook using your Google Account, the Gmail web app automatically connects to the email account for that Google Account, enabling you to send and receive email messages on that account without any further setup.

If you want, you can use the Gmail web app to check other email accounts. Doing so can help simplify your email management by removing the need to use multiple email apps or services. To check your other accounts via Gmail, you must add each account to your Gmail setup.

Add External Email Accounts to Gmail

1 Press **Shift** and click **Launcher** (⊙).

Note: If Gmail (M) appears on the shelf, click **Gmail** (M) and go to step **3**.

The Launcher screen appears.

2 Click **Gmail** (M).

The Gmail web app opens in a Chrome tab.

3 Click **Settings** (⚙).

The Quick Settings pane opens.

4 Click **See all settings**.

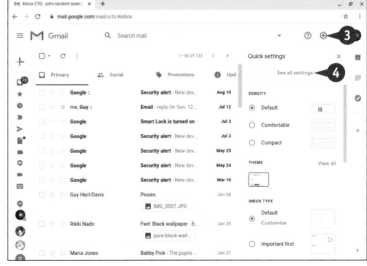

The Settings screen appears.

5 Click **Accounts and Import**.

The Accounts and Import tab appears.

6 On the Check Mail from Other Accounts row, click **Add a mail account**.

A new Chrome window opens, showing the Add a Mail Account screen.

7 In the Email Address box, type the email address for the account you want to add.

8 Click **Next**.

The Gmail – Add a Mail Account screen appears.

9 Click **Link accounts with Gmailify** (○ changes to ◉).

10 Click **Next**.

Note: If the Link Accounts with Gmailify option button is grayed out and the message *Gmailify is not available for this provider* appears, click **Import emails from my other account (POP3s)** (○ changes to ◉), and then click **Next**.

TIP

Should I use the Gmailify feature if it is available?

Normally, you will want to use the Gmailify feature for any account it supports, because Gmailify saves you time and effort by enabling you to manage other accounts from Gmail. However, bear in mind that using Gmailify makes your Google email account a more tempting and disruptive target for hackers — by taking control of your Google email account, a hacker can also take control of your connected accounts. If this is a concern, consider setting your other email accounts to automatically forward messages to your Gmail account, without linking the email accounts.

continued ►

Gmail can synchronize some types of email account using a connector feature called Gmailify. As of this writing, Gmailify works for Yahoo! accounts, AOL accounts, Hotmail accounts, Outlook accounts, and a few other types.

For email account types that Gmailify cannot synchronize, Gmail can import messages from the email account, enabling you to read the messages in Gmail. But it cannot synchronize the messages, so you will still need to use another email app or service to manage the messages — for example, to file, archive, or delete them.

Add External Email Accounts to Gmail (continued)

The Chrome window shows the password challenge screen for the account, such as the Enter Password screen for Microsoft's Live service.

⑪ Type your password.

⑫ Click **Sign in**.

Depending on the email service, a confirmation screen may appear, such as the Let This App Access Your Info? screen.

⑬ Look through the permissions in the Gmail Needs Your Permission To list.

⑭ Click **Yes**.

Ⓐ The You've Been Gmailified! screen appears, confirming that you can manage the account from Gmail.

⑮ Click **Close**.

The You've Been Gmailified window closes.

Ⓑ In the When Replying to a Message area, click **Reply from the same address the message was sent to** (○ changes to ◉) or **Always reply from default address** (○ changes to ◉), as needed.

⑯ To change the name used for your account, click **edit info**.

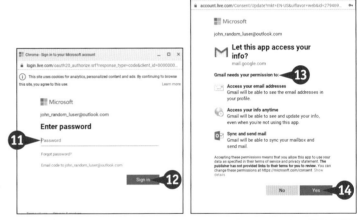

A new Chrome window opens, showing the Edit Email Address dialog box.

17 Edit the name, as needed.

18 Click **Save Changes**.

The new window closes.

C The Last Sync readout shows the sync status for the account you linked.

D You can click **Check mail now** to check mail immediately rather than waiting till the next automatic check.

E You can click **Add a mail account** to add another email account.

19 When you finish adding email accounts, click **Inbox** (☐ changes to ☐).

Your Inbox appears, showing your messages from your Google email account and all the accounts you have added.

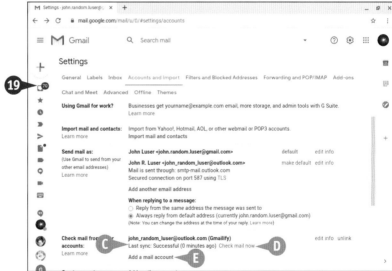

TIP

How do I remove an external email account?

Click **Settings** (⚙) to open the Quick Settings pane, and then click **See all settings** to display the Settings screen. Click **Accounts and Import** to display the Accounts and Import tab. Go to the Check Mail from Other Accounts row, and then click **unlink** to the right of the appropriate account. In the Unlink Account dialog box, click **Keep a copy of the imported messages in Gmail** (○ changes to ◉) or **Delete the copied emails** (○ changes to ◉), as needed; and then click **Unlink**.

Navigate the Gmail Interface

The Gmail web app packs a lot of functionality into a single Chrome tab. As well as giving you access to all your email, Gmail enables you to take actions such as starting meetings in Google Meet; communicating via Google Hangouts; and managing your calendar, tasks, and notes.

By default, Gmail filters out spam — junk mail — and divides the remaining incoming messages into four categories in your Inbox: Primary for significant messages; Social for messages relating to social media; Promotions for advertising and marketing messages; and Updates for service notifications, bills, and receipts.

Navigate the Gmail Interface

1 Press **Shift** and click **Launcher** (⚬).

Note: If Gmail (✉) appears on the shelf, click **Gmail** (✉) and go to step **3**.

The Launcher screen appears.

2 Click **Gmail** (✉).

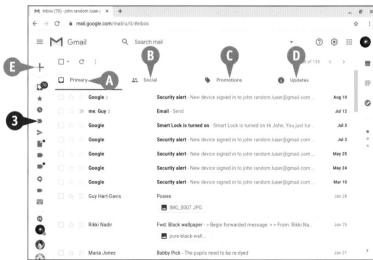

The Gmail web app opens in a Chrome tab.

A Gmail normally displays the Primary tab of the Inbox at first.

B You can click **Social** (👥 changes to 👥) to display the Social tab.

C You can click **Promotions** (🏷 changes to 🏷) to display the Promotions tab.

D You can click **Updates** (ⓘ changes to ⓘ) to display the Updates tab.

E You can click **Compose** (➕) to start a new message.

3 Move the cursor over the navigation bar, the column of icons on the left.

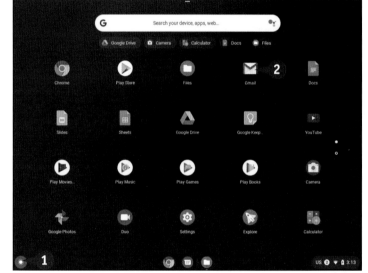

The navigation bar expands.

F In the upper section, you can click a label to display messages assigned that label. For example, click **Starred** (⭐) to display all messages assigned the Starred label.

G In the Meet section, you can start or join a meeting in Google Meet.

H In the Hangouts section, you can interact with a Google Hangouts contact. For example, you can start a video chat or send an email message.

I You can click **Settings** (⚙) to display the Quick Settings pane.

J You can click **Calendar** (📅) to expand the side panel to show a Calendar pane.

K You can click **Keep** (📝) to expand the side panel, showing your notes in Google Keep.

L You can click **Tasks** (✓) to expand the side panel, showing your tasks in Google Tasks.

M You can click **Hide side panel** (❯) to hide the side panel.

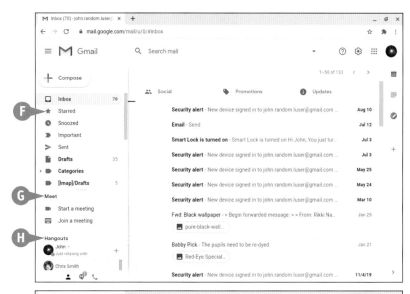

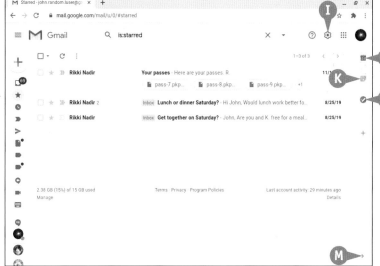

TIP

How do I change the tabs displayed at the top of the default Inbox?
Click **Settings** (⚙) to open the Quick Settings pane, go to the Inbox Type section, and then click **Customize** under the Default item. In the Select Tabs to Enable dialog box, select (☑) the check box for each tab you want to show, and deselect (☐) each other check box. Select (☑) **Include starred in Primary** if you want to include starred messages in the Primary Inbox. Click **Save** to close the Select Tabs to Enable dialog box.

Receive and Read Your Email Messages

Gmail enables you to receive your incoming messages easily and read them in whatever order you prefer. A message sent to you goes to Google's email servers. To receive the message, you cause the Gmail web app to connect to the email servers so that it can display the message.

Google's division of the Inbox into four categories — Primary, Social, Promotions, and Updates — helps you to focus on particular types of messages. For example, you might choose to deal with all messages in the Primary category before going on to the Social category.

Receive and Read Your Email Messages

1 Press **Shift** and click **Launcher** ( ).

Note: If Gmail ( ) appears on the shelf, click **Gmail** ( ) and go to step **3**.

The Launcher screen appears.

2 Click **Gmail** ( ).

The Gmail web app opens in a Chrome tab.

A Gmail displays the Inbox ( ) at first.

B Within the Inbox, Gmail displays the Primary category (also).

C You can click another category, if necessary. For example, click **Social** (changes to) to display the Social category.

D Boldface on the sender and the subject indicates an unread message.

3 Click a message you want to open.

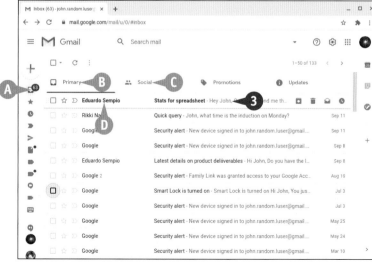

The contents of the message appear.

Ⓔ You can click **Archive** (🗅) to archive the message, removing it from your Inbox.

Ⓕ You can click **Delete** (🗑) to delete the message.

Ⓖ You can click **Mark as unread** (✉) to mark the message as not having been read, so it still appears to be new.

Ⓗ You can click **Older** (‹) to display the next older message.

④ Click **Newer** (›).

The next older message appears.

Ⓘ Gmail displays the Be Careful with This Message dialog box if the sender's email address is new to you.

Ⓙ You can click **Report phishing** to report the message as phishing, which is an attempt to scam you.

Ⓚ Once you establish the sender's address is genuine, click **Looks safe** to close the Be Careful with This Message dialog box.

⑤ Click **Back** (←).

Your Inbox appears again.

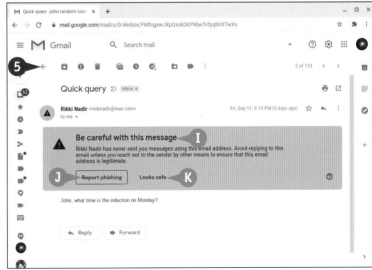

When I have read a message, why would I mark it as unread?

You might want to mark a read message as unread to indicate to yourself that you need to read it more closely or devote more time to it. Doing so is especially helpful if you tend to "triage" your incoming messages to determine which you must deal with first.

Many productivity methods recommend instead looking at each incoming item only once and dealing with the item at that point. For example, following the 4 Ds approach, you would Do, Defer, Delegate, or Delete each message you open, where "Do" might encompass actions such as replying, creating a task, or archiving the message.

Send an Email Message

The Gmail web app enables you to send an email message to anybody whose email address you know. After starting a new message, you can specify the recipient's address either by typing the whole address into the To field or by accepting a suggestion that Gmail displays as you start typing the address.

You can send an email message to a single recipient or to multiple recipients. You can send copies to Cc, or carbon-copy, recipients or send hidden copies to Bcc, or blind carbon-copy, recipients.

Send an Email Message

1 Press **Shift** and click **Launcher** (⊙).

Note: If Gmail (📧) appears on the shelf, click **Gmail** (📧) and go to step **3**.

　The Launcher screen appears.

2 Click **Gmail** (📧).

　The Gmail web app opens in a Chrome tab.

3 Click **Compose** (➕).

Ⓐ A New Message window opens as a pop-up window within the Gmail window.

Note: The window is called New Message at first, but the name changes briefly to Draft Saved each time Gmail saves your changes.

Ⓑ You can click **Full screen** (▣) to expand the New Message window; if necessary, click **Exit full screen** (▣) to reduce it again.

Ⓒ If you have configured Gmail with more than one email account, you can click **From** (▼) and then click the email address from which to send the message.

4 Click **To** and start typing the recipient's address.

　A list of matches from your contacts appears.

5 To see more information, move the cursor over a contact.

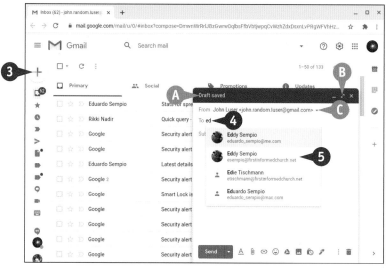

220

A pop-up panel displays more information about the contact.

6 Click the appropriate contact.

The contact's name appears in the To field as a button.

D You can click **Remove** (✖) to remove the recipient.

You can now add another recipient to the To field by following steps **4** to **6**.

E To add a Cc recipient, click **Cc**.

F To add a Bcc recipient, click **Bcc**.

7 Click **Subject**.

8 Type the subject.

9 Click the body area. Alternatively, press `Tab`.

G The title bar shows the subject.

10 Type the body of the message.

11 Click **Send**.

Gmail sends the message.

Note: When you send a message, a *Message sent* pop-up appears for a few seconds. You can click **Undo** on this pop-up to undo the sending. You can adjust the time delay by clicking **Settings** (⚙), clicking **See all settings**, clicking **Send cancellation** (⌄) in the Undo Send section of the General tab, and then clicking the time.

TIP

Can I write a message in a separate window from the main Gmail window?

Yes. Press `Shift`+click **Full screen** (⬛) or press `Shift`+click **Exit full screen** (⬛) to switch the pop-up New Message window to a separate Chrome window titled Compose Mail. Doing so gives you more flexibility in positioning the window so that you can see other windows and apps, which can be useful for reference.

After switching the message to a separate window, you can click **Pop-in** (⬛) to switch the message back to a pop-up window in the main window.

Reply to a Message

Gmail makes it easy to reply to any message you receive. When you reply, you can include either the whole of the original message or just parts of it.

If the message had multiple recipients, you can choose between replying only to the sender and replying to both the sender and all the other recipients other than Bcc recipients. You can also customize the list of recipients manually, removing existing recipients and adding other recipients, as needed.

Reply to a Message

1 Press **Shift** and click **Launcher** (⊙).

Note: If Gmail (M) appears on the shelf, click **Gmail** (M) and go to step **3**.

The Launcher screen appears.

2 Click **Gmail** (M).

The Gmail web app opens in a Chrome tab.

3 Click the message to which you want to reply.

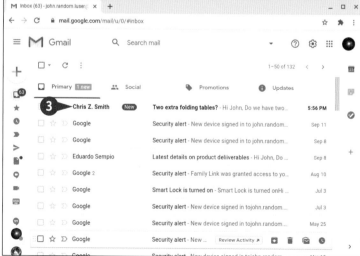

The message opens.

(A) The Reply All button appears if the message had multiple recipients, either To recipients or Cc recipients.

The To readout shows the recipients.

(B) You can click **to** (▼) to display a pop-up panel containing more information, including the names and email addresses of the recipients.

(4) Click **Reply** (↩) or **Reply All** (↩), as appropriate.

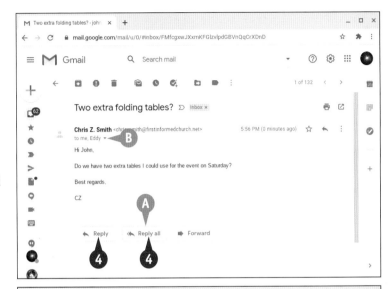

The Reply panel opens.

(C) You can click **more** to expand the address area so that you can see the recipients.

(5) Type your reply to the message.

(D) You can click **Pop-out reply** (☑) to move the reply pane to a pop-up window.

(6) Click **Send**.

Gmail sends the reply.

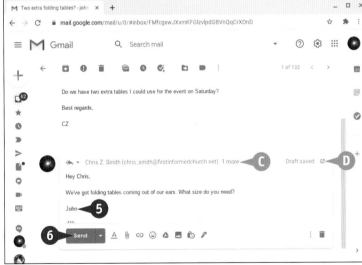

TIPS

How do I change the subject line when I reply to a message?

Click **Type of response** (such as ↩) to display the Type of Response pop-up menu, and then click **Edit subject**. The reply message opens in a pop-up window with the subject line selected. You can then edit the existing subject line or type a new subject line.

How do include only part of the original message in my reply?

Start your reply, and then click **Show trimmed content** (⋯). Gmail shows the original content in an editable format, and you can delete the parts you do not want to include. You can also reply inline — for example, putting an answer straight after a question in the original message.

Forward a Message

Rather than replying to the sender of a message, you may sometimes want to forward the message to other people. Gmail enables you to forward either an entire message or only those parts you choose.

When you forward a message, you can add your own comments to the message. For example, you might want to tell the recipient something about the person or organization that sent you the original message, why you are forwarding it, and what action — if any — you expect the recipient to take.

Forward a Message

1 Press **Shift** and click **Launcher** (●).

Note: If Gmail (M) appears on the shelf, click **Gmail** (M) and go to step **3**.

The Launcher screen appears.

2 Click **Gmail** (M).

The Gmail web app opens in a Chrome tab.

3 Right-click the message you want to forward.

The contextual menu opens.

4 Click **Forward** (➡).

Note: You can also click the message to open it and then click **Forward** (➡) to start the forwarding process.

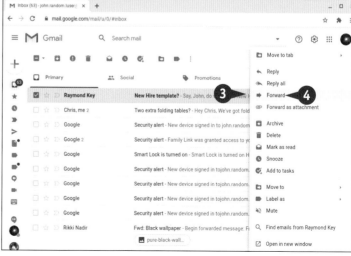

Gmail displays the message to be forwarded in a pop-up window.

Ⓐ You can click **Full screen** (▣) to switch the pop-out window to full screen.

Note: You can press Shift +click **Full screen** (▣) to open the message in a separate Chrome window.

⑤ Click **To** and start typing the recipient's email address.

The list of matches appears.

⑥ Click the appropriate match.

Note: At this point, you can add further recipients, including Cc or Bcc recipients.

⑦ Click the body area or press Tab .

The body area becomes active.

⑧ Type any message needed to the recipient.

For example, you might explain why you are forwarding the message.

⑨ Click **Send**.

Gmail forwards the message to the recipient.

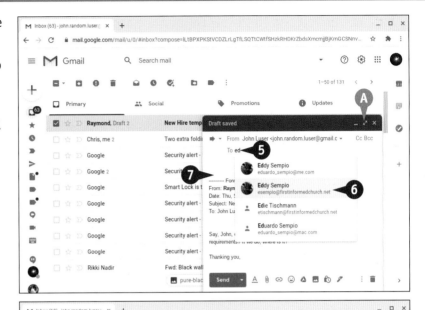

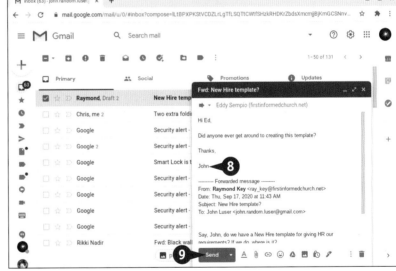

TIP

What does the Forward as Attachment command on the contextual menu do?

The Forward as Attachment command enables you to send a copy of the message as an attachment to a message instead of in the message itself. This command is useful when you want to forward a formatted message in a plain-text message.

Include Formatting, Emojis, and Pictures in Messages

You can communicate effectively via email by using nothing more than unformatted text in your outgoing messages. But Gmail enables you to include a wide variety of formatting, should you need it. You can also add emoji icons to help convey your meaning. When you need to convey a graphical concept without using a thousand words, you can insert a picture — or indeed several pictures — in a message.

First, open the Gmail web app and start a new message. For example, press Shift+click **Launcher** (⬤), click **Gmail** (✉) on the Launcher screen, and then click **Compose** (➕).

Add Formatting to a Message

Click **Full screen** (⬚) to switch the new message window to full screen; when you do this, Gmail automatically displays the Formatting Options bar. If you prefer to work in the smaller window, click **Formatting options** (**A**) to display the Formatting Options bar.

You can then use the controls on the Formatting Options bar to apply formatting:

Font (Sans Serif ▾). Select the font or font family, such as **Sans Serif** or **Tahoma**.

Size (𝕋▾). Select the font size: **Small**, **Normal**, **Large**, or **Huge**.

Bold (**B**). Click to toggle boldface on or off.

Italic (*I*). Click to toggle italics on or off.

Underline (U̲). Click to toggle underlining on or off.

Text color (A▾). Click to display the Text Color panel, and then click the background color or text color you want to apply.

Align (≡▾). Click to display the Align toolbar, and then click **Align left** (≡), **Align center** (≡), or **Align right** (≡), as needed.

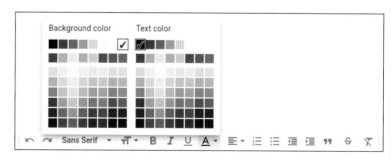

Numbered list (≟). Click to toggle list numbering on or off.

Bulleted list (≔). Click to toggle list bulleting on or off.

Indent less (≤). Click to reduce the indent.

Indent more (≥). Click to increase the indent.

Quote (❞). Click to indent the paragraph both left and right.

Add Formatting to a Message (continued)

Strikethrough (S). Click to toggle strikethrough on or off.

Remove formatting (T). Click to remove formatting from the selection.

Click **Undo** (↶) to undo a change. Click **Redo** (↷) to redo a change.

Insert Emojis in a Message

When you want to insert an emoji at the cursor position, click **Insert emoji** (☺) to display the Emoji pane. Display the emoji category you want by clicking **Show face emoticons** (☺), **Show object emoticons** (♔), **Show nature emoticons** (❉), **Show transportation emoticons** (🚗), or **Show symbol emoticons** (▲). You can then browse to locate the emoji you want and click the emoji to insert it.

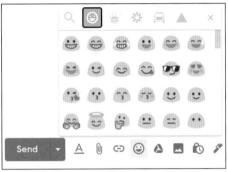 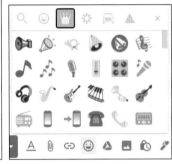

Alternatively, click **Search** (🔍) to display the Search pane, and then type a keyword describing what you want to find.

Insert Pictures in a Message

To insert a picture in a message at the cursor position, click **Insert photo** (🖼). In the Insert Photo dialog box that opens, click the appropriate category — **Photos**, **Albums**, **Upload**, or **Web Address (URL)** — on the tab bar. Within the category, click the photo you want to insert. In the Insert images area, click **Inline** (🖼) if you want to insert the photo as a display element in the message; click **As attachment** (📎) if you want to attach the photo as a file. Then click **Insert**.

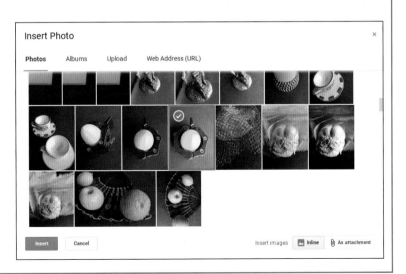

Send an Email Message Using Confidential Mode

When including sensitive information in an email message, you may want to enable Gmail's Confidential Mode for that message. Confidential Mode prevents the recipient from forwarding, copying, printing, or downloading the message. You can also specify an expiry date for the message and choose whether the recipient must use an SMS passcode.

Before using Confidential Mode, be aware that the protections it offers are largely "security theater" rather than effective protection; they do not meet serious information-security requirements, such as those of HIPAA. For example, the recipient can take screenshots or photographs of the content, transcribe it, or simply memorize it.

Send an Email Message Using Confidential Mode

1 Open the Gmail web app and start the message as usual.

Note: See the section "Send an Email Message," earlier in this chapter, for details on how to start a message in Gmail.

2 Address the message.

3 Enter the subject.

4 Enter the body of the message.

5 Click **Confidential Mode** (🔒).

The Confidential Mode dialog box opens.

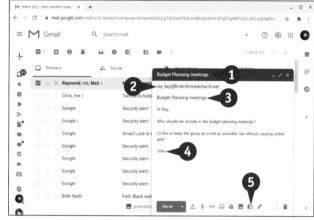

6 Click **Set expiration** (▼), and then click **Expires in 1 day**, **Expires in 1 week**, **Expires in 1 month**, **Expires in 3 months**, or **Expires in 5 years**, as appropriate.

7 In the Require Passcode area, select **No SMS passcode** (◉) or **SMS passcode** (◉), as needed.

8 Click **Save**.

The Confidential Mode dialog box closes.

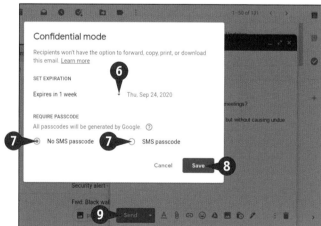

9 Click **Send**.

Note: If you chose to use an SMS passcode, type the recipient's phone number in the Confirm Phone Numbers dialog box, and then click **Send**.

Gmail sends the message.

Schedule a Message for Sending Later

Normally, Gmail sends each outgoing message when you click **Send** — or, more precisely, Gmail sends each message after a five-second delay that gives you the chance to not only recognize you have made a dreadful mistake but also recover from it.

Sometimes, however, you may want to write a message and have Gmail send it later. Gmail makes scheduled sending easy.

Schedule a Message for Sending Later

1 Open the Gmail web app and start the message as usual.

Note: See the section "Send an Email Message," earlier in this chapter, for details on how to start a message in Gmail.

2 Address the message.

3 Enter the subject.

4 Enter the body of the message.

5 Click **Send** (▢).

The Send pop-up menu opens.

6 Click **Schedule send** (▧).

The Schedule Send dialog box opens.

7 If the appropriate time appears in the list, click it. Otherwise, click **Pick date & time** (▥).

The Pick Date & Time dialog box opens.

8 Click the date.

9 Click the time readout, and then adjust it as needed.

10 Click **Schedule send**.

The Pick Date & Time dialog box closes.

The message pop-up window closes.

Gmail schedules the message for sending at the time and date you specified.

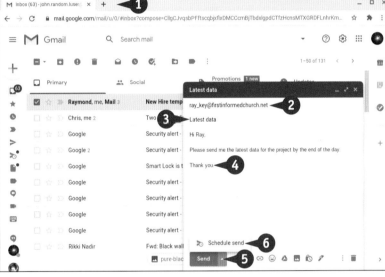

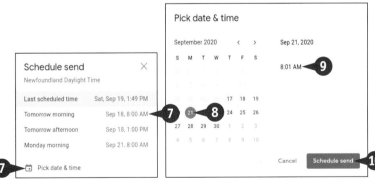

Send a File or a Link via Email

A part from enabling you to communicate via email messages, Gmail provides an easy way to transfer files to other people. You can attach one or more files to an email message so that the files travel as part of the message. The recipient can then save the file on their computer, open the file, and work with it.

When the file you want to send is stored on Google Drive, you can choose between sending the file as an attachment and sending a link to the file. Sending a link keeps down the message size and reduces Internet traffic.

Send a File or a Link via Email

1 Open the Gmail web app and start the message as usual.

Note: See the section "Send an Email Message," earlier in this chapter, for details on how to start a message in Gmail.

2 Address the message.

3 Enter the subject.

4 Enter the body of the message.

5 Click **Attach files** (📎).

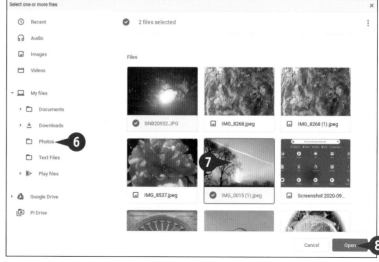

The Select One or More Files dialog box opens.

6 Navigate to the folder that contains the file or files you want to attach.

7 Select the file or files.

8 Click **Open**.

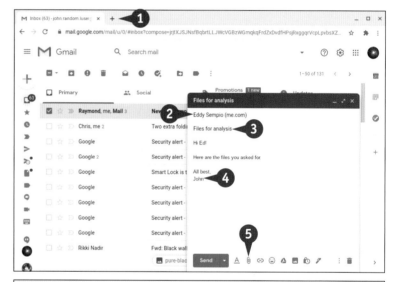

230

The Select One or More Files dialog box closes.

Ⓐ A button for each attachment appears in the message window.

Ⓑ You can click **Remove attachment** (✕) to remove an attachment.

⑨ Click **Insert files using Drive** (△).

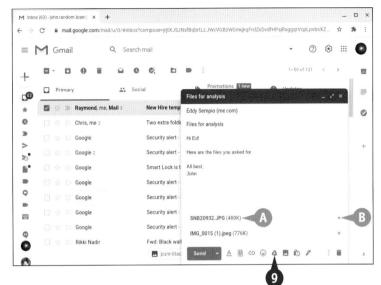

The Insert Files Using Google Drive dialog box opens.

⑩ Select the file or files you want to send.

⑪ In the Insert As area, click **Drive link** (△) or **Attachment** (🖇), as needed.

⑫ Click **Insert**.

Gmail adds the file or link to the message.

⑬ Click **Send**.

Note: If the Someone Needs Access to the File dialog box opens, click **Turn link sharing on**, and then click **Send**.

Gmail sends the message with the items you have attached.

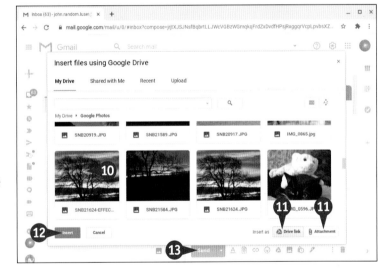

Why is the Attachment button grayed out for a Google Sheets file?
Gmail enables you to share Google Sheets, Google Docs, and Google Slides files stored on Google Drive only via links — Gmail does not let you share such files as attachments. When you select one of these files in the Insert Files Using Google Drive dialog box, the Attachment button is grayed out to indicate that it is not available.

Receive a File or a Link via Email

When you receive a file via email, it appears as an attachment to a message in your Inbox. Similarly, when you receive a link via email, it appears as a button in an email message. Gmail makes it easy to view the attached files and the links you receive. You can even preview an attached file or open a linked file directly from your Inbox, without having to open the message.

Receive a File or a Link via Email

Open Gmail and View a File from the Inbox

1 Press **Shift** and click **Launcher** (⬤).

Note: If Gmail (✉) appears on the shelf, click **Gmail** (✉) and go to step **3**.

The Launcher screen appears.

2 Click **Gmail** (✉).

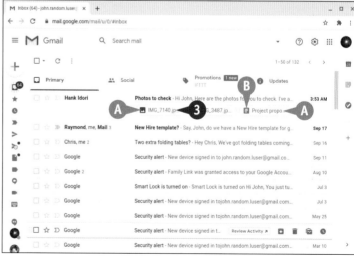

The Gmail web app opens in a Chrome tab.

A Any attachments or links appear as buttons in the Inbox.

3 To see an attached file, such as an image, without opening the message, click the file's button.

B You can click the button for a linked file to open that file in the associated app. In this example, the linked file is a Google Docs document (📄), so clicking the button opens the file in Google Docs.

The image opens.

C You can click **Add to My Drive** (🖉) to add the image to your Google Drive.

D You can click **Download** (⬇) to download the file to your Chromebook's Downloads folder.

4 Click **Back** (⬅).

Your Inbox appears again.

Open a Message and Work with Files and Links It Contains

1 In your Inbox, click the message.

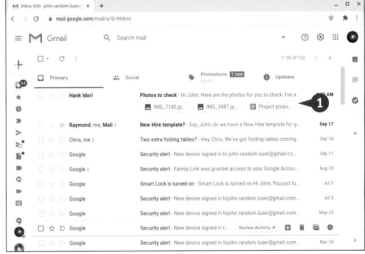

TIP

Is it better to download a file or to save it to my Google Drive?

That depends on what you want to do with the file. Downloading the file to your Chromebook is convenient if you will need to work with the file while your Chromebook is offline — but if you save the file to your Google Drive, you can make it available for offline usage, as discussed in the section "Enable and Use Google Drive's Offline Mode" in Chapter 7. Saving the file to Google Drive also makes it available to other computers and devices you use with your Google Account.

continued ▶

Receive a File or a Link via Email (continued)

Sending and receiving files via email can be highly convenient, but because each attached file is included in the message, it increases the amount of data that needs to be transmitted. It also increases the amount of storage needed for your messages on Google's servers. Making matters worse, Gmail does not provide a way to remove an attached file from a message. For these reasons, sending file links is preferable to sending attached files whenever practicable.

Receive a File or a Link via Email (continued)

The message opens.

E A linked file appears as a button.

F The Attachments area shows both attached files, such as the two photos in this example, and linked files, such as the Google Docs document (⊟).

2 To open a linked file, click its button in the message body or in the Attachments area.

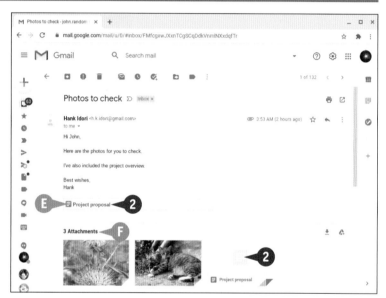

G The file opens in a new tab in the Chrome browser.

You can view the file's contents.

H If you want to edit the file, you may need to click **Request edit access** to get editing permission.

3 When you are ready to return to the message, click **Close** (✕).

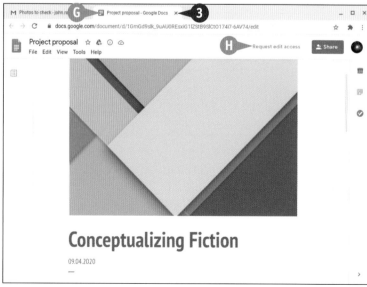

The Chrome tab containing the file closes.

Your Inbox appears again.

④ Move the cursor over an attached file.

Details and controls appear.

Ⓘ The file name appears.

Ⓙ The file size appears.

Ⓚ You can click **Download** (🔽) to download the file to your Chromebook's Downloads folder.

Ⓛ You can click **Add to My Drive** (🔼) to add the file to your Google Drive.

⑤ Click a file you want to view.

Gmail displays the file in the same Chrome browser tab.

Ⓜ You can click **Add to My Drive** (🔼) to add the file to your Google Drive.

Ⓝ You can click **Download** (🔽) to download the file to your Chromebook's Downloads folder.

⑥ When you finish viewing the file, click **Back** (⬅).

The message appears again.

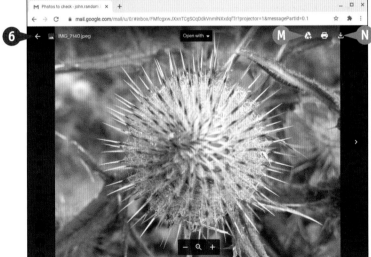

TIP

Pictures in incoming messages sometimes appear as blank boxes. How do I fix this?
You need to turn on the display of external images. Click **Settings** (⚙) to open the Quick Settings pane, and then click **See all settings** to display the Settings screen. On the General tab, which appears by default, go to the Images section, and then click **Always display external images** (◯ changes to ◉).

View Email Messages by Conversations

Gmail enables you to view an exchange of email messages as a conversation instead of viewing each message as a separate item. Conversations, also called *threads*, let you browse and sort messages on the same subject more easily by separating them from other messages in your mailboxes.

Conversation View is enabled by default in Gmail. But if you prefer not to use Conversation View, you can disable it easily; see the tip for instructions.

View Email Messages by Conversations

1 Press **Shift** and click **Launcher** (○).

Note: If Gmail (✉) appears on the shelf, click **Gmail** (✉) and go to step **3**.

    The Launcher screen appears.

2 Click **Gmail** (✉).

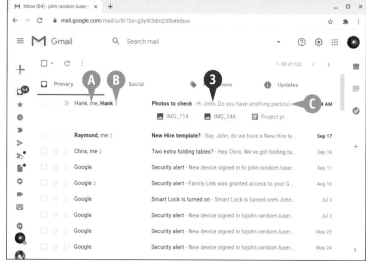

    The Gmail web app opens in a Chrome tab.

Ⓐ The readout summarizes the people involved in the conversation, in sequence.

Ⓑ The number shows how many messages the conversation contains.

Ⓒ The preview shows the beginning of the most recent message.

3 Click the conversation.

The conversation appears.

D The latest message in the conversation appears in full.

E Each earlier message in the conversation appears reduced to its minimal length.

F If Gmail's Smart Compose feature is on, buttons for suggested quick replies appear.

4 To view the full text of a particular message, click it.

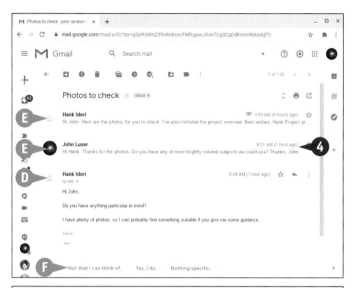

G The full text of the message appears.

H You can click the sender bar to reduce the message to its summary again.

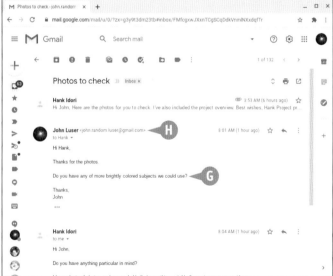

Block and Unblock Senders

If you receive unwanted messages in Gmail, you can block the message's sender. After you implement the blocking, Gmail directs any incoming messages from that sender to your Spam folder, so they do not appear in your Inbox. You can then review the messages in your Spam folder at your leisure to make sure the folder has not caught any useful messages.

If you decide that you do want to receive messages from a blocked sender after all, you can unblock the sender easily.

Block and Unblock Senders

1 Press **Shift** and click **Launcher** (⬜).

Note: If Gmail (M) appears on the shelf, click **Gmail** (M) and go to step **3**.

The Launcher screen appears.

2 Click **Gmail** (M).

The Gmail web app opens in a Chrome tab.

3 Click a message from the sender you want to block.

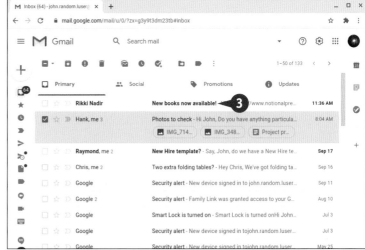

The message opens.

④ Click **Menu** (⁝).

The menu opens.

⑤ Click **Block "[sender]"**.

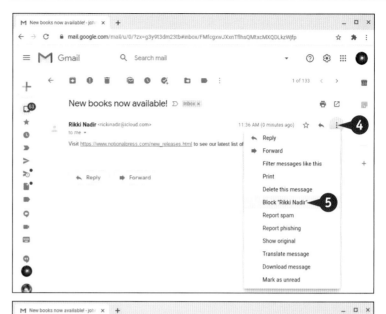

The Block This Email Address dialog box opens.

⑥ Click **Block**.

The Block This Email Address dialog box closes.

The Email Address Blocked readout appears briefly in the lower-left corner of the Gmail screen, confirming the blocking.

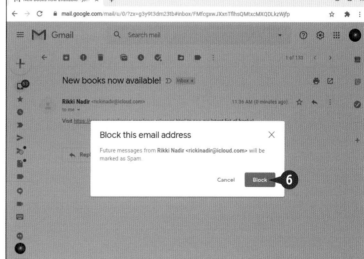

TIP

How do I unblock a sender I have blocked?
In the Gmail web app, click **Settings** (⚙) to open the Quick Settings pane, and then click **See all settings** to display the Settings screen. On the tab bar at the top, click **Filters and Blocked Addresses** to display the Filters and Blocked Addresses tab. Go to the "The Following Email Addresses Are Blocked" section, and then click **unblock** on the right side of the row for the sender you want to unblock.

Create Email Filters

An *email filter* is a rule for automatically processing email messages. Gmail uses a wide range of filters automatically — for example, to weed out as much spam as possible and to sort your remaining incoming messages into the Primary, Social, Promotions, and Updates categories.

Gmail also enables you to create custom filters of your own. For example, you might create a filter to apply a particular label to high-priority messages or to forward such messages to a colleague — or to do both.

Create Email Filters

Display the Filters and Blocked Addresses Tab in Gmail Settings

1 Press **Shift** and click **Launcher** (⊙).

Note: If Gmail (M) appears on the shelf, click **Gmail** (M) and go to step **3**.

The Launcher screen appears.

2 Click **Gmail** (M).

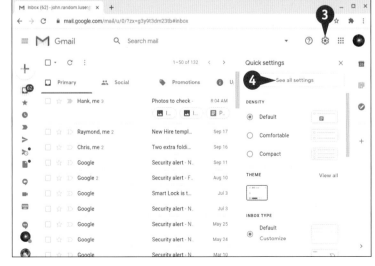

The Gmail web app opens in a Chrome tab.

3 Click **Settings** (⚙).

The Quick Settings pane opens.

4 Click **See all settings**.

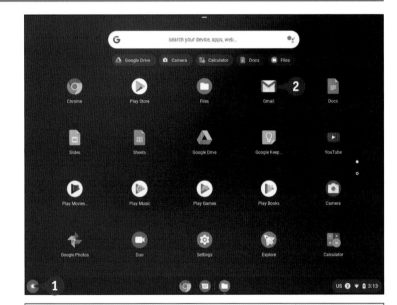

The Settings screen appears.

5 Click **Filters and Blocked Addresses**.

The Filters and Blocked Addresses tab appears.

A The "The Following Filters Are Applied to All Incoming Mail" list shows your existing filters. If you are just getting started with filters, this list may be empty.

B You can click **Create a new filter** to start creating a new filter.

C The "The Following Email Addresses Are Blocked" list shows email addresses you have blocked.

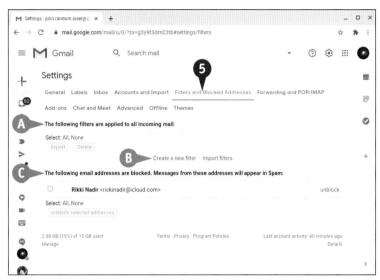

Create a New Filter

1 On the Filters and Blocked Addresses tab, click **Create a new filter**.

The Create Filter dialog opens.

2 Click the first field you want to use in the filter.

For this example, you would click **From**.

3 Enter the data required to specify your first criterion.

For this example, you would type or paste the appropriate email address.

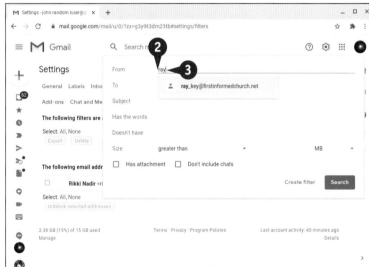

Note: If Gmail suggests the appropriate item when you start typing, click the item to enter it.

How else can I start creating a filter?
You can start creating a filter in various other ways. For example, open a message from a sender whose email address you want to use in a filter, click **Menu** (⋮) to open the menu, and then click **Filter messages like this** to open the Filter dialog box with the sender's email address entered in the From field.

continued ▶

Your home base for working with filters is the Filters and Blocked Addresses tab on the Settings screen for Gmail. From this tab, not only can you start creating a new filter of your choosing, but you can also manage, edit, and delete the filters you create.

You can also start the process of creating a filter from other points in Gmail. This section gives a couple of examples of starting filters in such ways.

Create Email Filters (continued)

The criterion appears.

4 Specify other criteria, as needed.

For example, you might click **Subject** and specify a keyword.

D You can use the controls on the Size row to specify a minimum size or a maximum size for messages.

E You can select **Has attachment** (☑) to include only messages that have attachments.

F You can select **Don't include chats** (☑) to exclude Hangouts chats from the filter.

5 When you finish specifying your criteria, click **Create filter**.

A screen for specifying the filter actions appears.

6 Use the controls in the When a Message Is an Exact Match for Your Search Criteria list to specify what to do with the message.

For example, select **Apply the label** (☑), click ▼, and then click the label you want to apply.

7 Click **Create filter**.

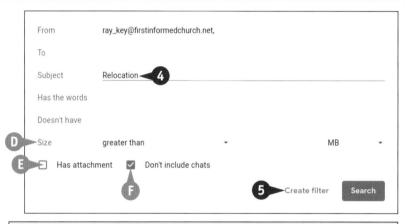

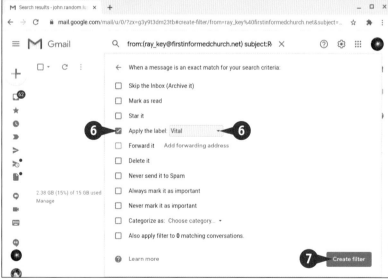

The filter appears in the "The Following Filters Are Applied to All Incoming Mail" list.

8 Select the check box (☑) for the filter.

The filter becomes active.

G You can click **edit** to edit a filter you have created.

H You can click **delete** to delete a filter you have created.

I You can click **Create a new filter** to start creating another filter.

9 When you finish creating filters, click **Inbox** (☐ changes to ☐).

Your Inbox appears.

The filter or filters that you created and applied are now in effect.

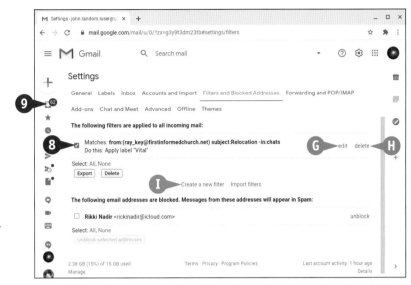

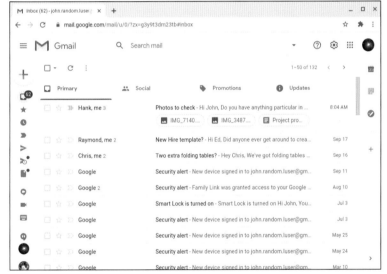

TIP

How can I quickly implement a standard set of filters?

Usually, the quickest way to implement a standard set of filters is to import the filters. For example, if your company or organization has created filters and saved them to a file, you can import them by clicking **Import filters** on the Filters and Blocked Addresses tab of the Settings screen, clicking **Choose file** to display the Select a File to Open dialog box, selecting the file, and then clicking **Open**.

CHAPTER 10

Chatting and Calling

Your Chromebook gives you a wide range of options for chatting with others online. The Google Hangouts service enables you to chat via text or via video; you can start a chat either from Gmail or by going to the Google Hangouts website. You can also connect via video chat using Google Duo and other services. Another chat option is to set up Google Messages for Web on your Chromebook and then send messages using your Android phone's cellular connection.

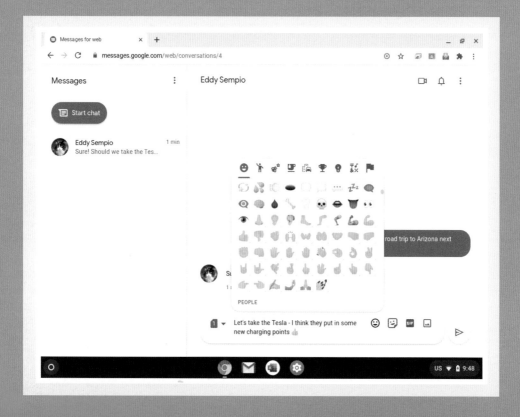

Chat via Google Hangouts from Gmail

Starting from the Gmail web app, you can quickly start a chat with another Google Account holder through the Google Hangouts service. The chat is primarily text-based, but you can also send emoji and photos. You can turn a private chat into a group chat by adding more members to it.

From the text chat, you can also launch a Hangouts video chat in the Hangouts web app. See the section "Video Chat via Google Hangouts," later in this chapter, for information on video chat.

Chat via Google Hangouts from Gmail

1 Open the Gmail web app.

For example, press **Shift**+click **Launcher** (○) to open the Launcher full screen, and then click **Gmail** (M).

2 In the left pane, click **New conversation** (⊕).

A A pop-up panel opens.

3 Click **Enter name, email address or telephone number**.

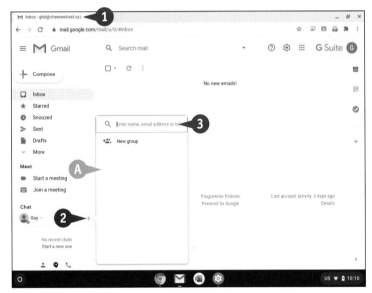

4 Type the contact's name, Google Account address, or phone number.

B Matching entries appear.

5 Click **Invite**.

The first pop-up panel closes.

C Another pop-up panel appears.

6 Click **Send a message**.

Note: To communicate with a contact who does not have a Google Account, you can use other services — for example, Skype — in the Chrome browser.

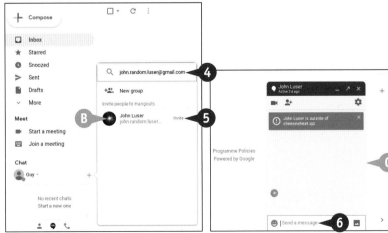

7 Type the message you want to send.

D You can click **Add an emoji or sticker** (☺) to display a panel containing a wide range of emoji and stickers that you can send.

8 Press Enter.

Chrome sends the message.

E The message appears in the chat window.

F If you want to send a photo, click **Attach a photo** (▨), select the photo in the dialog box that opens, and then click **Select**. Then press Enter to send the photo.

G When your contact sends a reply, the message appears in the chat window.

H The contact's account picture or initials appear in a circle to the left of the message.

9 When you want to manage the conversation, click **Options** (⚙).

The Options dialog box opens.

I You can click **Archive conversation** (⊡) to archive the conversation.

J You can click **Delete conversation** (🗑) to delete the conversation.

10 Click **OK**.

The Options dialog box closes.

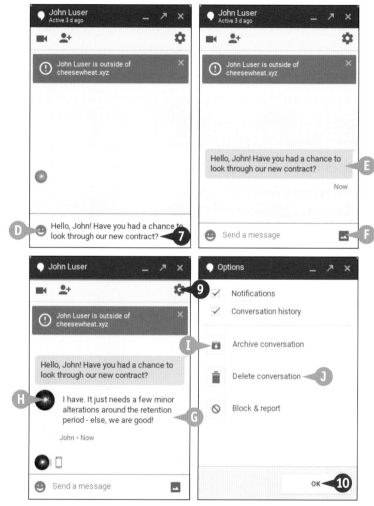

TIPS

Is there an easy way to send a photo via chat?

Yes. Open a Files window to the folder that contains the photo, and then drag the photo to the chat window.

What does the Block & Report button do?

Click **Block & report** (⊘) to open the Block & Report dialog box. Click **Also report** (☐ changes to ✓) if you want to report the contact, sending a copy of their last 10 messages to Google. Then click **Confirm** to confirm the blocking and reporting.

Chat via Google Hangouts

As you saw in the previous section, "Chat via Google Hangouts from Gmail," you can start a chat on the Google Hangouts service directly from Gmail. This method of starting a chat is useful when you are working in Gmail, but at other times, you may want to start a chat from Hangouts itself. To do so, you simply open a Chrome tab to the Hangouts service.

A Hangouts chat can be either with a single contact or with a group of contacts.

Chat via Google Hangouts

1 Open a Chrome tab.

For example, click **Chrome** (🌐) on the shelf; or press Shift+click **Launcher** (⬤) to display the Launcher full screen, and then click **Chrome** (🌐).

2 Click the omnibox.

3 Type *hangouts.google.com* and press Enter.

4 Click **New conversation** (➕).

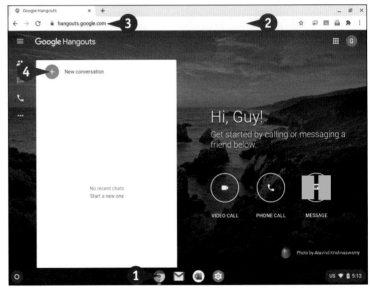

The New Conversation pane opens.

5 Type the contact's name, Google Account address, or phone number.

Ⓐ Matching entries appear.

6 Click the appropriate entry.

Ⓑ You can also click **Invite** to the right of the appropriate entry.

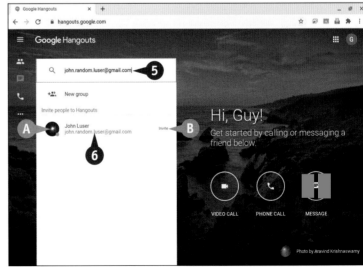

C A conversation window opens for the chat.

7 Click **Send a message**, type your message, and press Enter.

D Your message appears right-aligned in the conversation window.

E The Conversations pane shows the latest message sent in each of your current conversations.

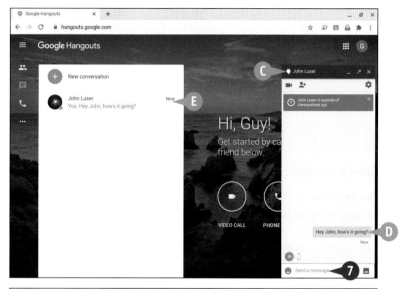

F Your contact's messages appear left-aligned in the conversation window.

8 To send an emoji, click **Add an emoji or sticker** (☺).

The Emoji and Sticker panel opens.

9 Click the emoji you want to include.

10 Press Enter to send the message.

11 When you finish the chat, click **Close** (✕).

The conversation window closes.

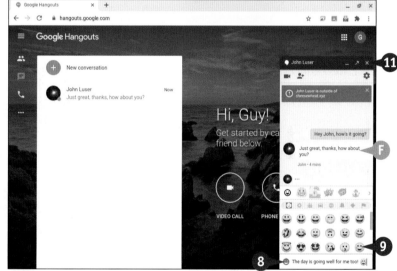

TIP

How do I start a group chat in Google Hangouts?

Open a Chrome tab and go to hangouts.google.com, as usual. Then click **New group** (+👥) in the Conversations pane, optionally assign a name to the group, and then add contacts to the To field. When you finish, click the check mark icon (✓) to open the conversation window for the group. You can click **Send a message**, type the message, and then press Enter to send the message to the group. To add or remove group members, click **People** (👤) at the top of the conversation window, and then work on the People in Conversation screen that appears.

Video Chat via Google Hangouts

Google Hangouts enables you to chat not only via text but also via audio or video. This section shows you how to chat via video via Hangouts. To start a chat, you open a Chrome tab to the Hangouts service, choose the contact or contacts for the chat, and then click the Video Call button in the conversation window.

During video chat via Google Hangouts, you can also send text chat messages to participants.

Video Chat via Google Hangouts

1 Open a Chrome tab.

For example, click **Chrome** (⬤) on the shelf; or press **Shift**+click **Launcher** (⬤) to display the Launcher full screen, and then click **Chrome** (⬤).

2 Click the omnibox.

3 Type *hangouts.google.com* and press **Enter**.

4 Click **New conversation** (⊕).

The New Conversation pane opens.

5 Type the contact's name, Google Account address, or phone number.

Ⓐ Matching entries appear.

6 Click the appropriate entry.

Ⓑ A conversation window opens for the chat.

7 Click **Video call** (🎥).

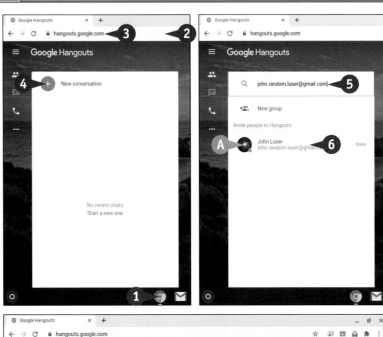

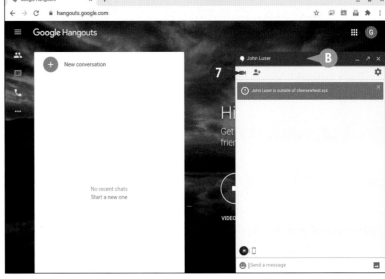

C A Hangouts Video Call window opens in Chrome.

D Your video preview appears.

E Hangouts displays a progress readout as it places the call.

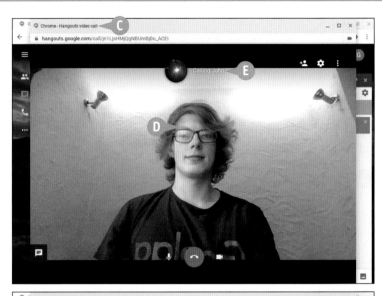

F If your contact accepts the call, your contact's video appears in the main part of the window.

G Your video appears as a thumbnail.

Note: The controls disappear after a few seconds if you do not use them. To display them again, move the cursor over the video.

H You can click **Mute** (🎤) to mute your audio.

I You can click **Video off** (▢) to stop sending video.

8 When you are ready to end the call, click **End call** (📞).

What does the Chat icon in the lower-left corner of the video chat window do?

Click **Chat** (▣) to display a text chat field in to the lower-left corner of the video chat window. You can type a message in the text chat field, and then click **Send** (▶) to send it. Click **Show messages** (▲) to expand the text-chat field so that you can see messages and replies. Click **Hide messages** (▼) when you want to collapse the text-chat field again.

Be aware of one limitation: Video chat participants using Google Hangouts on Android phones can view the text messages you send but cannot reply to them.

Make Video Calls via Google Duo

nother option for making video calls on your Chromebook is the Google Duo service. Unlike Google Hangouts, which also enables you to chat via text, chat in groups, and make audio calls without video, Google Duo is a video-only service. You may find you get better performance for video calls on Google Duo than on Hangouts. Google Duo also enables you to set up group video calls with up to 12 participants.

Make Video Calls via Google Duo

1 Open a Chrome tab.

For example, click **Chrome** (🟢) on the shelf; or press **Shift** + click **Launcher** (⭕) to display the Launcher full screen, and then click **Chrome** (🟢).

2 Click the omnibox.

3 Type *duo.google.com* and press **Enter**.

The Google Duo website appears.

4 Click **Start a call**.

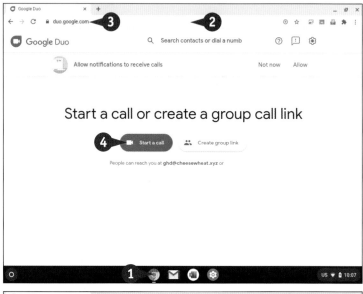

The Starting a Video Call dialog box opens.

5 Type the Google Account address or the phone number of the contact you want to call.

6 Click **Video call**.

Ⓐ The first time you use Google Duo on your Chromebook, Chrome prompts you to give duo.google.com permission to use the Chromebook's microphone and camera. Click **Allow**.

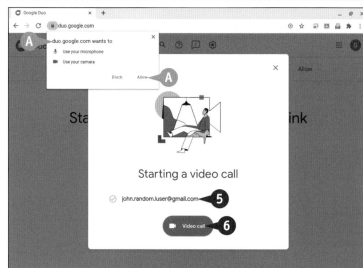

Google Duo attempts to place a video call to the contact.

Ⓑ The Camera or Microphone Active icon (⦿) indicates that the webcam or the microphone is active in this Chrome tab.

Ⓒ The *Knock Knock is on — your video is visible* message tells you that the contact will be able to see your video preview.

If your contact accepts the call, their video appears, and you can start chatting.

Ⓓ Move the cursor over the window to display the controls.

Ⓔ Click **Mute microphone** (🔊 changes to 🔇) to mute the microphone.

Ⓕ Click **Turn off camera** (📷 changes to 📷) to turn off the camera.

Ⓖ Click **Send wide video** (▣) or **Send narrow video** (▣) to control the video format.

Ⓗ This example shows wide video on the thumbnail.

Ⓘ Click **Enter full screen mode** (⛶) to switch to full-screen view. Click **Exit full screen mode** (⛶) to switch back.

Ⓙ Click **Show settings** (⚙) to open the Settings dialog box.

❼ Click **End call** when you are ready to end the call.

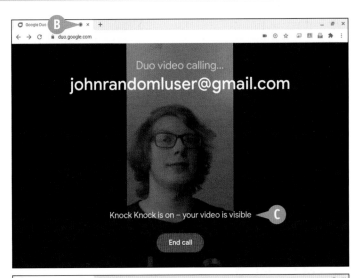

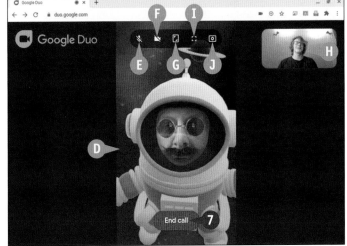

How do I add another participant to an existing video call?
You cannot add another participant to an existing call. Instead, you need to set up a link for a group call. On the Google Duo website, click **Create group link** (👥), and then follow the prompts to create a group link that you can share with all the contacts you want to include in the call.

How do I apply special effects to my Google Duo video calls on my Chromebook?
As of this writing, you can apply special effects to Google Duo video calls only on Android, not on Chrome OS.

Set Up Google Messages for Web

As you have seen earlier in this chapter, you can chat via text directly from the Gmail app on your Chromebook. But you can also set up your Chromebook to send and receive SMS messages via your Android phone on the Google Messages service. Chat via Messages can be convenient when you are out and about.

Your Android phone may already have Messages set up as the default SMS messaging app. But if it does not, you will need to install the Messages app on the phone and make it the default SMS messaging app.

Install Google Messages on Your Android Phone

If your Android phone does not use the Google Messages app by default, you will need to install the app and make it the default. Phones such as Google's Pixel series and Nokia's Android phones normally use Google Messages by default, but Android phones from other manufacturers — such as Samsung, Xiaomi, and Huawei — typically use other, custom messaging apps by default. Confusingly, most of these apps are also called Messages; although they have different icons from Google Messages, the icons may appear similar at first glance.

To install Google Messages, open the Play Store app by tapping **Play Store** (▶) on the Home screen or the Apps screen. Tap **Search** (🔍), type *messages*, locate the Messages entry (🟦) marked "Google LLC," and then tap **Messages** (🟦). On the Messages screen, tap **Install**. When installation finishes, you can run the app by tapping **Open** on the installation screen or tapping **Messages** (🟦) on the Apps screen.

The first time you run Messages, you need to set it up. On the Messages screen, tap **Set default chat app**; tap **Messages** (🟦) in the Set Messages As Your Default SMS App dialog box (○ changes to ◉); and then tap **Set as default**. On the Messages for Web screen, tap **QR code scanner**, and then use the QR Code Scanner screen to scan the code your Chromebook displays.

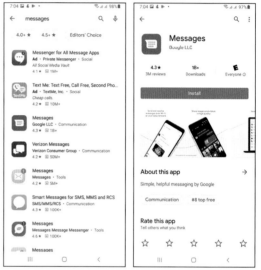

Set Up Your Chromebook to Use Google Messages

To set up your Chromebook to use Google Messages on your Android phone, open a new Chrome tab — for example, click **Chrome** () on the shelf or on the Launcher screen. Click the omnibox, type *messages.google.com*, and then press **Enter** to display the Text on Your Computer with Messages for Web page. If you want to save the link between your Chromebook and your Android phone, set the **Remember this computer** switch to On (⬤). Then use the Messages app on your phone to scan the QR code displayed on the page.

If the "messages.google.com Wants To" dialog box opens, prompting you to allow notifications, click **Allow**.

You can then start a chat as explained in the following section, "Chat from Your Chromebook Using Messages."

Chat from Your Chromebook Using Messages

After connecting your Chromebook to your Android phone, as explained in the previous section, "Set Up Google Messages for Web," you can send and receive SMS messages on the Chromebook.

You can start a conversation with a single contact or with multiple people. You can add emoji, stickers, GIFs, or small files to the messages you send. You can mute a conversation if you need peace. And when you finish a conversation, you can archive it or simply delete it.

Chat from Your Chromebook Using Messages

1 Open a Chrome tab.

For example, click **Chrome** (🟢) on the shelf; or press Shift+click **Launcher** (○) to display the Launcher full screen, and then click **Chrome** (🟢).

2 Click the omnibox.

3 Type *messages.google.com* and press Enter.

The Google Messages website appears.

4 Click **Start chat**.

The New Conversation pane appears.

5 Click the contact number you want to use.

The pane for the conversation appears.

A You can click **Add more people** to add more people to the chat.

6 Type your message in the message box.

7 Click **Send** (▷) or press Enter.

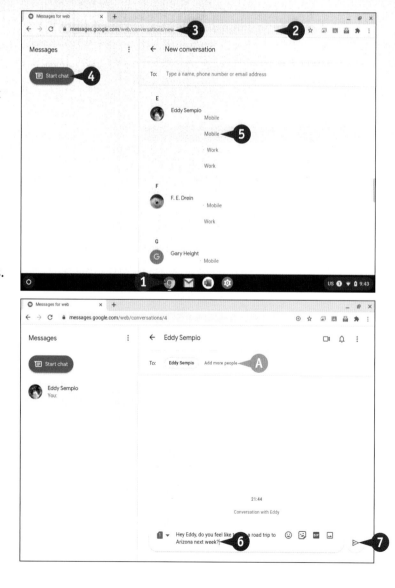

Messages sends the message to the contact.

Ⓑ When your contact replies, the message appears in a bubble on the other side of the screen.

⑧ To include an emoji in a message, click **Select an emoji** (☺).

Ⓒ You can click **Select a sticker** (☺) to display the Sticker panel and choose a sticker.

Ⓓ You can click **Select a GIF** (GIF) to display the GIF panel and select a GIF.

Ⓔ You can click **Select attachments** (🖼) to display the Select One or More Files dialog box and select files to attach.

The Emoji panel appears.

⑨ Click the emoji you want to send.

Ⓕ The emoji appears at the cursor position.

⑩ Click **Send** (▷) or press Enter.

Messages sends the message.

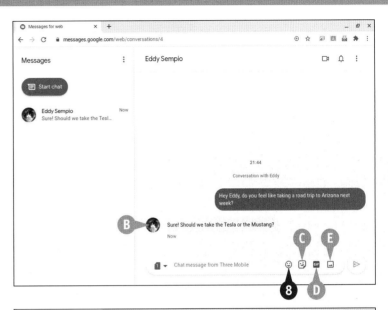

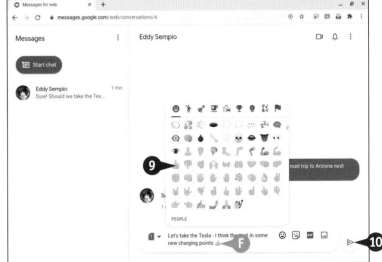

How do I manage my conversations in Messages for Web?

Click **Menu** (⋮) in the upper-right corner of the conversation pane to display the menu. You can then click **Details** to display the Details dialog box for the contact, in which you can set the **Mute conversation** switch to On (⚫) to mute the conversation or click **Add people** to add others to the conversation; click **Done** when you are ready to close the Details dialog box. Also on the menu, you can click **Archive** to archive the conversation; or you can click **Delete** to open the Delete This Conversation? dialog box, and then click **Delete** to delete the conversation.

CHAPTER 11

Organizing Your Life

In this chapter, you learn to use some of the key tools that Google provides for organizing your life on your Chromebook. First, you explore how to manage and configure your Google Account. Next, you organize your schedule with Google Calendar, your contact data with Google Contacts, and your tasks with Google Tasks. Last, you use Google Maps to get directions.

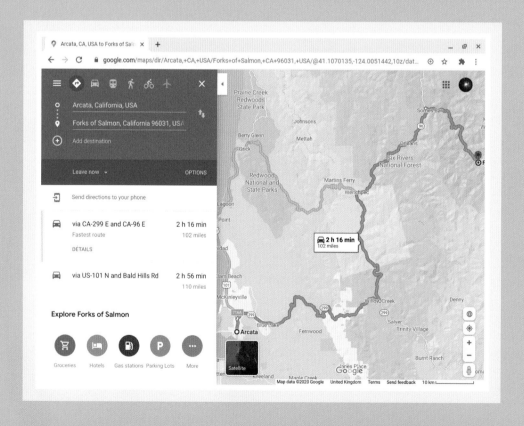

Your Google Account is essential to you using your Chromebook effectively and extensively. Google enables you to sync a wide variety of data across your Google Account, making this data available to not only your Chromebook but also any other computer or device you sign in to using your Google Account.

In this section, you learn how to control which items your Google Account syncs. Your first step is to display the Sync and Google Services screen, which you find in the Chrome browser's settings.

Manage Your Google Account

Display the Sync and Google Services Screen in Chrome Settings

1 Click **Chrome** (🌐) on the shelf.

Note: If Chrome (🌐) does not appear on the shelf, press Shift+click **Launcher** (●) to display the Launcher screen, and then click **Chrome** (🌐).

A Chrome window opens.

2 Click **Menu** (⋮).

The menu opens.

3 Click **Settings**.

The Settings screen appears.

Ⓐ You can click **Open** (☑) on the right side of the button for your user account to open a Settings app window showing the My Accounts page. Here, you can click **Add account** to add another Google Account, if necessary.

4 In the You and Google section, click **Sync and Google services**.

The Sync and Google Services screen appears.

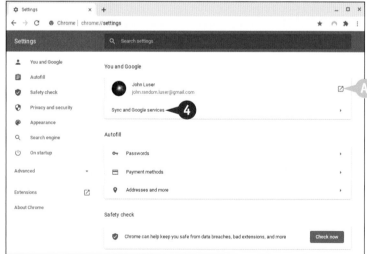

Choose Which Items to Sync Through Your Google Account

1 On the Sync and Google Services screen, click **Manage what you sync**.

The Manage What You Sync screen appears.

2 If you want to sync all your data, click **Sync everything** (○ changes to ◉), and then go to step **14**. Otherwise, click **Customize sync** (○ changes to ◉), and continue with the following steps to specify which items to sync across your devices.

3 Set the **Apps** switch to On (●●) to sync your apps.

4 Set the **Bookmarks** switch to On (●●) to sync your Chrome bookmarks.

5 Set the **Extensions** switch to On (●●) to sync your Chrome extensions.

6 Set the **History** switch to On (●●) to sync your Chrome browsing history.

7 Set the **Settings** switch to On (●●) to sync your settings.

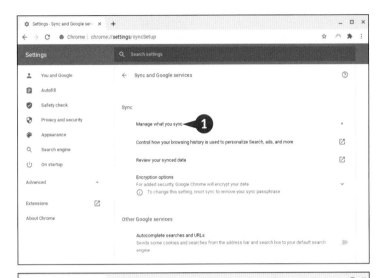

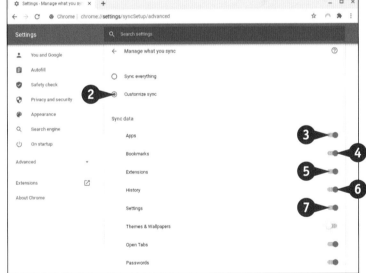

TIP

Which data should I sync through my Google Account?
Sync whatever data you will find most useful. The easiest solution is to select **Sync everything** (◉) to make sure you do not miss out on syncing something that would be beneficial. All the data you sync is encrypted against snooping, but to keep your data secure, you need to maintain security on all the devices that use your Google Account. If you feel that some data is too sensitive to risk syncing, select **Customize sync** (◉), and then set the appropriate switch in the Sync Data area to Off ( ).

continued ▶

The data you can sync via your Google Account includes the apps and Chrome extensions you have installed; your open tabs, the Chrome browser, your browser bookmarks, and your browsing history; and the themes and wallpapers that give your Chrome and Chromebook sessions their preferred look. You can also sync passwords, addresses, and phone numbers; payment methods and addresses using the Google Pay service; and details of Wi-Fi networks.

Manage Your Google Account (continued)

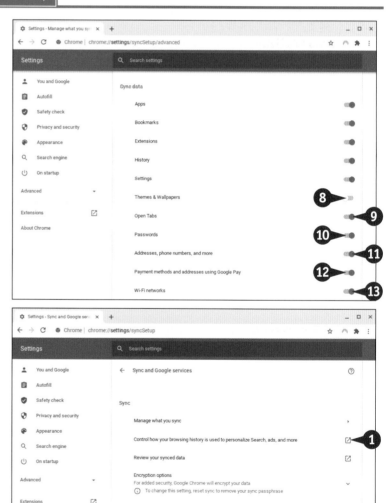

8 Set the **Themes & Wallpapers** switch to On (⬤) to sync your themes and wallpapers.

9 Set the **Open Tabs** switch to On (⬤) to sync your open tabs in the Chrome browser.

10 Set the **Passwords** switch to On (⬤) to sync your saved passwords.

11 Set the **Addresses, phone numbers, and more** switch to On (⬤) to sync data including addresses and phone numbers.

12 Set the **Payment methods and addresses using Google Pay** switch to On (⬤) to sync this Google Pay information.

13 Set the **Wi-Fi networks** switch to On (⬤) to sync data about Wi-Fi network connections.

14 Click **Back** (←) to the left of the Manage What You Sync heading.

The Sync and Google Services screen appears again.

Control How Google Uses Your Browsing History for Personalization

1 Click **Control how your browsing history is used to personalize Search, ads, and more** (☑).

A new tab opens in the same Chrome window, showing the Activity Controls screen in your Google Account settings.

Ⓑ If you want to pause Google's Web & App Activity across all sites and devices with which you use your Google Account, click the **Web & App Activity** switch, which is set to On (⬤) by default. In the Pause Web & App Activity? dialog box that opens, click **Pause**. The dialog box closes, and Chrome sets the Web & Activity switch to Off (   ).

② Select **Include Chrome history and activity from sites, apps, and devices that use Google services** (☑) to include this data in your web and app activity.

③ Select **Include audio recordings** (☑) if you want to include audio recordings from you speaking to Google services such as Search and Google Assistant. These recordings are excluded by default.

④ Click **Auto-delete** (🗑).

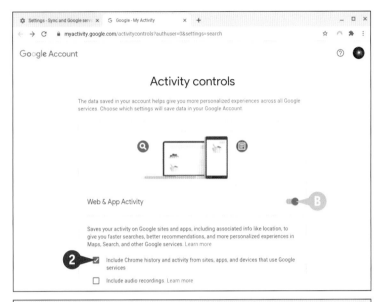

continued ▶

TIP

Should I include audio recordings in my Web & App Activity?

This is up to you, but before including them in your Web & App Activity, determine what value including them would bring to you. These audio recordings include audio captured when you are using Google Assistant via voice on your Chromebook, on your phone, or on other devices, such as Google Home speakers. Because Google Assistant must listen to you constantly to detect when you are invoking it, it can easily capture audio that you have not directed to it.

You can set your Google Account to automatically delete all the activity from your Web & App Activity list after a set period of time, such as 3 months or 36 months. You can also delete items from your Web & App Activity list manually at any time; for example, you might want to remove details of a potentially embarrassing site you stumbled upon.

You can also control how Google uses your browsing history to personalize your searches.

Manage Your Google Account (continued)

The Choose an Auto-Delete Option for Your Web & App Activity dialog box opens.

5 Click the appropriate option button (○ changes to ◉). Your choices are **Auto-delete activity older than 3 months**, **Auto-delete activity older than 18 months**, **Auto-delete activity older than 36 months**, or **Don't auto-delete**.

6 Click **Next**.

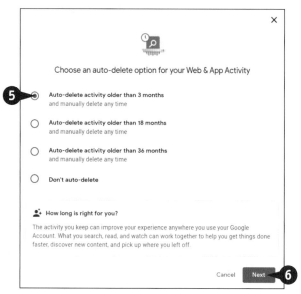

A dialog box opens to confirm your choices — for example, the Confirm Your Preference to Auto-Delete Activity Older Than 3 Months dialog box opens.

7 Look at the Automatically Deleting in the Future (🗑) box and the Deleting Now (🗑) box to verify the details.

8 Click **Confirm**.

The Preference Saved dialog box opens.

9 Click **Got It**.

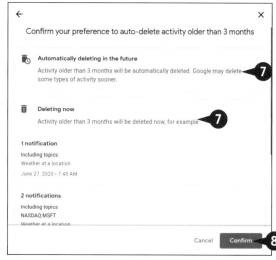

The Activity Controls screen appears again.

🔟 Click **Manage activity** (🕔).

The Web & App Activity screen appears.

Ⓒ You can click **Search your activity** (🔍) and type one or more terms by which to search.

Ⓓ You can click **Filter by date & product** to open the Filter dialog box, in which you can apply filters to locate the data you want to view. For example, you might filter by *Last 7 days* and *Gmail* to display recent messages.

⓫ To browse the data instead of filtering or searching, scroll further down the screen.

Ⓔ Boxes such as the Today box or the Yesterday box show your activities in specific time periods.

Ⓕ You can click **Delete** (🗑) to delete all the activity in a box.

Ⓖ You can click **Menu** (⋮) for an entry, and then click **Details** or **Delete**, as appropriate.

⓬ When you finish working on the Activity Controls screen, click **Close** (✖).

The tab closes.

The Sync and Google Services screen appears again.

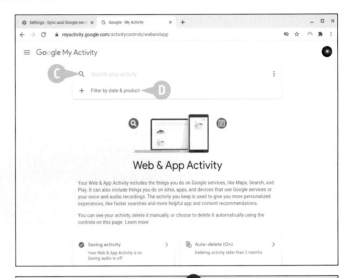

TIP

How long should I keep my Web & App Activity?
You choose. The longer you keep your Web & App Activity, the more closely Google can use the activity's data to tailor search results, ads, and so on to your apparent needs and interests. But if you feel that improved search results and less-irrelevant ads are poor reward for entrusting Google with your valuable usage data, you can delete your Web & App Activity after a short period. You may be able to improve your search results by using more precise search terms and by adding search operators, from basics such as AND and OR to more specialized ones such as *site:*, *intext:*, and *inurl*.

continued ▶

Google enables you to review your synced data stored on its servers and to clear the data by resetting synchronization. Clearing the data from the servers is a move you would normally make to resolve sync issues. It does not remove the data from your devices, which will resume syncing when you sign back in to Chrome.

When reviewing the data, you can see how many items are in each category of data — for example, how many apps, address bar history items, and passwords. But you cannot see the individual items.

Manage Your Google Account (continued)

Review Your Synced Data

1 On the Sync and Google Services screen, click **Review your synced data** (⬛).

A new tab opens in the same Chrome window, showing the Data from Chrome Sync screen in your Google Account settings.

Ⓗ For each category, you can see the number of items.

Ⓘ 🔒 indicates that the data is encrypted.

2 If you want to reset sync, click **RESET SYNC** at the bottom of the Data from Chrome Sync screen.

The Reset Sync dialog box opens.

3 Click **OK**.

The Reset Sync dialog box closes.

Chrome clears the data.

Note: After clearing the data, you can click the **sign into your Chrome browser** link at the bottom of the Data from Chrome Sync screen to sign in to Chrome again.

4 Click **Close** (✖).

The Data from Chrome Sync tab closes.

The Sync and Google Services screen appears again.

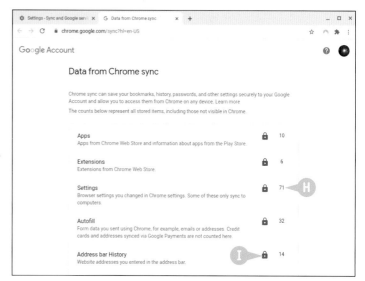

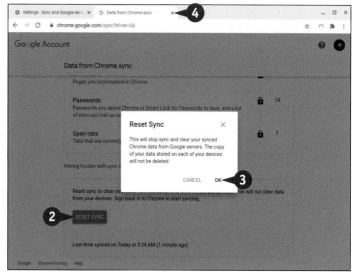

Choose Options for Encryption and Other Google Services

1 On the Sync and Google Services screen, click **Encryption options** (✔).

The Encryption Options section expands.

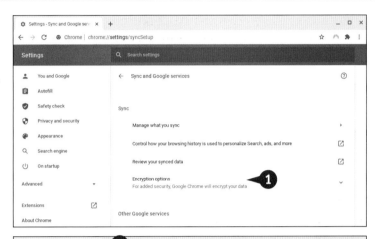

2 Click **Encrypt synced passwords with your Google username and password** (○ changes to ⦿) or **Encrypt synced data with your own sync passphrase** (○ changes to ⦿), as needed. See the tip for more information.

3 Set the **Autocomplete searches and URLs** switch to On (➍) or Off ( ), as needed.

4 Set the **Help improve Chrome's features and performance** switch to On (➍) or Off ( ), as needed, to control whether Chrome automatically shares usage statistics and crash reports.

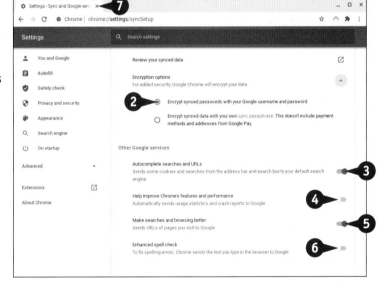

5 Set the **Make searches and browsing better** switch to On (➍) or Off ( ), as needed.

6 Set the **Enhanced spell check** switch to On (➍) or Off ( ), as needed.

7 When you finish choosing options on the Sync and Google Services page, click **Close** (✕).

The Chrome tab or Chrome window closes.

TIP

Which method should I use for encrypting my synced passwords?

For encrypting your passwords, the Sync and Google Services screen lets you choose between using your Google username and password and using a custom sync passphrase.

Normally, using your Google username and password is the better choice, because it provides for more complete syncing of your data. Creating a custom sync passphrase can add another layer of security, but you are likely to be better off ensuring that the password for your Google Account is strong enough to ensure security.

Open Google Calendar and Create a Shortcut

G oogle Calendar is a web-based calendaring service that enables you to manage multiple calendars and create events, reminders, and tasks. By default, Google Calendar does not have an icon on the Launcher screen; instead, you access Calendar from its icon in the side panel in web apps such as Gmail or from the Google Apps pop-up panel in any Google web app, as explained in this section.

If you will use Google Calendar extensively, you will likely want to create a Launcher screen shortcut for it. This section explains how to create such a shortcut.

Open Google Calendar and Create a Shortcut

Open Google Calendar from Gmail

1 Open Gmail as usual. For example, press **Shift**+click **Launcher** (⊙), and then click **Gmail** (M) on the Launcher screen.

Note: If the side panel is hidden, click **Show side panel** (‹) to display it.

2 Click **Calendar** (📅) in the side panel.

Google Calendar opens in a new tab.

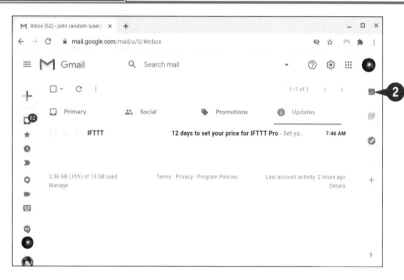

Open Google Calendar from the Google Apps Panel

1 In one of the Google apps, such as Docs or Sheets, click **Google Apps** (⋮⋮⋮).

The Google Apps panel opens.

2 Click **Calendar** (📅).

Google Calendar opens in a new tab.

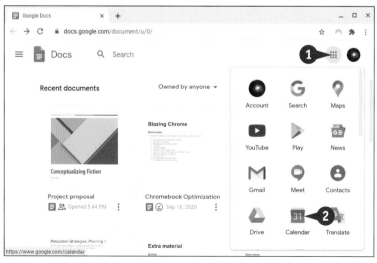

Create a Shortcut to Google Calendar

1 After opening Google Calendar in one of the ways explained earlier in this section, click **Menu** (⋮).

The menu opens.

2 Click or highlight **More tools**.

The More Tools submenu opens.

3 Click **Create shortcut**.

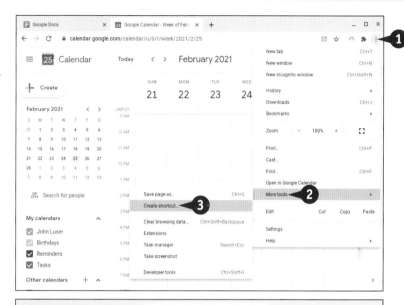

The Create Shortcut? dialog box opens.

4 Edit the suggested name, if needed.

5 Select **Open as window** (☑) if you want Google Calendar to open in a new Chrome window rather than as a tab in the current Chrome window.

6 Click **Create**.

The Create Shortcut? dialog box closes.

Chrome OS adds the shortcut to the Launcher screen.

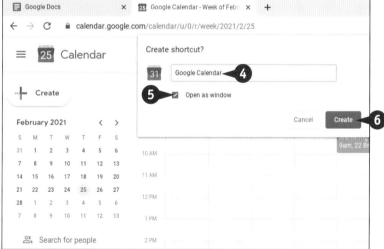

TIP

Should I set Google Calendar to open in a new window?
Having Google Calendar open in a new window is often more convenient than having Calendar on a tab in a Chrome window. When Google Calendar is open in its own window, a Google Calendar icon appears on the shelf, giving you a quick way to access your calendar data.

Navigate the Google Calendar Interface

Google Calendar packs a large amount of data into its interface. You can choose to display what period of time to display — one day, four days, one week, one month, or one year — or instead display a straightforward list of events.

You can choose whether to show weekend days or hide them to reduce the amount of information displayed. You can also choose whether to show events you have declined or to hide them.

Navigate the Google Calendar Interface

1 Press **Shift**+click **Launcher** (⊙).

The Launcher screen appears.

2 Click **Google Calendar** (📅).

Note: If Google Calendar (📅) does not appear on the Launcher screen, follow the instructions in the section "Open Google Calendar and Create a Shortcut," earlier in this chapter, to create a shortcut there.

Google Calendar opens.

Ⓐ The panel on the left is the main menu.

Ⓑ The calendar control enables you to navigate by date.

Ⓒ The Search for People box enables you to search your calendar by people.

Ⓓ The My Calendars list and Other Calendars list let you control which calendars appear.

Ⓔ Your calendar entries for the selected date range appear.

3 Click **Main menu** (≡).

The main menu closes, giving more space for the calendar entries.

F You can click **Hide side panel** (⟩) to hide the side panel, if needed.

4 Click **Show** (▼).

The Show pop-up menu opens.

5 Click **Day**, **Week**, **Month**, **Year**, **Schedule**, or **4 days**, as appropriate.

Note: Click **Schedule** to display a list of your upcoming events in date order.

G You can click **Show weekends** to display or hide weekend days.

H You can click **Show declined events** to display or hide events you have declined.

Google Calendar shows the time period you chose.

I You can click **Today** to display the current date.

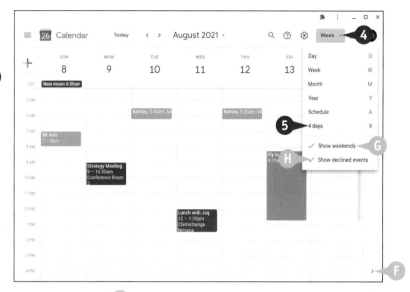

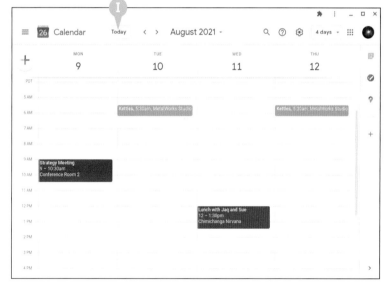

TIP

Should I allow Google Calendar to give me "better" notifications?
Better notifications contain more data, so they are usually helpful. If Google Calendar displays the Want to Get Better Notifications? dialog box, asking your permission to display notifications through the browser, click **Continue**. In the calendar.google.com Wants to Show Notifications dialog box that opens, click **Allow**.

Create a New Calendar

Google Calendar enables you to create as many calendars as you need to separate your events into logical categories. Google Calendar starts you off with four default calendars: a calendar that bears your name, a Birthdays calendar, a Reminders calendar, and a Tasks calendar. These calendars appear in the My Calendars list in the main menu in Google Calendar by default.

You can create other calendars as needed. For example, you may want to create separate calendars for work events, home events, and other categories of commitments that you will track in Google Calendar.

Create a New Calendar

1 Press **Shift** + click **Launcher** (o).

The Launcher screen appears.

2 Click **Google Calendar** (31).

Note: If Google Calendar (31) does not appear on the Launcher screen, follow the instructions in the section "Open Google Calendar and Create a Shortcut," earlier in this chapter, to create a shortcut there.

Google Calendar opens.

Note: If the main menu is not displayed on the left of the Google Calendar window, click **Main menu** (≡) to display it.

3 Click **Add other calendars** (+).

The pop-up menu opens.

4 Click **Create new calendar**.

The Settings screen appears, showing the Create New Calendar screen in the Add Calendar section.

5 Click **Name** and type the name for the calendar.

6 Click **Description** and type a description that will help you — and anyone with whom you share the calendar — grasp the calendar's contents.

7 Verify the time zone is correct. If not, click **Time zone** (⯆), and then click the appropriate time zone.

8 Click **Create calendar**.

A pop-up message appears, confirming the creation of the calendar.

A You can click **Configure** to configure further settings on the calendar.

9 Click **Back** (←).

The Calendar interface appears again.

B The new calendar appears in the My Calendars list.

C You can toggle the display of a calendar's events by clicking its check box (such as ☑ or ☑).

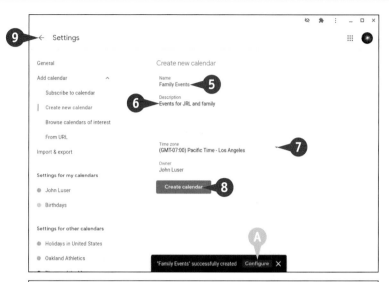

How do I import a calendar I have exported from another calendaring app?

You can import calendar files in Apple's iCal format or CSV — comma-separated values — format. Start by exporting the calendar to one of these formats.

Click **Add other calendars** (+) to open the pop-up menu, and then click **Import**. The Settings screen appears, showing the Import screen in the Import & Export section. Click **Select file from your computer** (⬆) to display the Select a File to Open dialog box, click the calendar file, and then click **Open**. Click **Add to calendar** (⯆), and then click the calendar into which you want to import the events. Click **Import**.

Create an Event in Google Calendar

Google Calendar enables you to create events for your time commitments, such as appointments, meetings, or trips. Your events appear as separate items on the grid, so you can see what you are supposed to do when.

You can create an event either for a specific length of time, such as 30 minutes or 2 hours, or for an entire day. You can create an event that occurs only once or an event that repeats one or more times on a schedule.

Create an Event in Google Calendar

1 Press **Shift**+click **Launcher** (⊙).

The Launcher screen appears.

2 Click **Google Calendar** (🗓).

Note: If Google Calendar (🗓) does not appear on the Launcher screen, follow the instructions in the section "Open Google Calendar and Create a Shortcut," earlier in this chapter, to create a shortcut there.

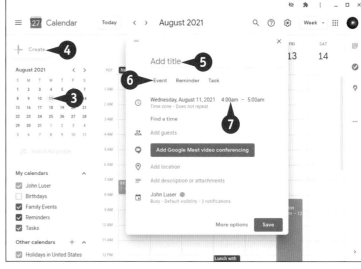

Google Calendar opens.

3 Click the date for the event.

4 Click **Create** (+).

The New Event dialog box opens.

5 Click **Add title** and type the title for the event.

6 On the tab bar, make sure Event is selected. If not, click **Event**.

7 In the time readout, click the start time.

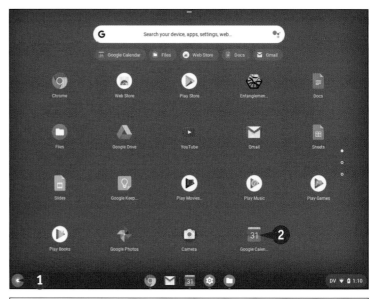

274

The time controls appear.

Note: Google Calendar sets the new event's length to the default duration. See the tip for how to change the default duration.

Ⓐ You can select **All day** (☑) to create an all-day event.

⑧ Click the start time.

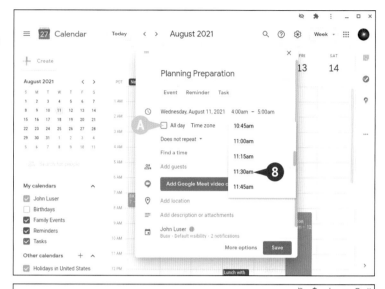

Google Calendar enters the new start time and updates the end time based on the default duration.

Ⓑ You can click the end time and change it, if needed.

⑨ Click **Location** and type the location.

Note: As you type the location, Google Calendar suggests matching locations from Google Maps. You can click a location to enter it.

⑩ Click **Save**.

The New Event dialog box closes.

The new event appears on your calendar.

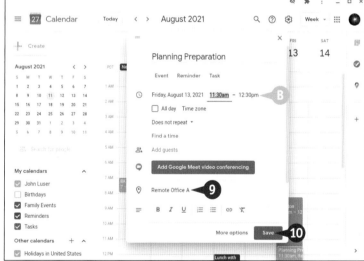

TIP

How do I change the default duration for new events?

In Google Calendar, click **Settings** (⚙) to open the Settings menu, and then click **Settings** to display the Settings screen. In the General section of the sidebar on the left, click **Event settings** to display the Event Settings section. Click **Default duration** (▼) to open the pop-up menu, and then click **15 minutes**, **20 minutes**, **30 minutes**, **45 minutes**, **60 minutes**, **90 minutes**, or **120 minutes**, as appropriate. Select **Speedy meetings** (☑) to trim 5 minutes off meetings of 45 minutes or shorter and to trim 10 minutes off longer meetings. Click **Back** (←) to return to the Calendar interface.

Share a Calendar with Other People

oogle Calendar enables you to share your main calendar, or a calendar you have created, with other people so that they can view its contents. The people you specify can then access the shared calendar by subscribing to it, as explained in the following section, "Subscribe to a Shared Calendar."

You can choose what level of access other people have to your shared calendar. For example, you can specify that one person can see all the details of events in a calendar, whereas another person can see only that you are busy during those events.

Share a Calendar with Other People

1 Press **Shift**+click **Launcher** (⬡).

The Launcher screen appears.

2 Click **Google Calendar** (📅).

Note: If Google Calendar (📅) does not appear on the Launcher screen, follow the instructions in the section "Open Google Calendar and Create a Shortcut," earlier in this chapter, to create a shortcut there.

Google Calendar opens.

Note: If the main menu is not displayed on the left of the Google Calendar window, click **Main menu** (≡) to display it.

Note: If the My Calendars list is collapsed, click **My calendars** (∨ changes to ∧).

3 Move the cursor over the calendar you want to share.

Pop-up controls for that calendar appear.

4 Click **Menu** (⋮).

The menu opens.

5 Click **Settings and sharing**.

Ⓐ You can click a color button to change the color assigned to the calendar.

The Settings screen appears, showing the Calendar Settings screen for the calendar.

6 Click **Share with specific people**.

The Share with Specific People screen appears.

Note: You cannot share your Birthdays calendar, your Reminders calendar, or your Tasks calendar.

7 Click **Add people** (**+**).

The Share with Specific People dialog box opens.

8 Click **Add email or name**, and then click the person with whom you want to share the calendar.

Ⓑ A button shows the person's name.

9 Click **Permissions** (▼), and then click the appropriate permission. See the tip for advice.

10 Click **Send**.

The Share with Specific People dialog box closes.

11 Click **Back** (←).

The calendar interface appears again.

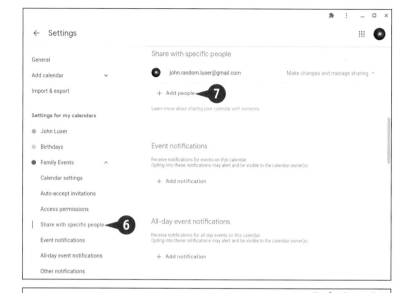

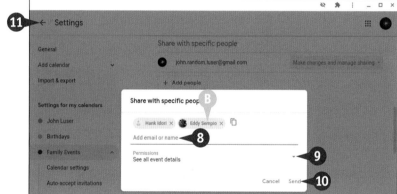

Which permissions should I assign when I share a calendar?

Normally, you would assign the See All Event Details permission, enabling the person to see the event's details but not change them. If you are sharing the calendar only so that the person can see whether you are free or busy at a particular time, assign the See Only Free/Busy (Hide Details) permission instead.

If the person will help you manage your calendar, assign the Make Changes to Events permission. And if you want to let the person not only make changes but also share the calendar with others, assign the Make Changes and Manage Sharing permission.

Subscribe to a Shared Calendar

Just as you can share a calendar with others, you can subscribe to a calendar that one of your contacts has shared with you on Google Calendar. Your contact gets to control the level of access you receive, from being able to see only when the contact is free or busy to being able to see all the details of events, making changes to events, or even making changes and managing sharing.

Google Calendar also enables you to add published calendars, such as those for sports teams or public bodies.

Subscribe to a Shared Calendar

1 Press **Shift**+click **Launcher** (⭘).

The Launcher screen appears.

2 Click **Google Calendar** (🗓️).

Note: If Google Calendar (🗓️) does not appear on the Launcher screen, follow the instructions in the section "Open Google Calendar and Create a Shortcut," earlier in this chapter, to create a shortcut there.

Google Calendar opens.

Note: If the main menu is not displayed on the left of the Google Calendar window, click **Main menu** (≡) to display it.

3 Click **Add other calendars** (+).

The pop-up menu opens.

4 Click **Subscribe to calendar**.

The Settings screen appears, showing the Subscribe to Calendar screen in the Add Calendar section.

5 Click **Add calendar**.

A pop-up menu opens showing available contacts.

6 Click the contact who is sharing the calendar.

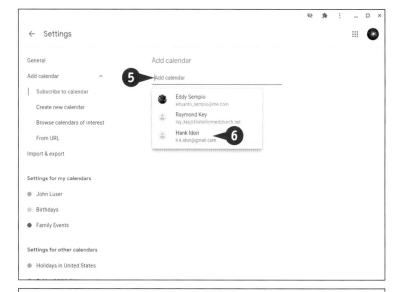

The contact's email address appears in the Name box.

7 Optionally, type a description of the calendar to make it easier to identify.

A In the Permissions Settings area, the You Can readout shows your permissions for the calendar, such as *See all event details*.

8 Click **Back** (←).

The calendar interface appears again.

The calendar you added appears in the Other Calendars list in the main menu.

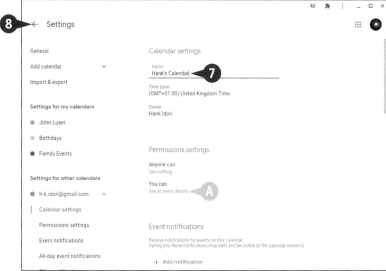

 TIP

How do I add a sports team's calendar to Google Calendar?
You can add a published calendar, such as a sports team's calendar or a holidays calendar, by using the Browse Calendars of Interest feature. In the main menu, click **Add other calendars** (+) to open the pop-up menu, and then click **Browse calendars of interest**. The Browse Calendars of Interest screen in the Add Calendar category of Settings appears. Go to the Holidays list, the Sports list, or the Other list; locate the calendar; and then select its check box (☑). The calendar then appears in your Other Calendars list.

Google Contacts is a web-based database that enables you to store information about your contacts. By default, Google Contacts does not have an icon on the Launcher screen in Chrome OS; instead, you access Contacts from the Google Apps pop-up panel in any Google web app, as explained in this section.

If you will use Google Contacts extensively, you will likely want to create a Launcher screen shortcut for it. This section explains how to create such a shortcut. You can set the shortcut to open Google Contacts either in a new Chrome tab or in a separate window.

Open Google Contacts and Create a Shortcut

Note: This example uses the Gmail web app, but you can use any of the Google web apps. For example, if you have the Google Drive web app or the Google Calendar web app open in a Chrome tab, activate that Chrome tab and go to step **3**.

1. Press **Shift**+click **Launcher** (⊙).

   The Launcher screen appears.

2. Click **Gmail** (✉).

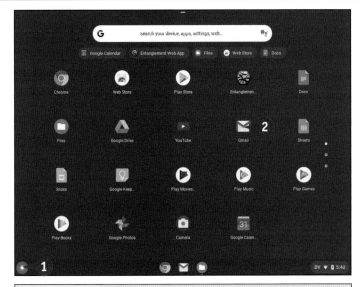

   The Gmail web app opens in a Chrome tab.

3. Click **Google Apps** (⠿).

   The Google Apps panel opens.

4. Click **Contacts** (☻).

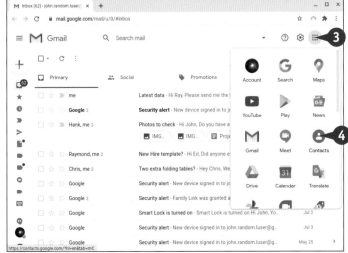

Google Contacts opens in a new tab in the same Chrome window.

5 Click **Menu** (⋮).

The menu opens.

6 Click or highlight **More tools**.

The More Tools submenu opens.

7 Click **Create shortcut**.

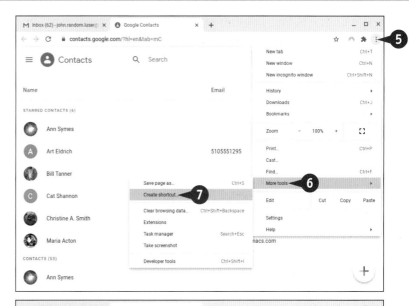

The Create Shortcut? dialog box opens.

8 Edit the suggested name, if needed.

9 Select **Open as window** (☑) if you want Google Contacts to open in a new Chrome window rather than as a tab in the current Chrome window.

10 Click **Create**.

The Create Shortcut? dialog box closes.

Chrome OS adds the shortcut to the Launcher screen.

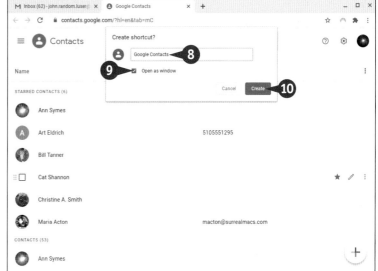

TIP

How do I make Google Contacts display more contacts in its window or tab?
In Google Contacts, click **Menu** (⋮), and then click **Display density** to open the Display Density dialog box. On the tab bar at the bottom, click **Compact** to switch to the Compact View from Comfortable View, which is more spacious. Then click **Done** to close the Display Density dialog box.

oogle Contacts helps you to track and manage your contacts. Google Contacts stores the data for each contact in a contact record that contains storage slots for many different items of information, from the person's names and phone numbers to their email addresses and photo.

To add a contact, you create a new contact record and enter the person's data on it.

Add Someone to Your Contacts

1 Press **Shift**+click **Launcher** (⬚).

The Launcher screen appears.

2 Click **Google Contacts** (☻).

Note: If Google Contacts (☻) does not appear on the Launcher screen, follow the instructions in the previous section, "Open Google Contacts and Create a Shortcut," to create a shortcut there.

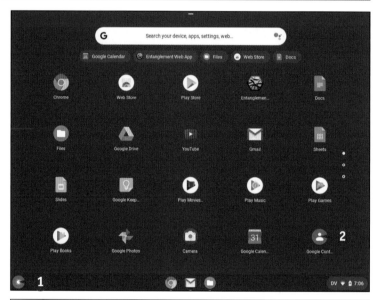

Google Contacts opens.

Ⓐ The Starred Contacts list contains contacts you have marked with a star — for example, to designate them as being important.

Ⓑ The Contacts list contains all your contacts, including starred contacts.

3 Click **New** (╋).

The New pop-up menu opens.

4 Click **Create a contact** (☺).

Ⓒ You can click **Create multiple contacts** (☺) to create multiple contacts in a single move.

The Create New Contact dialog box opens with the First Name field selected.

5 Enter the contact's first name.

6 Click **Last name** and enter the contact's last name.

Note: You can press `Tab` to move from one field to another in the Create New Contact dialog box. Press `Shift` + `Tab` to move backward.

7 Enter other information, as needed.

8 To assign the contact to one or more labels, click **Label** (▢).

Note: The Label button shows No Label when no label is assigned to the contact.

The Add to Label pop-up panel opens.

9 Click each label to which you want to add the contact.

10 Click outside the Add to Label panel.

The Add to Label panel closes.

11 Click **Save**.

The Create New Contact dialog box closes.

The contact appears in the Contacts list.

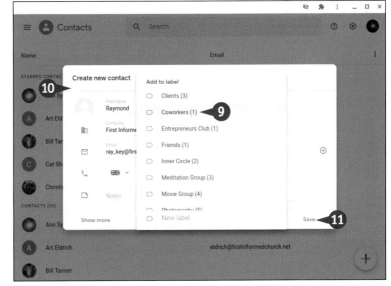

TIP

What other way can I start adding a contact?
In Gmail, open a message from a sender who you want to add to your contacts, and then move the cursor over the sender name. In the pop-up panel that appears, click **Add to Contacts**. Gmail adds the contact information to Google Contacts. The Edit Contact button replaces the Add to Contacts button. You can click **Edit contact** to open the Edit Contact dialog box in Google Contacts. The Edit Contact dialog box is essentially the Create New Contact dialog box with a different title.

Change a Contact's Information

Google Contacts enables you to easily edit the information for a contact. So when you learn that a contact's details have changed or you need to add extra information, you can open the contact record and make the changes needed.

You can edit any of the contact record's fields, which provide prebuilt storage for information from the contact's birthday to their website. If you need to add information that does not fit neatly in any of the existing fields, you can put it either in the custom field or in the notes field.

Change a Contact's Information

1 Press **Shift** + click **Launcher** (⬤).

The Launcher screen appears.

2 Click **Google Contacts** (🧑).

Note: If Google Contacts (🧑) does not appear on the Launcher screen, follow the instructions in the section "Open Google Contacts and Create a Shortcut," earlier in this chapter, to create a shortcut there.

Google Contacts opens.

(A) You can locate a contact by clicking **Search** (🔍) and starting to type the contact's name or other identifying information.

3 Click the contact you want to edit.

The contact record opens.

4 Click **Edit** (✏️).

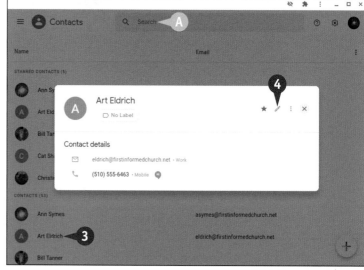

The Edit Contact dialog box opens.

5 Edit the contact data, as needed.

B Field names appear in blue where you have added or changed information.

C You can click **Add** (⊕) at the right side of a line to add another item of the same type.

D To delete the information in a field, move the cursor over the field, and then click **Remove** (⊗).

6 To display the full set of fields in the contact record, click **Show more**.

The Edit Contact dialog box displays the remaining fields.

E You can scroll down to display other fields.

7 Enter additional information, as needed.

8 Click **Save**.

Google Contacts saves your changes.

The Edit Contact dialog box closes.

The contact record appears, showing the updated information.

9 Click **Close** (✖) in the upper-right corner of the contact record.

The contact record closes.

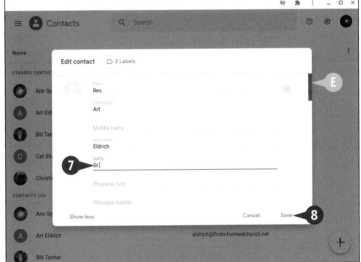

TIP

How do I delete a contact?

Move the cursor over the contact's record so that it becomes highlighted and the Edit button (✏) and Menu button (⋮) appear at its right side. Click **Menu** (⋮) to open the menu, and then click **Delete** (🗑). In the Delete This Contact? confirmation dialog box, click **Delete**.

Import Contacts into Google Contacts

I f you have contact information stored in another contact-management app or service, you do not need to enter them laboriously into Google Contacts one at a time. Instead, you can import the contact data quickly and easily. Google Contacts can import data in either the widely used vCard format or the even more widely used comma-separated values format, often referred to as CSV.

Before you take the following steps, export your data from your existing contact-management app or service to either a vCard file or a CSV file.

Import Contacts into Google Contacts

1 Press Shift+click **Launcher** (⊙).

The Launcher screen appears.

2 Click **Google Contacts** (⊖).

Note: If Google Contacts (⊖) does not appear on the Launcher screen, follow the instructions in the section "Open Google Contacts and Create a Shortcut," earlier in this chapter, to create a shortcut there.

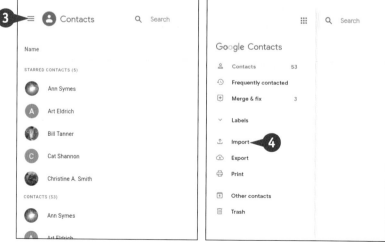

Google Contacts opens.

3 Click **Main menu** (≡).

The main menu opens.

4 Click **Import** (⬆).

The Import Contacts dialog box opens.

5 If you want to mark all the imported contacts with the same label or labels, click **Label** (⬜), and then click the label or labels.

6 Click **Select file**.

The Select a File to Open dialog box opens.

7 Navigate to the location or folder that contains the file.

8 Click the file.

9 Click **Open**.

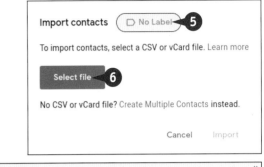

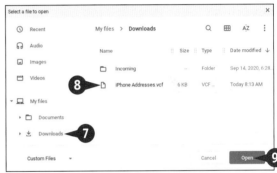

The Select a File to Open dialog box closes.

The filename appears in the Import Contacts dialog box.

10 Click **Import**.

Google Contacts imports the contact data.

A pop-up message saying All Done appears when the import is complete.

Note: If Google Contacts displays a banner prompting you to look for duplicate contact records, click **Dismiss** or **Find duplicates**, as appropriate. See the following section, "Merge and Fix Contacts," for coverage of removing duplicates.

TIP

How do I export my contact data from the People app in Windows 10?
As of this writing, you cannot export data directly from the People app. Instead, open a browser to **outlook.live.com**, and then sign in to your Microsoft account. Click **App launcher** (▦), click **All apps**, and then click **People** (👤) to switch to the People app. Select the contacts you want to export. In the upper-right corner of the window, click **Manage** (⌄) to open the Manage menu, and then click **Export contacts** to launch the Export Contacts Wizard.

Merge and Fix Contacts

When you create many contact records, it is easy to get duplicate records — two or more records that contain information for the same contact. Having duplicate records can cause confusion, especially when they contain conflicting data or out-of-date information. Duplicate records are especially likely to occur when you import existing contacts into Google Contacts.

Google Contacts provides the Merge & Fix feature to help you get rid of duplicate records quickly and easily. You access the Merge & Fix feature from the main menu in Google Contacts.

Merge and Fix Contacts

1 Press **Shift**+click **Launcher** (⊙).

The Launcher screen appears.

2 Click **Google Contacts** (👤).

Note: If Google Contacts (👤) does not appear on the Launcher screen, follow the instructions in the section "Open Google Contacts and Create a Shortcut," earlier in this chapter, to create a shortcut there.

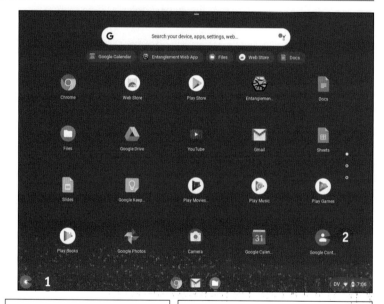

Google Contacts opens.

3 Click **Main menu** (≡).

The main menu opens.

4 Click **Merge & fix** (⊞).

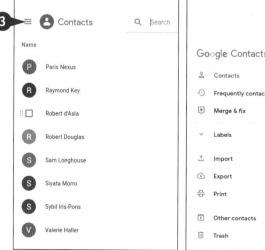

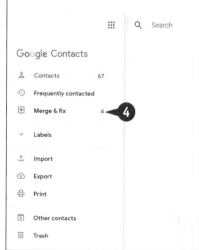

The Merge Duplicates list appears, showing apparent duplicate contact records.

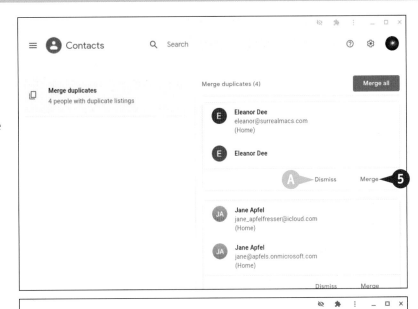

🅐 You can click **Dismiss** to dismiss the apparent duplicate.

5 Click **Merge** to merge a duplicate record.

🅑 A pop-up message appears, telling you that the contact has been merged.

🅒 You can click **Undo** to undo the merge.

6 If you want to merge all remaining duplicates, click **Merge all**.

Google Contacts merges all the contacts.

A pop-up message appears, telling you that the contacts have been merged. Here, too, you can click **Undo** to undo the merge, if needed.

Note: To return from Merge & Fix to viewing your contacts, click **Main menu** (☰), and then click **Contacts** (👤).

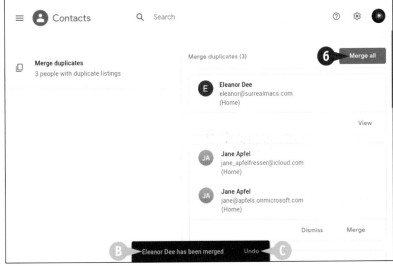

TIP

How can I recover my contacts after a merge operation goes wrong?

Google Contacts provides an Undo Changes command that can roll back your changes for up to 30 days. Click **Settings** (⚙), and then click **Undo changes** to display the Undo Changes dialog box. In the Undo Changes From list, select **10 min ago** (◉), **1 hr ago** (◉), **Yesterday** (◉), or **1 week ago** (◉); or click **Custom** (◉), and then use the Days, Hours, and Minutes controls to specify the period. Click **Undo** to make the changes.

Google Contacts enables you to organize your contacts into separate groups by applying labels to them. Creating groups makes it easier to find the contacts you need. For example, you might apply a label called Clients to your clients so you can quickly identify all your clients — or even send them a group email.

After applying labels, you can view a single label at a time or search within a label.

Organize Your Contacts into Groups

1 Press **Shift**+click **Launcher** (⊙).

The Launcher screen appears.

2 Click **Google Contacts** (●).

Note: If Google Contacts (●) does not appear on the Launcher screen, follow the instructions in the section "Open Google Contacts and Create a Shortcut," earlier in this chapter, to create a shortcut there.

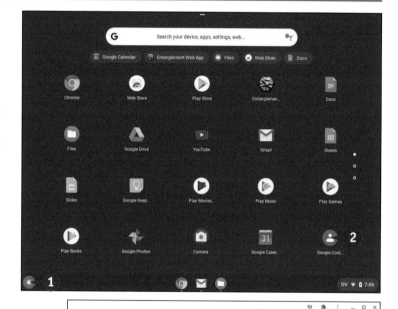

Google Contacts opens.

3 Move the cursor over the first contact to which you want to apply a label.

A check box (☐) replaces the contact's picture or letter circle.

4 Select the check box (☑).

5 Continue selecting contacts by moving the cursor over a contact, and then selecting the check box (☑).

6 When you have selected all the contacts you want to label, click **Label** (□).

The Manage Labels pop-up panel opens.

7 Click each label (✓) you want to apply.

8 Click **Apply**.

9 When you want to display a label, click **Main menu** (≡).

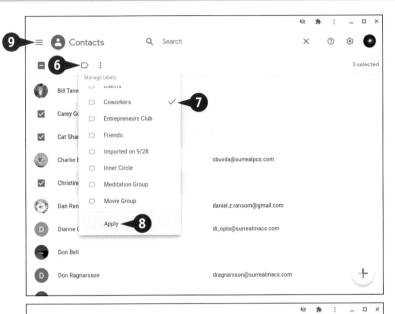

The main menu appears.

Note: If the Labels section of the main menu is collapsed, click **Labels** (⌄ changes to ⌃) to expand it.

10 Click the label you want to view.

The main menu closes.

The contacts in the label appear.

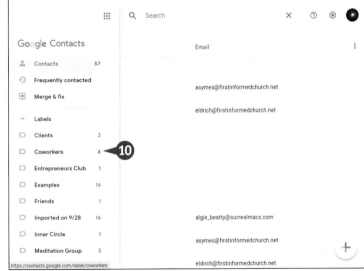

How many labels can I apply to a contact?
You can apply as many labels to your contacts as you need to be able to sort the contacts the way you wish.

Track Your Commitments with Google Tasks

To help you track your commitment, Google provides the Google Tasks service. Google Tasks runs in the side panel within Gmail or Google Calendar, giving you quick access to your tasks while you are working with email or your schedule.

You can create various lists to sort your tasks into different categories. For example, you might create a Work list, a Home list, a Family list, and an Errands list. After creating the lists you need, you can assign your tasks to lists, as appropriate.

Track Your Commitments with Google Tasks

Open Gmail and Display Google Tasks in the Side Pane

1 Press **Shift**+click **Launcher** (⊙).

The Launcher screen appears.

2 Click **Gmail** (✉).

Gmail opens in a Chrome tab.

Note: If the side panel is hidden, click **Show side panel** (❮) to show the side panel.

3 Click **Tasks** (◐).

The side panel expands and shows Google Tasks.

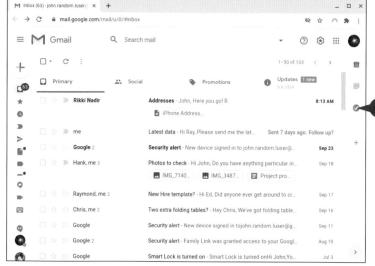

Set Up Your Task Lists

1 Under the Tasks heading, click ▼ to the right of the current list.

The Lists pop-up menu opens.

2 Click **Create new list**.

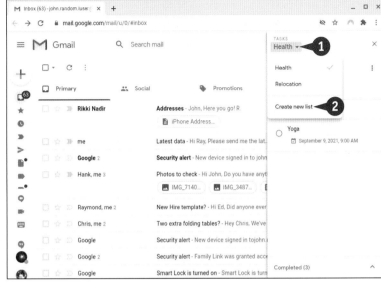

The Create New List dialog box opens.

3 Type the name for the new list.

4 Click **Done**.

The Create New List dialog box closes.

Google Tasks creates the new list and displays it in the task pane.

As the list contains no tasks yet, the pane contains a cartoon prompting you to add a task.

You can now set up the other lists you need by repeating steps **1** through **4**.

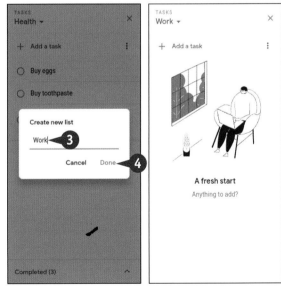

TIP

How do I change the order of my task lists?
Under the Tasks heading, click ▼ to the right of the current list to open the Lists pop-up menu. Move the cursor over the list you want to move so that the handle (⠿) appears. Click the handle (⠿), and then drag the list to where you want it on the Lists pop-up menu.

continued ▶

When you create a task, you can enter as little as the task name, or you can enter any details you have. You can assign a due date, which can include a due time, to the task. You can also add subtasks to a task, effectively dividing up the task into a series of steps that are easier — or perhaps just quicker — to complete.

After adding tasks to your lists, you can sort them into your preferred order. And once you finish a task, you can mark it as complete.

Track Your Commitments with Google Tasks (continued)

Create a Task

1 Under the Tasks heading, click ▼ to the right of the current list.

The Lists pop-up menu opens.

2 Click the list in which you want to create the new task.

The list you clicked appears.

3 Click **Add a task** (+).

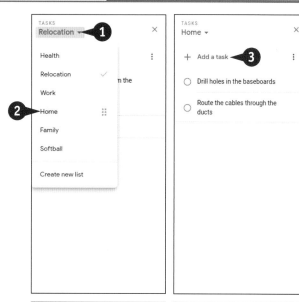

A blank line appears for the new task.

4 Type the task name.

Note: If you want to add no detail beyond the task name, you can press Enter to enter the task and start creating another task in the same list.

5 Click **Edit details** (✎).

The Details pane for the task appears.

6 Click **Add details** and type or paste any text details needed.

7 If needed, you can click **List** (▼), and then click a different list.

8 To schedule the task, click **Add date/time**.

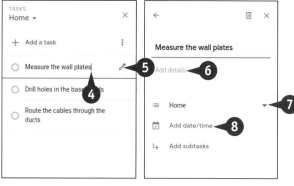

The date and time pane opens.

9 Click the date.

10 To assign a time, click **Time** (🕐).

The pop-up menu opens.

11 Click the appropriate time.

Ⓐ If you need to create a repeating task, click **Repeat** (⇄), and then specify the details in the Repeat dialog box that opens.

12 Click **OK**.

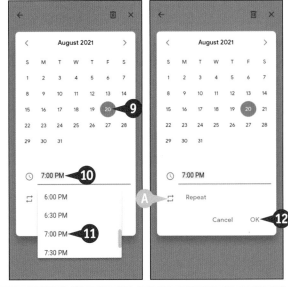

The date and time pane closes.

Ⓑ You can click **Add subtasks** (↳) to start adding subtasks to the task.

13 Click **Back** (←).

The task appears in your task list.

Ⓒ When you complete a task, click **Mark complete** (○ changes to ✓).

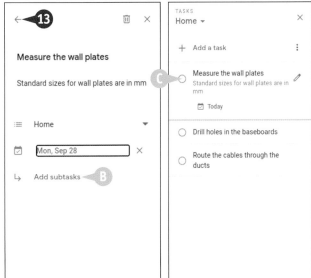

TIP

How do I change the order of the tasks?
You can display the tasks either in what Google Tasks calls My Order — in other words, the order you choose — or by date. To choose the order, click **Menu** (⋮) to open the menu, and then click **My order** or **Date** in the Sort By section of the menu.
If you use My Order, you can click a task and drag it up or down the task list to where you want it to appear.

Get Directions with Google Maps

Google Maps enables you to not only pinpoint your location but also get detailed directions from one place to another. You can get directions for various means of transport: driving, transit, walking, cycling, and flights.

You can switch the map between Map View, which shows roads and key geographical features, and Satellite View, which displays actual satellite imagery. The satellite images may be several years old, so do not expect reality to correspond exactly to them.

Get Directions with Google Maps

1 Right-click **Chrome** (🌐).

Note: If Chrome (🌐) does not appear on the shelf, press **Shift**+click **Launcher** (○) to display the Launcher screen, and then click **Chrome** (🌐).

The contextual menu opens.

2 Click **New window** (🗗).

A new Chrome window opens.

3 Click the omnibox, type **google.com/maps**, and press **Enter**.

Google Maps opens.

Ⓐ You can click **Satellite** to switch the map to Satellite View.

4 Click **Expand side panel** (▶).

The side panel opens.

5 Click **Directions** (◉).

The Directions panel appears.

6 Click **Starting point** and enter your starting point.

Ⓑ You can click **Reverse starting point and destination** (⇅) to swap the starting point and the destination.

7 Click **Choose destination, or click on the map** and start typing your destination.

Note: You can also click on the map to specify your destination.

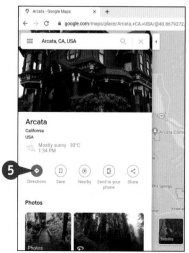

A list of matches appears.

⑧ Click the appropriate match.

⑨ Click **Search** (🔍).

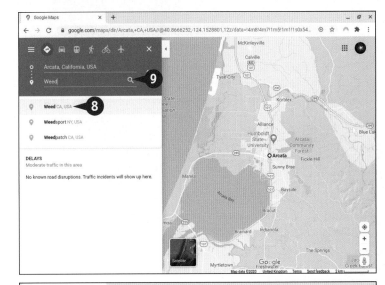

Suggested routes appear.

🅒 The blue route is the current route.

🅓 You can click an alternative route.

🅔 You can click **Send directions to your phone** (📲) to send directions to the Google Maps app on your Android phone or iPhone.

⑩ Click **Leave now** (🚗).

The Leave Now pop-up menu opens.

⑪ Click **Leave now**.

The first instructions for the journey appear.

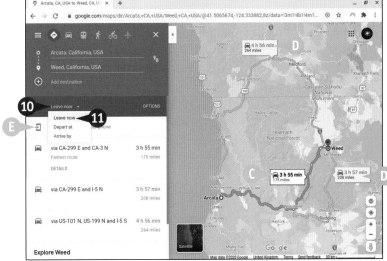

TIP

Can I create a Launcher shortcut for Google Maps?
Yes. Open a Chrome tab to Google Maps as explained in this section. Click **Menu** (⋮) to open the menu, click or highlight **More tools** to display the More Tools submenu, and then click **Create shortcut**. In the Create Shortcut dialog box that opens, select **Open as window** (☑), and then click **Create**. Chrome OS creates a Google Maps shortcut on the Launcher screen.

CHAPTER 12

Advanced Moves and Troubleshooting

This chapter shows you how to keep your Chromebook's operating system updated; how to connect to remote networks via virtual private networks, how to access other computers remotely, and how to get remote support; and how to perform essential troubleshooting maneuvers, from dealing with frozen Chrome tabs all the way up to recovering your Chromebook following major problems.

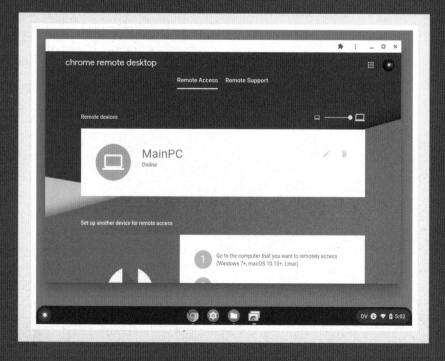

Keep Your Chromebook Current with Updates

To keep your Chromebook running well, it is a good idea to apply any updates to its operating system, Chrome OS. By default, Chrome OS checks for updates periodically, downloads any it finds, and prompts you to install them; but you can also check manually for updates at any point.

Updates may contain fixes for software bugs or patches for security problems that have been discovered. They may also make changes to existing features or add new features.

Keep Your Chromebook Current with Updates

Ⓐ When Chrome OS discovers an update for your Chromebook, an Update Available notification appears in the lower-right corner of the screen.

Ⓑ You can click **RESTART TO UPDATE** if you decide to simply apply the update immediately without learning more about it.

Ⓒ You can click **Collapse** (˄) to collapse the notification, hiding the Restart to Update button.

Ⓓ You can click **Update available** to open the Settings app to the About Chrome OS screen in the Settings app, where you can view information about the update. Go straight to step **4**.

If you dismiss the notification, or if you simply miss it, you can check for updates manually.

1 Click the status area.

The system menu opens.

2 Click **Settings** (⚙).

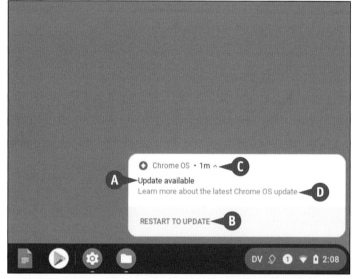

The Settings screen appears.

3 Click **About Chrome OS**.

The About Chrome OS screen appears.

E The Version readout shows the current version of Chrome. You may sometimes need to know the current version when troubleshooting problems or getting support.

4 Click **Check for updates**.

Chrome OS checks for updates.

F If an update is available, the About Chrome OS screen prompts you to restart your Chromebook to finish updating.

Note: If no update is available, the About Chrome OS screen shows the message *Your Chromebook is up to date*.

5 Click **Restart**.

Your Chromebook restarts and applies the update.

When the update is complete, the sign-in screen appears.

You can then sign in and resume work, as usual.

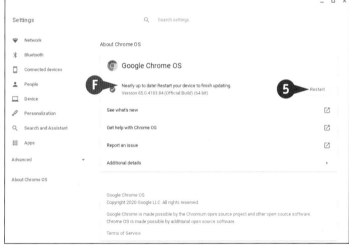

TIP

Is it wise to apply Chrome OS updates immediately, or is it better to wait a week or two?
If you have used, say, Windows, and experienced problems arising from updates not installing successfully or installing but not working, you may be leery of applying updates immediately. But Chrome OS rarely has problems with updates, partly because of successful quality control but also because Chromebooks use a much narrower set of hardware than Windows PCs.

Generally speaking, the advantages of having Chrome OS up to date and protected as fully as possible against bugs and security threats outweigh the chance of an update causing problems. If severe problems do occur, you can get your Chromebook working again by using moves such as Powerwash or recovery, both discussed later in this chapter.

Connect to a Remote Network via a VPN

A *virtual private network*, or VPN, is an encrypted connection that provides a secure link across a non-secure network. For example, if you use your Chromebook to connect remotely to your school or workplace across the Internet, you would usually use a virtual private network to secure the connection.

Virtual private networking also enables you to circumvent geographic restrictions on services. For example, if you use a geographically restricted movie service in your home country, you can use a VPN to make your Chromebook appear to be in your home country to access the service when abroad.

Choose a Suitable VPN Service Provider

Your first step is to choose the VPN service provider you will use. Many providers are available, and it is wise to spend a while researching the possibilities. You will need a provider that makes available a VPN extension for the Chrome browser.

If you already have a VPN service provider, you can skip this step. If you are getting VPN service for work or school, ask the administrators for their preferred VPN provider or — if they have none — for a shortlist of VPN providers they consider acceptable.

If you are choosing a VPN service provider on your own, the first key decision is whether to pay for a service or whether to use a free service. If you prefer not to pay, remember the standard Internet advice that if you are not paying for the product, you yourself are the product — the provider will be looking to make money from you via advertising or other means.

Whether you settle on a pay service or a free service, search online for evaluations and recommendations of VPN service providers. Make sure the advice you are reading is up to date.

Check the country or region where the VPN provider is domiciled, as this will decide which jurisdiction applies if companies or government bodies try to access your VPN usage data via legal means. For example, as of this writing, the IPVanish service is domiciled in the United States, the NordVPN service is domiciled in Panama, and the CyberGhost service is domiciled in Romania.

After making a shortlist of possible providers, open the Web Store and see which providers have extensions. Press **Shift**+click **Launcher** (◯), and then click **Web Store** (◉). Click **Extensions** (✹), click **Search Extensions**, type the provider's name, and then press **Enter**.

When you have chosen a suitable VPN provider, set up an account. Some providers offer trial periods to help you determine whether the service meets your needs.

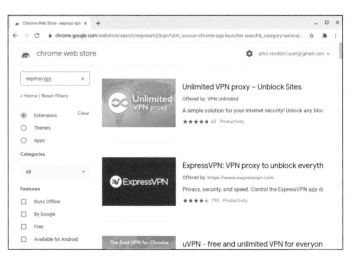

Install an Extension for Your VPN Provider

Once you have selected a VPN provider for which a Chrome extension is available, install that extension in Chrome. Be aware that multiple extensions may be available for some VPN providers; if so, the provider's official extension will normally be your best choice, unless you have read authoritative information demonstrating that a third-party extension gives better performance or security.

For example, open the Web Store app by **Shift**+clicking **Launcher** (🔘) and then clicking **Web Store** (🌐) on the Launcher screen. Locate the extension by clicking **Extensions** (🧩), clicking **Search Extensions**, typing the provider's name, and then pressing **Enter**. Click the search result for the extension to display its information screen, and then click **Add to Chrome**.

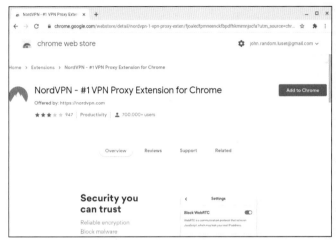

In the Add dialog box that opens, look at the It Can list to make sure that the permissions the extension requires are appropriate for VPN service. For example, the NordVPN extension requires these three permissions:

- **Read and Change All Your Data on the Websites You Visit.** This permission sounds threatening, but it is required for the VPN service to hide your IP address from the websites.

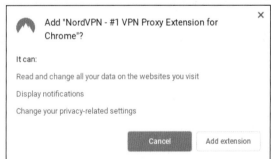

- **Display Notifications.** The VPN service needs to display notifications for various purposes, such as to inform you that it has established or ended a connection.

- **Change Your Privacy-Related Settings.** The VPN service needs to change your settings so as to route your data through a proxy server, a server that redirects the requests.

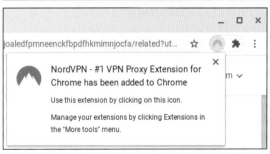

By contrast, a VPN service requiring permission to access your contacts would raise a red flag.

Assuming you decide the permissions list is acceptable, click **Add extension** to add the extension. A pop-up message confirms the addition and shows you the icon to click for configuring the extension.

continued ▶

After installing the extension for a VPN service, you need to configure the extension before you can use it. Typically, this means entering your account's credentials, such as a username and password, and then choosing usage settings.

Once you have configured the extension, you can start using the VPN service. To use the service, you simply establish a connection to the VPN service provider and then use the Chrome browser and other Internet-enabled software as usual. Your Internet traffic goes via the VPN service provider to its destination. When you finish using the VPN connection, you disconnect it.

Configure the Extension for the VPN Service

In a Chrome tab, click the icon for the VPN service's extension. If the icon does not appear on the section of the toolbar to the right of the omnibox, click **Extensions** (🧩) on this section to display the Extensions pop-up panel, and then click the VPN service's extension.

Use the controls in the pop-up panel for the extension to log in to the VPN service. For example, in the NordVPN pop-up panel shown here, you would type your email address or username, type your password, and then click **Log In**.

Once you have logged in, access the Settings screen or pane and choose suitable options for your needs. Continuing the example, you would click **Settings** (⚙) to display the Settings pane, where you could set the **Block WebRTC** switch and the **CyberSec** switch to On (⬤) or Off ( ), as needed.

Connect to the VPN

With the VPN service configured, you can start using it. In a Chrome tab, click the icon for the service's extension on the section of the toolbar to the right of the omnibox or on the Extensions pop-up panel. Then, in the extension's pop-up panel, give the command to connect.

For example, in the NordVPN pop-up panel shown here, you can click **Quick Connect** to make NordVPN quickly establish a connection to a VPN server that the service itself selects — for example, one that currently has plenty of capacity. Alternatively, you can click **Search for a specific country** (🔍) to display the Connect to Specific Country pane, in which you can either search for a country or browse to locate a country. Whichever method you use for finding the country, you click the country to establish a connection to a VPN server there.

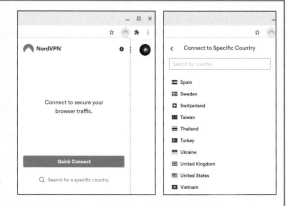

Work via the VPN

When the VPN service extension has established a connection to the VPN server, it displays information about the connection. For example, the NordVPN pop-up panel shows the country to which the VPN is connected and the message *Your browser traffic is now secured*.

Click outside the pop-up panel to close it. You can then work across the Internet connection much as usual.

Depending on the VPN service provider and the connection you have established, accessing websites may be somewhat slower than usual. Slowdowns are more likely to occur with free VPN services and with connections to busy countries.

Many Internet services use your connection's apparent location to detect security threats to user accounts, so you might want to avoid logging in to such services over a VPN connected to a new location.

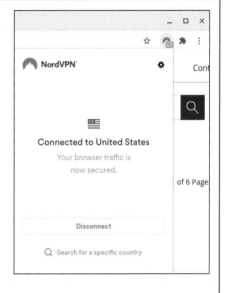

For example, if you are based in the USA and establish a VPN connection to, say, Bulgaria, trying to log into your email from there is likely to trigger a security alert.

Close the VPN Connection

When you finish using the VPN connection, close it. Click the extension's icon in the section of the toolbar to the right of the omnibox to display the extension's pop-up panel, and then give the command for closing the connection. For example, in the NordVPN pop-up panel, click **Disconnect**.

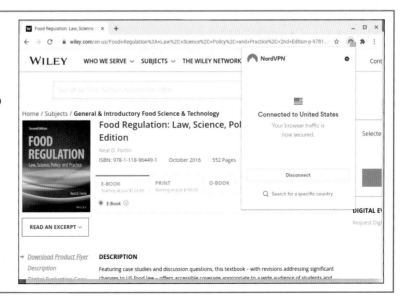

Using Remote Access and Remote Support

You can use your Chromebook to access and control a remote computer — such as a Windows PC, a Mac, or a Linux box — across a local network or the Internet. Various technologies are available for making this type of connection, but the easiest for Chromebook users is Google's Chrome Remote Desktop app, which you can install for free from the Chrome Web Store.

Chrome Remote Desktop also includes a Remote Support feature. When you need help on your Chromebook, you can use Remote Support to request and receive assistance from someone on a remote computer.

Install Chrome and Chrome Remote Desktop on Each Computer

To get the highest level of functionality in your remote connection, install the Chrome browser and the Chrome Remote Desktop app on each computer involved.

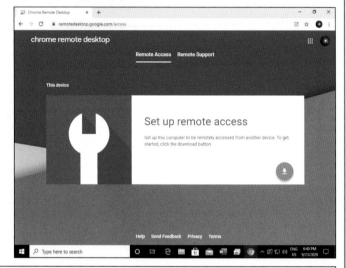

Your Chromebook already has the Chrome browser installed, and you can quickly install the browser on any Windows, macOS, or Linux PC. Open an existing browser and go to **chrome.google.com**, click **Download Chrome**, and follow the prompts that appear.

After installing Chrome, run the app and go to **g.co/crd/setup**, the Chrome Remote Desktop website. At the top of the page, make sure the Remote Access tab is displayed; if not, click **Remote Access**. Then go to the Set Up Remote Access box and click **Download** (⊙) to display the Chrome Remote Desktop extension's page in the Chrome Web Store.

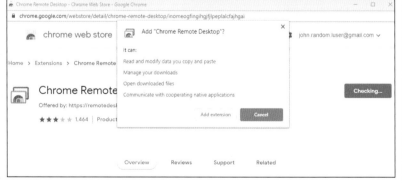

Click **Add to Chrome** to start installing the extension. In the Add "Chrome Remote Desktop"? dialog box that opens, click **Add extension**.

When the installation completes, the Chrome Remote Desktop Has Been Added to Chrome panel appears, highlighting the toolbar icon from which you can run the extension. Click **Close** (✖) to close the panel.

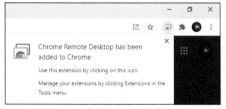

On the Ready to Install screen, click **ACCEPT & INSTALL**, and then click **Yes** in the Open Download confirmation message box.

In the Choose a Name dialog box, type the name you want to assign the computer for remote access, and then click **Next**.

In the Choose a PIN dialog box, type a PIN of six or more digits for securing your remote connections, and then click **START**. The Remote Access screen then appears again, showing an entry for the computer you just added.

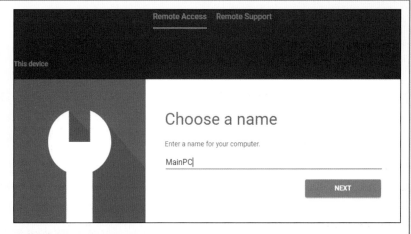

Take Control of Another Computer with Your Chromebook

On your Chromebook, launch Chrome Remote Desktop by pressing Shift +click **Launcher** (⊙) to display the Launcher screen and then clicking **Chrome Remote Desktop** (🖵).

In the Remote Devices box on the Remote Access tab, look at the button for the computer you want to access, and make sure that the *Online* readout appears. Then click the button to start the connection.

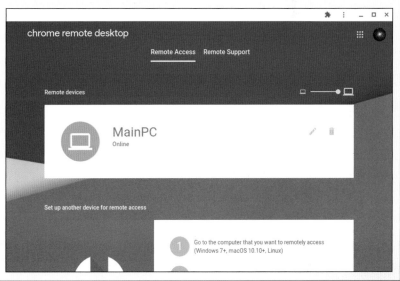

continued ▶

Once you have installed the Chrome browser and Chrome Remote Desktop on a computer, you can take control of it from your Chromebook — or indeed from Chrome on another computer.

When you need help on your Chromebook, you can use the Remote Support feature. To get support, you run Chrome Remote Desktop and generate a one-time code for connecting and authenticating. Your helper enters this code into Chrome Remote Desktop on their computer, enabling the app to establish the connection to your Chromebook.

Take Control of Another Computer with Your Chromebook (continued)

On the sign-in screen for the remote connection, type your remote-access PIN in the PIN field. Select **Remember my PIN on this device** (☑) if you want to store your PIN for the connection. Then click **Connect** (→) to establish the connection.

The remote computer's desktop then appears in the Chrome Remote Desktop window, and you can work on the computer much as if you were sitting at it.

To configure options for the connection, click **Options** (◄) at the right side of the window. The Options panel slides into view, and you can choose options in the Session Options section, the Enable Clipboard Synchronization section, the Input Controls section, the Displays section, the File Transfer section, and the Support section. When you finish, click **Close Options** (▶) to close the Options panel.

When you are ready to end the connection, click **Options** (◄) to display the Options panel, and then click **Disconnect** at the top of it.

Request and Receive Remote Support on Your Chromebook

When you need help on your Chromebook, identify someone who can help you remotely. This person's computer will need to have the Chrome browser and Chrome Remote Desktop installed. It is usually helpful to communicate with your helper via phone or audio chat.

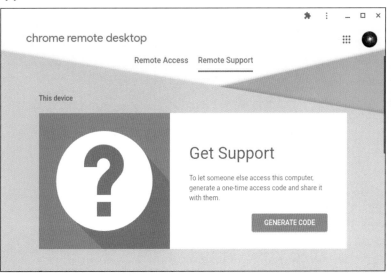

On your Chromebook, launch Chrome Remote Desktop by pressing [Shift] + click **Launcher** (🔘) to display the Launcher screen and then clicking **Chrome Remote Desktop** (🔲). Click **Remote Support** on the tab bar at the top of the screen to display the Remote Support tab, and then click **GENERATE CODE** in the Get Support box. Share the resulting code, which has a five-minute lifespan, with your helper.

Your helper also runs Chrome Remote Desktop and displays the Remote Support tab. They enter the access code in the Give Support box, and then click **CONNECT** to establish the connection.

When the Remote Assistance dialog box opens, verify the email address of the person connecting. Click **Share** if you want to share your screen and control of the Chromebook.

Once connected, your helper can help you solve the support issue. Both of you can move the cursor and use the keyboard — but only one of you at a time.

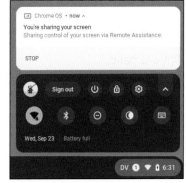

When you are ready to end the connection, click the status area to display the system menu and the You're Sharing Your Screen notification, which persists through the sharing session. Click **STOP** to end the connection.

Deal with Frozen Apps and Chrome Browser Tabs

Sometimes, a tab in the Chrome browser may *freeze* — in other words, stop responding — even though other tabs continue to work. You may be able to fix this problem by refreshing the tab.

Other times, the whole Chrome browser or another app may freeze. When this happens, you can use the Task Manager feature in Chrome to close the frozen tab. Task Manager is a system tool that displays a list of all the tasks — the computing processes — that the operating system is running. Using Task Manager, you can identify the offending process and terminate it.

Deal with Frozen Apps and Chrome Browser Tabs

Refresh a Frozen Chrome Browser Tab

A Chrome tab may sometimes freeze, becoming unresponsive.

Ⓐ The tab's content may display obvious visual problems, such as missing or incomplete images.

① Press Ctrl+click **Refresh** (C).

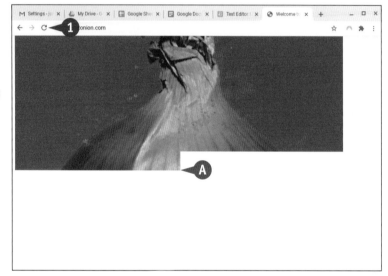

The Chrome browser reloads the tab.

Ⓑ Assuming the command works, the content appears in full, and the tab becomes responsive again.

Note: If the command does not work, you may need to close the Chrome browser using Task Manager, as explained next.

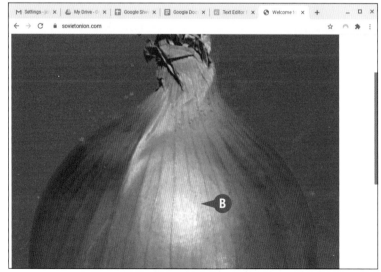

Using Task Manager to Close a Frozen App

C An app may sometimes freeze, becoming unresponsive.

Note: If the app contains unsaved work that you value, wait a minute or two to see if the app becomes responsive again. If it does, save your work immediately, and then close the app normally.

1 Press 🔍+Esc.

The Task Manager window opens.

Note: If the Task Manager window opens at a small size, drag a corner or side to enlarge the window so that you can view the contents easily.

2 Click **Task**.

Task Manager sorts the tasks by the Task column.

D Ascending Sort (▲) indicates the tasks are sorted in ascending order — alphabetically, for the Task column.

3 Click the app that has stopped responding.

4 Click **End process**.

Chrome OS forces the app to close.

5 Click **Close** (✖).

The Task Manager window closes.

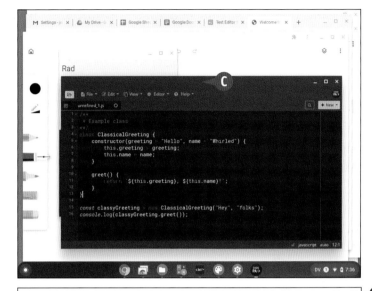

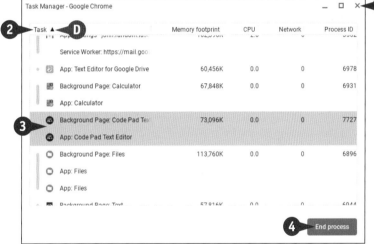

 TIP

How can I open Task Manager using the touchpad?
If you have a Chrome browser window open, switch to it by clicking **Chrome** (🌐) on the shelf; if not, open a Chrome browser window by pressing Shift+clicking **Launcher** (⊙) and then clicking **Chrome** (🌐) on the Launcher screen. Click **Menu** (⋮) to open the menu, click or highlight **More tools** to display the More Tools submenu, and then click **Task manager**.

Using Task Manager for Troubleshooting

As explained in the previous section, "Deal with Frozen Apps and Chrome Browser Tabs," the Task Manager feature enables you to close an app that has become unresponsive. You can also use the information available in Task Manager to identify other problems, such as apps or Chrome browser tabs that use large amounts of memory or processor time and so slow down your Chromebook.

After identifying an app that is causing problems, you can close the app either normally — if it is responding to commands — or by using the End Process command in Task Manager.

Using Task Manager for Troubleshooting

1 When your Chromebook starts to exhibit untoward behavior, such as running very slowly or stuttering while playing back audio or video, press ⊙ + Esc .

Task Manager opens.

Note: If the Task Manager window opens at a small size, drag a corner or side to enlarge the window so that you can view the contents easily. Alternatively, click **Maximize** (☐) to maximize the Task Manager window.

2 Click the heading of the column by which you want to sort.

A To change the columns displayed, right-click any column heading, and then click an item on the contextual menu to add it (✓) or remove it.

Note: See the tip for advice on which columns are most helpful.

Task Manager sorts the tasks by the column you specified.

B The Ascending Sort triangle (▲) indicates an ascending sort — in this case, from smaller numbers to larger numbers.

3 If necessary, click the same column heading again to reverse the sort order.

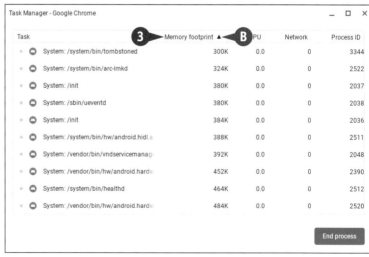

312

Task Manager sorts the tasks as specified.

C The Descending Sort triangle (▼) indicates a descending sort — in this case, from larger numbers to smaller numbers.

D In this example, you can see which apps are consuming the most memory.

4 To further investigate which apps are consuming most resources, click another column heading. For example, click **CPU**.

Task Manager sorts the tasks by the column you clicked.

E In this example, you can see which apps are consuming the most CPU — processor — cycles.

Note: The CPU percentages add up to more than 100% if the processor has multiple cores, as most Chromebook processors do.

5 When you finish using Task Manager, click **Close** (✖).

Task Manager closes.

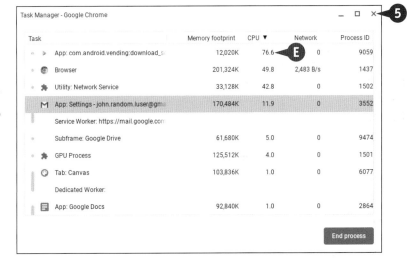

Which columns should I display in Task Manager?
Task Manager displays five columns of information by default: Task, which shows the task name; Memory Footprint, which shows the amount of active memory; CPU, which shows the percentage of processor cycles; Network, which shows the amount of network traffic; and Process ID, which shows the number of the system process. Adding the Swapped Memory column may help you identify apps that use large amounts of memory. Adding the Profile column — which shows the user ID, such as User 1 — may be useful when you have logged in multiple accounts. If space is tight, consider hiding the Process ID column, which is less helpful for nonspecialist troubleshooting; you may find the Process Priority column more helpful.

Troubleshoot Network Problems

Google has designed Chromebooks to use the Internet heavily, if not constantly, so any network problems that occur can put a serious crimp in your computing. When your Chromebook loses network connectivity, start with the essentials, making sure that Wi-Fi is enabled, that the Chromebook is connected to a Wi-Fi network — preferably the right one — and that the network is functioning. You may need to restart your Chromebook to resolve networking problems.

For further information about troubleshooting Wi-Fi connections, see the following section, "Troubleshoot Wi-Fi Connections."

Make Sure Wi-Fi Is Enabled

If your Chromebook loses network connectivity, look at the Wi-Fi icon in the status area to determine what the problem is. One of four icons appears:

- **Wi-Fi off** (⬇). This icon indicates that Wi-Fi is not enabled. When you move the cursor over this icon, the tooltip says *Disconnected*, which — while true — is misleading: "Disabled" or simply "Off" would be clearer.

- **Wi-Fi scanning** (▨). This icon indicates that Wi-Fi is enabled but is not currently connected to any network. When you move the cursor over this icon, the tooltip says *Disconnected*.

- **Wi-Fi connected** (▽). This icon indicates that Wi-Fi is enabled and connected to a network that is working. Moving the cursor over this icon displays a tooltip showing the network's name and the signal strength, such as *Connected to MyWiFiNetwork, Medium signal*.

- **Wi-Fi connected but with a problem** (▽). This icon indicates that Wi-Fi is enabled and connected to a network but that there is a problem with the network. Moving the cursor over this icon displays showing the network's name and the signal strength, such as *Connected to Wireless1, Medium signal*, but no information about the problem.

If ▽, ▨, or ▽ appears, click anywhere in the status area to display the system menu.

If the Wi-Fi icon shows ▽ and the label shows *Not connected: No networks*, click the Wi-Fi icon to enable Wi-Fi and to display the Network menu.

If the Wi-Fi icon shows any other icon, do not click it, because doing so will turn Wi-Fi off. Instead, click the Wi-Fi label — the text below the Wi-Fi icon — to display the Network menu.

Connect to the Right Network

You can determine the current network in any of three ways:

- Hold the cursor over the Wi-Fi icon in the status area.

- Open the system menu and look at the Wi-Fi label.

- Look at the *Connected* readout on the Network menu.

If the current network is the wrong one, click the right network on the Network menu.

Once Chrome OS has connected to the right network, verify that the Wi-Fi Connected () icon appears in the status area and that the network connection is working. For example, check your Gmail messages to verify that the network connection is working.

Forget Useless Networks and Set Preferred Networks

Once Chrome OS has connected to a Wi-Fi network successfully, it will connect to that network again in the future when it is available — even if the network has no connectivity and is useless to you. When this happens, you need to tell Chrome OS to forget the network.

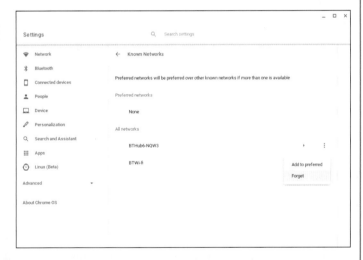

If you have connected to multiple Wi-Fi networks in the same location, you can tell Chrome OS which networks to prefer.

Click the status area to display the system menu, and click **Settings** (⚙) to open the Settings window. In the Network category, click **Wi-Fi** to display the Wi-Fi screen, and then click **Known networks** to display the Known Networks screen.

In the All Networks list, click **Menu** (⋮) for the network you want to affect. Then click **Add to preferred** to add the network to the Preferred Networks list, or click **Forget** to forget the network.

Using an Ethernet Connection

If you consistently have trouble with Wi-Fi, consider using a wired Ethernet connection. If your Chromebook model includes an Ethernet port, you can simply plug in a cable; if not, look into getting a USB-to-Ethernet adapter that will work with your Chromebook.

Troubleshoot Wi-Fi Connections

Wi-Fi connections generally work well on Chrome OS, but you may sometimes need to troubleshoot them. When problems occur, you may be able to resolve them by turning Wi-Fi off and then back on again or by restarting your Chromebook. If neither of these moves works, you may need to forget the existing entry for the network and set it up again from scratch. Creating a new entry for the network can resolve connectivity problems, even if the network's information — the network name, the security type, password, and so on — have not changed.

Turn Wi-Fi Off and Back On

If your Chromebook is connected to a Wi-Fi network that normally works well but is currently not working properly, try simply turning Wi-Fi off and back on. This move sounds almost too elementary to be worth mentioning — but it often works, and it takes only seconds, so you have little to lose by trying it.

Before you start, test the Wi-Fi network with another device if possible to make sure your Chromebook is the exception. For example, you might connect your phone to the Wi-Fi network and check your email to verify that the connection is working. If the Wi-Fi network is not working and you administer the network, try restarting the Wi-Fi router.

Click the status area to display the system menu, and then click **Wi-Fi** (such as [icon]) to turn Wi-Fi off. When the *Not connected: No networks* readout appears, click **Wi-Fi** ([icon]) to turn Wi-Fi back on and reconnect. This time, clicking the icon displays the Network menu.

Verify that the Chromebook has connected to the right Wi-Fi network. If not, click the right network.

Restart Your Chromebook

If turning Wi-Fi off and back on does not restore the connection to usability, try restarting your Chromebook by shutting it down and then starting it again. For example, press [icon] or **Power** momentarily to display the Power menu, and then click **Power off** ((!)). When the Chromebook has powered off, press [icon] or **Power** to start it again.

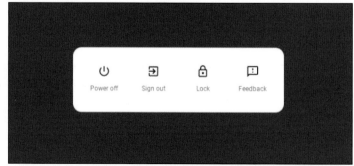

[icon] is the key in the upper-right corner of the keyboard on a nontouchscreen Chromebook, while Power is the physical power button on a touchscreen Chromebook.

Forget the Wi-Fi Network's Entry and Re-create It

If restarting your Chromebook does not get the Wi-Fi network working well, try making Chrome forget the Wi-Fi network and then creating a new entry for it.

Click the status area to display the system menu, and then double-click the network's name to display its screen in the Settings app. Make a note of the network's name; then expand the Advanced section and make a note of the security type as well. Once you have done that, click **Forget** to make Chrome OS forget the network.

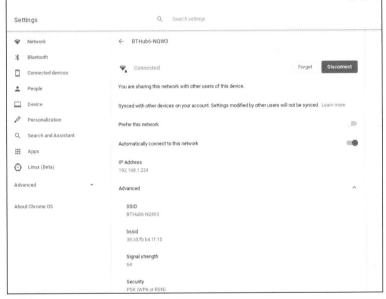

After forgetting the network, Chrome OS displays the main Settings screen. In the Network section at the top, click **Add connection** to expand the Add Connection section, and then click **Add Wi-Fi** to open the Join Wi-Fi Network dialog box.

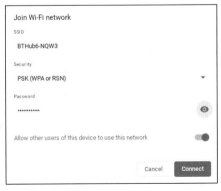

Click **SSID** and type the network's name, which is also called its service set identifier. Click **Security** (▾), and then click the security type, such as **PSK (WPA or RSN)**. Click **Password** and type the password. Set the **Allow other users of this device to use this network** switch to On (⚫) or Off ( ), as appropriate. Then click **Connect**.

After the Chromebook establishes a connection to the Wi-Fi network, make sure the connection works to your satisfaction.

Shut Down a Frozen Chromebook

If hardware or software glitches occur, your Chromebook may freeze so that the display stops changing and the computer does not respond to the keyboard, touchpad, or touchscreen. Sometimes a freeze lasts for just a few seconds, and the Chromebook then becomes responsive again. Other times, the Chromebook freezes until you force it to shut down.

Even if your Chromebook becomes responsive again after freezing for a few seconds, it is a good idea to shut it down and then restart it. This section explains the various ways to shut down a Chromebook.

Shut Down and Restart Your Chromebook Normally if Possible

If your Chromebook is currently responding well enough for you to shut it down normally, do so. For example, click the status area to open the system menu, and then click **Shut down** (⏻).

If the Chromebook is not responding to the touchpad — or the touchscreen, if it has one — but is responding to the keyboard, press Alt + Shift + N to open the system menu. Press Tab three times to move the focus to the Shut Down icon so that a light-blue selection circle appears around it. Then press Enter to give the Shut Down command.

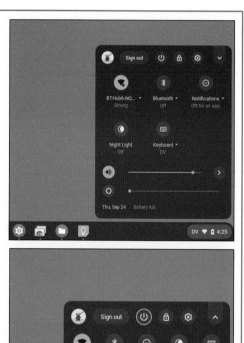

Shut Down Your Chromebook Using the Power Menu

If your Chromebook is not responding to the touchpad or keyboard, try using the Power menu to shut down the computer.

On a non-touchscreen Chromebook, press ⏻ in the upper-right corner of the keyboard. On a touchscreen Chromebook, press **Power**, which is usually a hardware button on the side of the Chromebook.

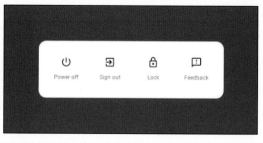

Shut Down Your Chromebook Using the Power Menu (continued)

If the Power menu appears, see if the Power command has made the touchpad, touchscreen, or keyboard responsive again. If the touchpad or touchscreen is working, click **Power off** (⏻). If the keyboard is working, press `Tab` or `➡` once to select the Power Off button, and then press `Enter` to give the command.

Shut Down Your Chromebook Using the Power Button

If you cannot display the status menu to reach the Shut Down button, try pressing and holding ⏻ or **Power** for 3 seconds. Doing so issues first the command for signing out of your Google account, causing it to save any unsaved work in your open apps, and then the command for shutting down the Chromebook.

Restart Your Chromebook with a Hard Reset

If holding down ⏻ or **Power** for 3 seconds does not sign you out and shut down your Chromebook, you will need to perform a *hard reset*. This move does not sign you out of your Google Account and save your work, so you may lose recent work in the apps you have been using.

To perform a hard reset on a Chromebook, hold down ↻ on the top row of the keyboard, and then press ⏻ or **Power**. Just a short press is enough — you do not need to press and hold the button. Keep holding down ↻ until the Chromebook restarts.

To perform a hard reset on a Chrome OS tablet, press and hold **Volume Up** and **Power** for 10 seconds until the tablet restarts.

Powerwash Your Chromebook

When you need to restore your Chromebook to its original state, you can run what Google calls a *powerwash*. Powerwashing the Chromebook removes all the user accounts and data from it, so you — or someone else — can set up as if it were a new device.

Normally, you would powerwash a Chromebook in only a few circumstances: to work around configuration issues that a factory reset cannot resolve, to change the owner account for the Chromebook, or to prepare for selling or giving the Chromebook to a new owner.

Powerwash Your Chromebook

Start a Powerwash from the Settings App

1 Click the status area.

The system menu opens.

2 Click **Settings** (⚙).

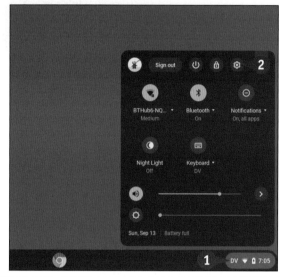

The Settings app opens in a window.

3 Click **Advanced**.

The Advanced section appears.

4 Click **Reset settings** (🕑).

The Reset Settings section of the Settings screen appears.

5 In the Powerwash box, click **Reset**.

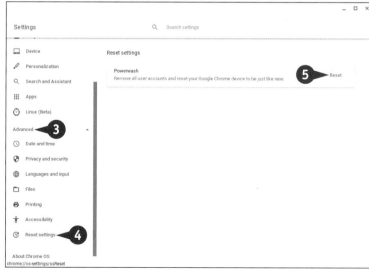

The Restart Your Device dialog box opens.

6 Click **Restart**.

The Chromebook restarts, and the powerwash operation begins.

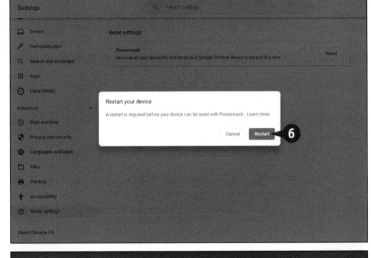

Start a Powerwash from the Sign-In Screen

1 On the Settings screen, press
`Ctrl`+`Alt`+`Shift`+`R`.

The Reset This Chrome Device dialog box opens.

2 Click **Restart**.

The Chromebook restarts, and the powerwash operation begins.

Note: When the powerwash operation ends, you can set up the Chromebook as if it were new. See the section "Set Up Your Chromebook" in Chapter 1 for details.

TIP

Why does the Powerwash button not appear on the Reset screen?
If the Reset screen does not include the Powerwash button, your Chromebook is managed through administration tools. This means you cannot powerwash the Chromebook. Instead, ask an administrator to powerwash it for you.

Recover Your Chromebook

If you go to use your Chromebook one day but find that, instead of starting, it displays the message *Chrome OS is missing or damaged*, you will need to recover the Chromebook using a recovery device. A *recovery device* sounds like a medical ventilator, or perhaps a tow truck, but for a Chromebook it is simply a USB flash drive or a microSD card with a copy of Chrome OS on it.

This section explains how to create a recovery device and how to use it to recover your Chromebook.

Choose the Computer for Creating the Recovery Device

First, choose the computer you will use to create the recovery device. You can use a Chromebook, a Windows PC, or a Mac:

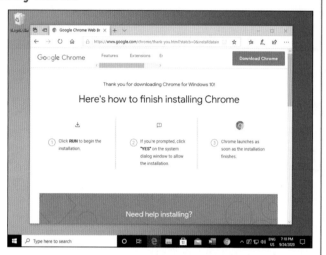

- **Chromebook.** A Chromebook is the easiest option. But if you are creating the recovery device to recover a Chromebook that is currently ailing, you will — obviously enough — need to use another Chromebook. If you are creating the recovery device just in case you need it in the future, you can use your prospective patient.

- **Windows PC or Mac.** The Windows PC or Mac needs to have the Chrome browser installed. You can install the Chrome browser by opening an existing browser, such as Microsoft Edge or Safari, to **chrome.google.com** and following the prompts.

Install the Chromebook Recovery Utility

Next, go to the Chrome Web Store and install the Chromebook Recovery Utility.

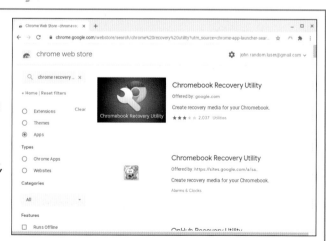

On a Chromebook, press Shift+click **Launcher** (🔘), and then click **Chrome Web Store** (🌐). Click **Apps** (▦); then click **Search the store** (🔍), type **Chromebook recovery utility**, and press Enter.

On a Windows PC or Mac, open the Chrome browser, and then search for the following two three-word phrases, **"Chrome web store" "Chromebook recovery utility"**, including the quotation marks.

Click the appropriate search result to display the page for the Chromebook Recovery Utility extension on the Chrome Web Store. Here, click **Add to Chrome**, and then click **Add app** in the confirmation dialog box that opens.

Launch the Chromebook Recovery Utility and Create the Recovery Device

Launch Chromebook Recovery Utility:

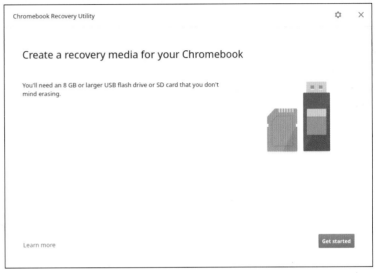

- **Chromebook:** Press **Shift**+click **Launcher**, and then click **Chromebook Recovery Utility** (🔄).

- Windows PC: Click **Start** (⊞), and then click **Chromebook Recovery Utility** (🔄).

- Mac: Click **Launchpad** (🚀), and then click **Chromebook Recovery Utility** (🔄).

The Chromebook Recovery Utility window opens and displays its first screen, which tells you that you will need an 8GB or larger USB flash drive or SD card whose contents you do not mind erasing.

Click **Get started** to display the Step 1 of 3: Identify Your Chromebook screen.

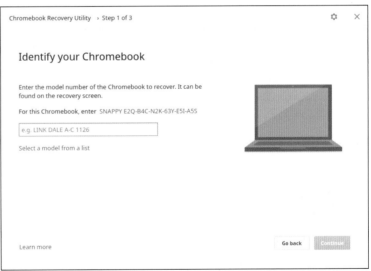

On this screen, you need to enter the model number of the Chromebook on which you will use the recovery device. You can find the model number in any of these three ways:

- Put the Chromebook into recovery by holding down **Esc**+**C** and pressing **⏻** or **Power** briefly. The model number appears at the bottom of the Recovery screen.

- Click **Select a model from a list** and browse to locate the number. Select the model to enter the number in the box.

- Enter the model number shown by the *For this Chromebook, enter* readout. Use this only if you are running Chromebook Recovery Utility on the model of Chromebook you will recover.

continued ▶

The recovery device you prepare with Chromebook Recovery Utility is customized to the model of Chromebook you want to recover. This customization ensures that the version of Chrome OS that recovery installs is configured correctly for the Chromebook.

After creating the recovery device, you put the Chromebook into Recovery Mode, connect the recovery device, and reinstall the operating system.

Launch the Chromebook Recovery Utility and Create the Recovery Device (continued)

Unless you browsed to the model number, start typing the model number into the box. When Chromebook Recovery Utility detects a match, it displays the *Found a match* readout and displays the make and model under the image of the generic Chromebook.

Click **Continue** to display the Step 2 of 3: Insert Your USB Flash Drive or SD Card screen.

Connect a USB flash drive or insert a microSD card with a capacity of 8GB or more.

Click **Select the media you'd like to use** (⬍), and then click the entry for the USB flash drive or microSD card on the pop-up menu.

Click **Continue** to display the Step 3 of 3: Create a Recovery Image screen. Then click **Create now** to start creating the recovery image on the recovery drive.

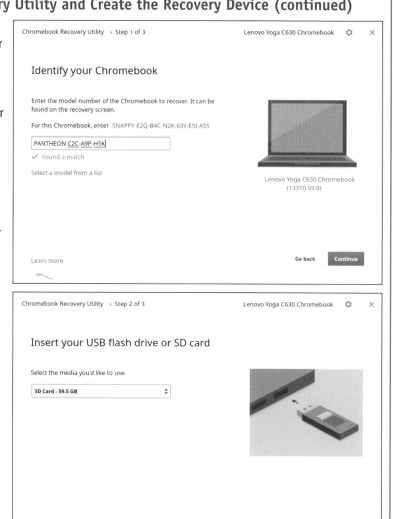

Chromebook Recovery Utility downloads a copy of Chrome OS for the Chromebook model you specified, verifies the download to make sure it is complete, unpacks the download's contents, and then writes those contents to the recovery device.

While Chromebook Recovery Utility performs these tasks, it displays the Help Us Improve Our Product section, in which you can describe what happened to the Chromebook to necessitate recovery. You can also choose whether to include the Chromebook model and information about how frequently you use it in your feedback.

When Chromebook Recovery Utility finishes writing the recovery image, click **Continue** to display the Success! Your Recovery Media Is Ready screen.

Click **Done** to close Chromebook Recovery Utility. You can then remove the USB flash drive or microSD card from the Chromebook.

Chromebook Recovery Utility › Step 3 of 3	Lenovo Yoga C630 Chromebook ⚙ ✕

Creating a recovery image

Don't remove your recovery media.

Writing. 26% completed. 5 minutes remaining.

(Optional) Help us improve our product.

Could you tell us what happened to your device?

☐ Include device model (Lenovo - Lenovo Yoga C630 Chromebook)?
How frequently do you use this tool?

Go to the Legal Help page to request content changes for legal reasons. Some account and system info will be sent to Google. We'll use the info you give us to address technical issues and improve our services, subject to our Privacy Policy and Terms of Service.

Learn more   Cancel   Continue

Chromebook Recovery Utility	Lenovo Yoga C630 Chromebook ⚙ ✕

Success! Your recovery media is ready

You can remove your recovery media now.

- To recover your Chromebook, plug the recovery media in to your Chromebook.
- After recovery, you can erase your recovery media using this utility.

(Optional) Help us improve our product.

Could you tell us what happened to your device?

☐ Include device model (Lenovo - Lenovo Yoga C630 Chromebook)?
How frequently do you use this tool?

Go to the Legal Help page to request content changes for legal reasons. Some account and system info will be sent to Google. We'll use the info you give us to address technical issues and improve our services, subject to our Privacy Policy and Terms of Service.

Learn more   Create another   Done

Put Your Chromebook into Recovery Mode and Install Chrome OS

Press 🔘 or **Power** to power on the Chromebook that needs recovery. It may put itself into Recovery Mode automatically; if not, hold down `Esc`+`↻` and pressing 🔘 or **Power** briefly.

Plug the recovery device USB flash drive or microSD card into the Chromebook. The Chromebook automatically begins reinstalling Chrome OS from the device. The System Recovery Is Complete screen appears when recovery finishes.

You can then remove the recovery device from the Chromebook, which restarts automatically and then displays the Welcome! screen.

Index

A

Accessibility features
    audio, 82–83
    keyboard, 78–79
    Magnifier, 76–77
    mouse, 80–81
    screen, 74–77
    text-to-speech, 84–85
    touchpad, 80–81
accessibility settings
    configuring, 8, 72–85
    displaying, 72–73
accounts, switching between, 125
actions
    allowing for extensions, 139
    Cookies screen, 207
    keyboard shortcuts for frequent, 22
    Other Site Data screen, 207
adding
    contacts to Google Contacts, 282–283
    emojis in email messages, 227
    external email accounts to Gmail, 212–215
    formatting to email messages, 226–227
    participants to video calls, 253
    pictures in email messages, 227
    sports team calendars to Google Calendar, 279
    users to whitelist, 117
advanced moves, keyboard shortcuts for, 23
Allow Other Users of This Device to Use
  This Network switch, 11
Android apps
    about, 129
    closing, 147
    configuring preferences for, 148–149
    installing, 144–145
    running, 146–147
Android phones
    about, 12
    adding Google Messages on, 254
    connecting, 102–103
    connecting to Internet via, 104–105

Apple iCal format, 273
applying
    browser themes, 68–69
    special effects to video calls, 253
apps
    about, 128–129
    Android, 129, 144–149
    availability of, 145
    comparing, 137
    controlling data usage, 149
    default, 169–171
    Files, 128
    frozen, 311
    Gallery, 168
    installing from Web Store, 136–137
    Microsoft Office, 129
    opening, 130–131
    organizing windows with desks, 134–135
    pinning, 43
    Remote Desktop, 306–309
    reviewing for children, 121
    running, 130–131, 137
    Settings, 128
    splitting screen between, 20
    switching between windows, 132–133
    unpinning, 43
    viewing data usage, 149
    web, 128
Apps & Notification screen, 148–149
Assistant command, 57
Attachment button, 231
audio
    changing volume for, 63
    configuring accessibility settings for, 82–83
    recordings of, 263
AUE (Auto Update Expiration) date, 5
authentication, two-factor, 115
Auto Update Expiration (AUE) date, 5
autohiding, configuring, 42
Automatic Click menu, 81

Index

Window Switcher, switching apps using, 132–133

windows

    closing, 20, 28–29

    displaying open, 20

    docking, 132, 133

    managing, 28–29

    navigating tabs in, 189

    opening, 28–29

    organizing, 134–135

    restoring open tabs, 65

    scaling, 133

    splitting screen between, 29

Windows 10, exporting contact data from Peoples app in, 287

Y

YouTube

    casting to Chromecast devices, 100–101

    playing, 194–195

    website, 195

Z

Zip files, 180–181

zooming

    with gestures, 20

    screen, 76–77